The International Money Market:
An Assessment of Forecasting
Techniques and Market Efficiency

**CONTEMPORARY STUDIES IN
ECONOMIC AND FINANCIAL ANALYSIS VOLUME 22**

Editors: Professor Edward I. Altman and Ingo Walter, Associate Dean
Graduate School of Business Administration, New York University

CONTEMPORARY STUDIES IN ECONOMIC AND FINANCIAL ANALYSIS

An International Series of Monographs

Series Editors: Edward I. Altman and Ingo Walter
                Graduate School of Business Administration, New York University

Volume 1. DYNAMICS OF FORECASTING FINANCIAL CYCLES:
Theory, Technique and Implementation
Lacy H. Hunt, II, *Fidelcor Inc. and the Fidelity Bank*

Volume 2. COMPOSITE RESERVE ASSETS IN THE INTERNATIONAL MONETARY SYSTEM
Jacob S. Dreyer, *Graduate School of Arts and Sciences, New York University*

Volume 3. APPLICATION OF CLASSIFICATION TECHNIQUES IN BUSINESS, BANKING AND FINANCE
Edward I. Altman, *Graduate School of Business Administration, New York University,* Robert B. Avery, *Graduate School of Industrial Administration, Carnegie-Mellon University,* Robert A. Eisenbeis, *Federal Deposit Insurance Corporation,* and Joseph F. Sinkey, Jr. *College of Business Administration, University of Georgia*

Volume 4. PROBLEM AND FAILED INSTITUTIONS IN THE COMMERCIAL BANKING INDUSTRY
Joseph F. Sinkey, Jr., *College of Business Administration, University of Georgia*

Volume 5 A NEW LOOK AT PORTFOLIO MANAGEMENT
David M. Ahlers, *Graduate School of Business and Public Administration, Cornell University*

Volume 6. MULTINATIONAL ELECTRONIC COMPANIES AND NATIONAL ECONOMIC POLICIES
Edmond Sciberras, *Science Policy Research Unit, University of Sussex*

Volume 7. VENEZUELAN ECONOMIC DEVELOPMENT:
A Politico-Economic Analysis
Loring Allen, *University of Missouri, St. Louis*

Volume 8. ENVIRONMENT, PLANNING AND THE MULTINATIONAL CORPORATION
Thomas N. Gladwin, *Centre d'Etudes Industrielles and New York University*

Volume 9. FOREIGN DIRECT INVESTMENT, INDUSTRIALIZATION AND SOCIAL CHANGE
Stephen J. Kobrin, *Sloan School of Management, Massachusetts Institute of Technology*

Volume 10. IMPLICATIONS OF REGULATION ON BANK EXPANSION:
A Simulation Analysis
George S. Oldfield, Jr., *Graduate School of Business and Public Administration, Cornell University*

Volume 11. IMPORT SUBSTITUTION, TRADE AND DEVELOPMENT
Jaleel Ahmad, *Concordia University, Sir George Williams Campus*

Volume 12. CORPORATE GROWTH AND COMMON STOCK RISK
David R. Fewings, *McGill University*

Volume 13. CAPITAL MARKET EQUILIBRIUM AND CORPORATE FINANCIAL DECISIONS
Richard C. Stapleton, *Manchester Business School and New York University*, and M. G. Subrahmanyam, *Indian Institute of Management and New York University*

Volume 14. IMPENDING CHANGES FOR SECURITIES MARKETS: What Role for the Exchanges?
Ernest Bloch and Robert A. Schwartz, *Graduate School of Business Administration, New York University*

Volume 15. INDUSTRIAL INNOVATION AND INTERNATIONAL TRADING PERFORMANCE
William B. Walker, *Science Policy Research Unit, University of Sussex*

Volume 16. FINANCIAL POLICY, INFLATION AND ECONOMIC DEVELOPMENT: The Mexican Experience
John K. Thompson, *Mellon Bank, N.A.*

Volume 17. *THE MANAGEMENT OF CORPORATE LIQUIDITY*
Michel Levasseur, *Centre d'Enseignement Superieur des Affaires, Jouy-en-Josas, France*

Volume 18. STABILIZATION OF INTERNATIONAL COMMODITY MARKETS
Paul Hallwood, *University of Aberdeen*

Volume 19. PROBLEMS IN EUROPEAN CORPORATE FINANCE: Text and Cases
Michel Schlosser, *Centre d'Enseignement Superieur des Affaires, Jouy-en-Josas, France*

Volume 20. THE MULTINATIONAL ENTERPRISE: International Investment and Host-Country Impacts
Thomas G. Parry, *School of Economics, University of New South Wales*

Volume 21. POLICY RESPONSES TO RESOURCE DEPLETION: The Case of Mercury
Nigel Roxburgh, Management Studies Division, The Economist Intelligence Unit Limited

Volume 22. THE INTERNATIONAL MONEY MARKET: An Assessment of Forecasting Techniques and Market Efficiency
Richard M. Levich, *Graduate School of Business Administration, New York University*

Volume 23. TRANSNATIONAL CONGLOMERATES AND THE ECONOMICS OF DEPENDENT DEVELOPMENT: A Case Study of the International Electric Oligopoly and Brazil's Electrical Industry
Richard Newfarmer, *University of Notre Dame*

Volume 24. THE POLITICAL ECONOMY OF ENVIRONMENTAL PROTECTION
Horst Siebert, *University of Mannheim,* and Ariane Berthoin Antal, *International Institute for Environment and Society, Berlin*

The International Money Market:

An Assessment of Forecasting Techniques and Market Efficiency

by RICHARD M. LEVICH
Graduate School of Business Administration
New York University

Foreword by ROBERT Z. ALIBER
University of Chicago

JAI PRESS INC.
Greenwich Connecticut

Library of Congress Cataloging in Publication Data

Levich, Richard M
   The international money market.

(Contemporary studies in economic and financial analysis; v. 22)
Bibliography: p.
Includes index.
1. Forward exchange. 2. Foreign exchange.
3. Money market. I. Title. II. Series.
HG3853.F6L45   332.4'5   78-13841
ISBN 0-89232-109-1

Copyright © 1979 JAI PRESS INC.
165 West Putnam Avenue
Greenwich, Connecticut 06830

All rights reserved. No part of this publication may be reproduced, stored on a retrieval system, or transmitted in any form or by any means, electronic, mechanical, photocopying, filming, recording or otherwise without prior permission in writing from the publisher.

ISBN NUMBER: 0-89232-109-1
Library of Congress Catalog Card Number: 78-13841
Manufactured in the United States of America

CONTENTS

List of Tables	xi
List of Figures	xiii
Foreword	xv
Acknowledgements	xix

I.	**Introduction and Overview**	**1**
	Introduction	1
	Overview	2
II.	**Review of the Literature**	**7**
	Transaction Costs	7
	Covered Interest Arbitrage	10
	Time Series Behavior of Exchange Rates	11
	Foreign Exchange Forecasting	14
	Structural Models	14
	Forecasting Based on Interest Rates and Forward Rates	15
III.	**Estimates of Transaction Costs in International Money Markets**	**23**
	Purpose	23
	Estimating Currency Transaction Costs	24
	The Bid-Ask Spread Approach	24
	The Triangular Market Approach	28

	Estimating Security Transaction Costs	33
	Theory and Methodology	33
	Empirical Results	35
	Conclusions	35
IV.	**The Efficiency of Short-Term Covered Arbitrage Flows**	**39**
	Purpose	39
	Transaction Costs and Interest Rate Parity	40
	Data Considerations and Interest Rate Parity	43
	Transforming the Data to Fit the Model	43
	Asset Selection and Interest Rate Parity	44
	Empirical Results	44
	Accounting for the Residual—The Role of Timing	46
	Conclusions	49
	Covered Interest Arbitrage in the Period 1967/75	49
	Analysis	60
V.	**Approaches to Forecasting Foreign Exchange Rates—Theory**	**65**
	Purpose	65
	Arbitrage and Speculation Models	65
	Interest Rate Based Forecasts	65
	Forward Exchange Rate Based Forecasts	70
	Pure Forecasting Models	77
	Time Series Analysis	77
	Composite Forecasting	78
	Three Issues in Methodology	79
	On Selecting a Time Series for Analysis	79
	On Analyzing the Performance of Forecasting Models	81
	Quoted Yields, Realized Yields, and Risk	83
VI.	**Time Series Behavior of Spot and Forward Exchange Rates**	**87**
	Purpose	87
	Descriptive Statistics of the Spot Exchange Rates	88
	The Box-Jenkins Technique for Analyzing Time Series Data	102
	Diagnostic Tests for Selecting a Time Series Model	104
	Empirical Results	106
	Spot Exchange Rate Series	106
	Forward Exchange Rate Series	110

	Conclusions	113
	Time Series Analysis of Exchange Rates in Three Periods	113
	Time Series Analysis of Canadian Exchange Rates 1950/62	116
VII.	**Forecasting Models—Empirical Results**	**123**
	Purpose	123
	An Overview of the Statistical Methodology	124
	Statistical Properties of the Forecast Errors	125
	Forecasting Performance and Forecasting Model	125
	Forecasting Performance and Currency	127
	Forecasting Performance and Currency Preference	131
	Forecasting Performance and Horizon	134
	Forecasting Performance and Time	136
	Forward Rate Forecasts—Test for Bias	147
	Composite Models	151
	Conclusions	154
VIII.	**Forecasts and Risky Investment Opportunities**	**157**
	Purpose	157
	Traditional Methodology for Analyzing Unusual Profits	157
	An Alternative Methodology for Testing the Profitability of Forecast Rules	159
	Empirical Results	161
	Conclusions	163
IX.	**Conclusions and Suggestions for Future Research**	**165**
	Conclusions	165
	Descriptive Statistics for the International Money Markets	166
	International Money Market Efficiency	167
	Implications for Financial Managers	168
	Suggestions for Future Research	170

Appendix	**171**
Data Sources	171
References	176
Index	181

LIST OF TABLES

2.1	Interest Rates and Forecasts of the Rupee Exchange Rate	16
2.2	Fisher's Analysis of Interest Rates and Exchange Rates	17
2.3	Summary Statistics for Yearly Forecast Errors	17
3.1	Bid-Ask Spread in Foreign Exchange Markets	26
3.2	Sample Data in Triangular Arbitrage	28
3.3	Estimates of the Percentage Cost of Transactions in the Market for Foreign Exchange	32
3.4	Estimates of the Percentage Cost of Transactions in the Markets for 90-Day Securities	33
4.1	Summary of Transactions in Covered Arbitrage Outflow	42
4.2	Transaction Costs and Neutral Band for 90-Day Covered Arbitrage	45
4.3	Mean Percentage Profits of a Simple Trading Rule (Traditional Pair)	48
4.4	Frequency Distribution for Deviations from Interest Rate Parity and Other Summary Statistics: Weekly Observations 1967/75	50
4.5	Country Comparisons—Percentage of Deviations from Interest Parity Within ± .25%	61
4.6	Maturity Comparisons—Percentage of Deviations from Interest Parity Within ± .25%	61
4.7	Instrument Comparisons—Percentage of Deviations from Interest Parity Within ± .25%	62

List of Tables / **xi**

5.1	Summary of Transactions in a Speculative Purchase of Forward Exchange	71
5.2	A Time Series of Spot and Forward Exchange Rates to Simulate the Time Pattern of Forecast Bias	75
6.1	Minimum, Maximum, and Ending Values of Transformed Spot Rates	90
6.2	Ending Dates for Sample Periods Peg I, Float I, Peg II	91
6.3	Summary Statistics for Standardized Spot Rates ($S_{i,t}$)	91
6.4	Summary Statistics for Weekly Percentage Changes ($X_{i,t}$)	102
6.5	Parameter Estimates for Alternative ARIMA (P,D,Q) Models of the Spot Rate	107
6.6	Likelihood Ratio Analysis of Alternative ARIMA (P,D,Q) Models Versus the Random Walk Model	109
6.7	Parameter Estimates for Alternative ARIMA (P,D,Q) Models of the 90-Day Forward Rate	111
6.8	Likelihood Ratio Analysis of Alternative ARIMA (P,D,Q) Models Versus the Random Walk Model of the 90-Day Forward Rate	112
6.9	Time Series Models for Spot Exchange in Three Periods	114
6.10	Time Series Models for Forward Exchange in Three Periods	115
6.11	Parameter Estimates for Alternative ARIMA (P,D,Q) Models of Canadian Spot Rate, 1950/62	117
6.12	Likelihood Ratio Analysis of Alternative ARIMA (P,D,Q) Models Versus the Random Walk Model for Canada—1950/62	120
7.1	MSE Across Forecasting Horizons—1967/75	126
7.2	MSE by Year and Horizon—Germany	128
7.3	Lowest MSE and Ranking for Country and Horizon	129
7.4	Percentage of 3-month Forward Rate Forecasts within 0.5%, 1.0%, and 2.0% of Future Spot Rate	130
7.5	Mean Forecasting Error Across Forecasting Horizon—1967/75	132
7.6	Time Pattern of Forecasting Bias with the Fisher External Model, Three-Month Horizon	133
7.7	Q-Statistic to Test Serial Correlation of Forecast Errors	134
7.8	Ratio of MSE for Pairs of Forecast Horizons	135

7.9	Percentage of Forward Rate Forecast Errors within Neutral Bands	136
7.10	Forward Rate Bias in Germany—One-Month Horizon	151
7.11	Summary of χ^2 Tests for Forward Bias	151
7.12	Ratio of Mean Squared Forecasting Error—Composite Model/Forward Rate Model	152
7.13	Ratio of Mean Squared Forecasting Error—Composite Model/Lagged Spot Model	153
8.1	Mean Percentage Profit from Speculation Following Alternative Rules	161
8.2	A Test for Unusual Speculative Returns	162
A.1	Deviations from Triangular Parity Using Daily Range of Prices and True Prices	173
A.2	Overview of Data Sources in Chapter IV	174

LIST OF FIGURES

3.1	Market Clearing Prices with Transaction Costs	24
3.2	Weekly Observations of the Ratio of 90-Day Forward to Spot Exchange Rates	31
3.3	Monthly Estimates of Transaction Costs in the U.S. Treasury Bill Market	34
3.4	Weekly Estimates of Transaction Costs in the 90-Day U.S. Treasury Bill Market and in the Euro-Currency Market	36
4.1	Interest Parity and the Neutral Band	41
5.1	The Fisher Open Effect	67
5.2	Jensen's Inequality and Forecasting Bias	84
5.3	Equilibrium in the Forward Market	74
5.4	A Time Series of Spot and Forward Exchange Rates to Simulate the Time Pattern of Forecast Bias	76
5.5	Frequency Distribution of a Biased Forecast and an Unbiased Forecast	82
6.1	Weekly Spot Exchange Rates—Canada (C), England (E), Belgium (B), France (F), Germany (G)	88
6.2	Weekly Spot Exchange Rates—Italy (I), Netherlands (N), Switzerland (S), Japan (J)	89
6.3	Weekly Percentage Change in Spot Rate—Canada	93
6.4	Weekly Percentage Change in Spot Rate—England	94
6.5	Weekly Percentage Change in Spot Rate—Belgium	95
6.6	Weekly Percentage Change in Spot Rate—France	96
6.7	Weekly Percentage Change in Spot Rate—Germany	97

6.8	Weekly Percentage Change in Spot Rate—Italy	98
6.9	Weekly Percentage Change in Spot Rate—Netherlands	99
6.10	Weekly Percentage Change in Spot Rate—Switzerland	100
6.11	Weekly Percentage Change in Spot Rate—Japan	101
7.1	Forecast Errors, Forward Rate 3-Month—Canada	137
7.2	Forecast Errors, Forward Rate 3-Month—England	138
7.3	Forecast Errors, Forward Rate 3-Month—Belgium	139
7.4	Forecast Errors, Forward Rate 3-month—France	140
7.5	Forecast Errors, Forward Rate 3-Month—Germany	141
7.6	Forecast Errors, Forward Rate 3-Month—Italy	142
7.7	Forecast Errors, Forward Rate 3-Month—Netherlands	143
7.8	Forecast Errors, Forward Rate 3-Month—Switzerland	144
7.9	Forecast Errors, Forward Rate 3-Month—Japan	145
7.10	Germany, Spot Rate and Forward Rate Forecast—1-Month Horizon	148
7.11	Germany, Spot Rate and Forward Rate Forecast—3-Month Horizon	149
7.12	Germany, Spot Rate and Forward Rate Forecast—6-Month Horizon	150

FOREWORD

The move to a system of floating exchange rates in the early 1970s raised a new problem for corporate managers—could changes in exchange rates be predicted and could unusual profits be systematically earned from predicting these changes. For most of the previous century, currencies had been pegged to gold or to the U.S. dollar. When parities of particular currencies appeared threatened there was never any doubt about the direction of the possible change Investors had a one-way option: they could alter the currency mix of their portfolios to profit from any possible change in a parity with a minimal loss if the anticipated change did not occur. Many investors made substantial profits anticipating changes in the parities, and almost always at the expense of central banks.

The question that became immediate once central banks no longer pegged their currencies was whether investors could still earn unusual profits. Although exchange rates are free to move in response to changes in supply and demand, exchange rates differ from most other market prices in that central banks frequently intervene to buy and sell their own currencies. Intervention usually appears intended to dampen the movements in the rates, for at times—over a period of several days or weeks—such movements have been especially sharp.

Since an exchange rate is the price of two monies or securities, movements in exchange rates might be considered similar to movements in prices in other financial markets. In the last decade, analysis of price movements in equity markets and various debt markets has led to the efficient market theory. One tenet of this theory is that investors react immediately to exploit any new information which may affect security prices, so that the prices of securities move immediately to their anticipated future values. A second tenet is that some new information will tend to lead to higher security prices and other new information will lead to lower security prices, so that, in the absence of any pattern to the flow of information, the pattern of movements in the price of any security will resemble the pattern of heads-and-tails in the coin-tossing experiments.

One implication of this theory is that success in securing higher-than-average profits from investing in securities requires insights into the forces that generate the new information and lead to changes in security prices. Competition among investors for these insights means that those who have them are likely to sell them dearly. Even then, as the new information becomes more widely available the value of these insights will decline.

Richard Levich's book examines whether investors in foreign exchange are likely to make higher than average profits from predicting changes in exchange rates. A major element is how well interest rate differentials and the forward exchange rates "predict" future spot exchange rates. The test of any forecasts is whether they "beat the market," in the sense that their predictions of the future spot exchange rates are better than the predictions inferred from the forward exchange rates.

Many investors believe that systematic profits can be realized from predicting changes in exchange rates. Some of these investors are the customers of the fifteen or twenty firms which have been recently established to sell exchange rate forecasts. The owners of some of these firms may have special insights into the factors that drive exchange rates. It may, however, be significant that the owners choose to sell these insights for amounts which would appear to be nominal relative to the profits available from predicting exchange rate movements.

In any one quarter, or year, some predictions will be very good. Just as the coin-tossing experiments will result in a number of successive heads, so some investors may do better than average for some time. The effective test, however, is whether the forecaster can beat the average in the long run. For every investor who does better than the average, someone else must do worse than the average—as shareholders of Herstatt Bank and Franklin National learned to their great cost.

Levich analyzes alternative approaches to exchange rate forecasting, including those based on interest rates and forward exchange rates. He develops a composite forecast which incorporates both the information in the forward rates and the interest rates in an attempt to predict future rates from the past time series of exchange rates.

Levich concludes that the international money market is efficient in that new information that will affect future exchange rates is quickly reflected in the forward exchange rates and interest rates. Unusual profits can not be made from using the forward exchange rates to predict future spot rates. His study is a significant contribution in the analysis of the operation of the foreign exchange market.

Robert Z. Aliber
University of Chicago

ACKNOWLEDGMENTS

This research was supported by many people and institutions which deserve my thanks. Robert Aliber devoted many hours and made valuable critical comments at all stages of the research. Jacob Frenkel worked with me closely throughout the project and especially in the writing of Chapters III and IV. The other members of my committee—Charles Nelson, Rudiger Dornbusch, Harry Johnson, Arthur Laffer, and Myron Scholes—made many useful suggestions to help sharpen and focus the empirical results and their interpretation. John Bilson, Christine Hekman, Charles Plosser, and William Schwert also contributed their expertise as well as moral support. I also wish to thank Lisa Polsky for proofreading the final manuscript and for constructing the index.

The Harris Trust and Savings Bank deserves my special thanks for supplying the data base. I am grateful for financial support from the Oscar Meyer Foundation and the Chicago Mercantile Exchange. Additional research support was provided by New York University. The computer graphs were completed while I was a Visiting Scholar at the Board of Governors of the Federal Reserve System.

Chapter I

Introduction and Overview

INTRODUCTION

Over the last twenty years, a substantial research effort has been directed toward developing and testing the efficient market hypothesis. Stated simply, an efficient market is one "in which prices always 'fully reflect' available information" (Fama 1970). Investors collect and process information in order to assess the value of an asset. Trading occurs so that market prices continuously reflect the information set; as a consequence, unusual profit opportunities are quickly eliminated.

The main laboratory for testing the efficient market hypothesis has been the market for financial claims (primarily equities) in the United States. The motivation for the research presented in this dissertation is to test the efficient market hypothesis on a uniform set of data from the international money market. Stated in this manner, the hypothesis is too general for empirical testing.

Therefore, three more specific hypotheses are formulated: 1) Unusual profit opportunities in covered interest arbitrage are quickly eliminated. 2) Prices of particular financial claims imply accurate and consistent forecasts of future spot exchange rates. 3) Unusual speculative profits should not be earned by investors who use exchange rate forecasts based on publicly available information.

The first hypothesis is a restatement of the interest rate parity theorem in an efficient market context. Efficiency here rests on the relatively simple process of policing an arbitrage boundary condition.

When the assumptions of the model are satisfied, risk-free arbitrage profits should be quickly eliminated.

The second hypothesis draws on the assumption that prices reflect information. Since investors' expectations of the future spot exchange rate are part of the information set, observed prices of spot rates, forward rates, and interest rates, for example, should reflect the market's consensus estimate of the future spot rate. A test of this hypothesis can be based on the statistical properties of exchange rate forecasts implied by market prices. Under the null hypothesis that the international money market is efficient, these statistical properties should agree with our theoretical expectations.

The third hypothesis considers the usefulness of exchange rate forecasts based on publicly available information. One risky investment opportunity is speculation in forward contracts. Market efficiency suggests that publicly available forecasts of the future spot rate should not lead to unusual profits in forward speculation.

These ideas are definitely not new. Statements describing the speed of foreign exchange traders and the efficiency of foreign exchange markets can be found in Ricardo (1811), Goschen (1864), and Walras (1874). This monograph makes its contribution by applying a thorough statistical analysis on a large, uniform data base covering nine major industrial countries in the same period 1967/75.

Overall this research suggests that we cannot reject any of the three specific hypotheses for the following reasons. First, when transaction costs are included and the financial assets are comparable in terms of risk, unusual arbitrage profits are quickly eliminated. Second, although exchange rate forecasts based on market prices are not perfect, they do display many statistical properties consistent with efficient use of available information. Third, publicly available forecasts do not lead to unusual profits in forward speculation. This research, therefore, cannot reject the hypothesis that the international money market is efficient.

OVERVIEW

The primary goal of this research is to test the three hypotheses stated above. To support these tests, it will be necessary to formulate several precise theoretical models. To supplement these tests, descriptive analysis of the raw data and statistical analysis of related hypotheses are a part of this monograph. The three, specific hypotheses proceed from simple to more complicated tests of market efficiency. Similarly, the statistical analysis in this paper is structured so that we proceed from simple to more complicated tests.

An analysis of research dealing with foreign exchange forecasting, international capital market efficiency, and other related topics is presented in Chapter II.

The purpose of Chapter III is to measure the cost of transacting in the international money market. Estimates of transaction costs are required to measure the success of foreign exchange forecasting models and to measure the degree of international money market efficiency. Two major groups of transactions are considered—foreign exchange and security market transactions. Foreign exchange transaction costs are first analyzed using the bid-ask spread approach. Next, a measure based on triangular arbitrage is developed and tested. This technique exploits a simple efficient market principle—that arbitrage among currencies should not yield profits in excess of transaction costs. The final empirical section of Chapter III estimates security market transaction costs.

A major conclusion of Chapter III is that the years 1962/75 cannot be treated as a single period. The data suggest that sample periods based on the discount or premium in the forward market may be more appropriate than a division into pegged rate and floating rate periods. The sample periods which emerge are 1) 1962/67, the quiet peg period, 2) 1968/69, the turbulent peg, and 3) 1973/75, the managed float. The results show that the cost of transacting in the foreign exchange market has risen dramatically from the quiet peg period to the managed float period. Similarly, the cost of transacting in US Treasury Bills has increased by a factor of three over the same period.

The primary purpose of Chapter IV is to test hypothesis one. In an efficient market, unusual profits from covered interest arbitrage should be quickly eliminated. Since covered arbitrage is between pairs of equally risky investments, any differential rate of return is unusual. Unusual profits in this case are computed given the *current* price of spot and forward exchange, the rate of return on comparable assets and transaction costs. Policing this boundary condition is therefore more complicated than policing the triangular arbitrage relationship which relies only on foreign exchange prices. Hypothesis one is, however, less demanding than hypotheses two and three, which presume that the market forms relatively accurate and consistent expectations of the *future* spot exchange rate. This suggests that the deviations from covered arbitrage could be considered as an acceptable lower bound for analyzing forecast errors or analyzing profits from forward speculation.

Chapter IV begins by developing a model of covered interest arbitrage which explicitly accounts for transaction costs. This model leads to the notion of a neutral equilibrium band. Since arbitrage is a one-period analysis, we then describe how reported data should be transformed to correspond with the model. Using the transformed data and transaction cost estimates from Chapter III, the model is tested in three periods (1962/67, 1968/69, and 1973/75). There are three important conclusions: 1) external securities appear more nearly comparable in terms of risk than domestic securities; 2) the structure of the first and third periods appear more alike than the middle, turbulent peg period; and 3) overall, we cannot reject hypothesis one—the market seems efficient in the sense that unexploited arbitrage profits are quickly eliminated.

Chapter V is a survey of forecasting theories and their application to the foreign exchange market. The purpose of this chapter is to develop a set of alternative forecasts for testing hypothesis two. We concentrate on two classes of models—arbitrage based models and pure forecasting models.

The arbitrage based models suggest that interest rate differentials or forward rates will forecast the future spot rate. The accuracy of these models depends on transaction costs and risk premia. Once again the models suggest a neutral band analysis for analyzing forecast errors. These models can lead to a forecasting bias if investors have systematic currency preferences or demand systematic risk premia for bearing exchange risk.

The pure forecasting models are based on time series analysis and composite forecasting. Only univariate time series models of the kind developed by Box and Jenkins (1970) are considered. In an efficient market where prices reflect available information—structural information as well as other information—time series models are expected to produce minimum mean squared error forecasts.

The theory of composite forecasting is to combine several alternative forecasts of the future spot rate. The composite forecast can increase accuracy if the correlation of forecast errors across models is less than one. In the case where information is costless, composite forecasting will have no beneficial effect, since all information is simultaneously reflected in all markets. In an alternative case where information is costly, or there are market inefficiencies (e.g., resulting from government intervention) prices will never fully reflect all information (see Grossman and Stiglitz 1976). In this case, composite forecasting may be beneficial since an analysis of more markets may exploit more information.

Chapter V concludes by analyzing three methodological issues that are raised by the forecasting models in this chapter.

In Chapter VI we analyze the time series behavior and distributional properties of the spot exchange rates for nine currencies. The purpose of this analysis is, first, to present descriptive statistics on the series which we desire to forecast, and second, to examine the stationarity of these series to determine if time series analysis is an appropriate forecasting technique.

The descriptive material includes graphs of the level and percentage change in the spot rate, which illustrate the varied behavior of the spot exchange rate over the sample period. With only few exceptions, exchange rates have become more volatile over time, where volatility is measured by the standard error of the mean and standard error of the mean percentage change in the spot exchange rate.

The analysis of stationarity relies on graphs since there are no formal tests for stationarity. In the most recent floating period, exchange rates appear to exhibit a stationary behavior. Accordingly, time series models are estimated for each series in this period. The Box-Jenkins time series model and the Zellner-Palm identification technique are described. In a strict sense, there are many cases where the random walk model is rejected. This result should be taken as purely descriptive of the data—and not an indication that the foreign exchange market is inefficient.

A comparison of time series models across three sample periods (1962/67, 1968/69, 1973/75) indicates that the process generating exchange rates is more similar during two periods (1962/67, 1973/75) with different exchange rate systems than during two periods (1962/67, 1968/69) with the same exchange rate system. This again supports the view that the level of the forward discount or premium, not the formal exchange rate system, may be the correct criterion for classifying sample periods.

The results of the forecasting models are presented in Chapter VII. The purpose of this chapter is to examine the evidence on hypothesis two. The statistical properties of the forecast errors are analyzed across several dimensions—forecasting model, currency, horizon, and sample time period. Composite models and tests for bias in the forward rate forecasts are discussed in separate sections.

The most important overall results are that 1) forecast errors appear to be serially uncorrelated; 2) while forecasting bias or currency preference does appear significant for the total sample period, it does not appear to be predictable within the sample period; and 3) Mean Squared forecasting Error (MSE) rises in proportion to the forecasting horizon. These results are consistent with the view that the market efficiently reflects information concerning future exchange rates. Thus, we cannot reject hypothesis two.

Another important finding in this chapter is that a composite forecasting model can significantly reduce forecast errors. The gain exists because individual forecasts are not perfectly correlated. Imperfect correlation may be the result of information costs, search costs, or government intervention which tend to separate financial markets. More generally, the model provides a framework for analyzing prospective forecasting techniques.

The purpose of Chapter VIII is to test hypothesis three. The null hypothesis is that investors who use an exchange rate forecast based on publicly available information should not earn unusual speculative profits. The chapter begins by describing a procedure to test this hypothesis in the spirit of a two parameter portfolio model. However, because of data limitations, an alternative methodology is proposed to measure the profits from using a currency forecast in forward speculation. A statistic called *perfect information profits* is devised and incorporated in the alternative test.

The data indicate that profits from forward speculation are small relative to a risk-free yield and relative to perfect information profits. Therefore, we cannot reject hypothesis three. These results should be considered only as indicative since we have abstracted from a portfolio measure of risk.

The monograph concludes with suggestions for further research in Chapter IX. A description of data sources is presented in the Appendix.

Chapter II

Review of the Literature

TRANSACTION COSTS

A recent paper by Barnea and Logue (1975) surveys three theories which describe an important component of transaction costs—the market maker's spread. In Barnea and Logue's taxonomy, these theories are the liquidity theory, the adversary theory, and the dynamic price/inventory adjustment theory.

The liquidity theory is developed in Demsetz (1968) and extended in Tinic (1972). Demsetz notes that the spread is only one component in the total cost of transaction.

> Transaction cost may be defined as the cost of exchanging ownership titles.... It is possible to increase or decrease this cost by a more or less inclusive definition of which activities are to be counted as transaction activities. From one viewpoint the cost of producing assets is necessary to the exchange of assets.... And one could include in transaction cost the cost of being informed about the general nature of the market—the cost of making phone calls to one's broker or of reading the financial pages... (Demsetz 1968, p. 35).

In this theory, the spread represents the cost of making a quick exchange of a financial claim for money, i.e., the cost of liquidity services.

Demsetz hypothesizes that the spread is a positive function of average security price and a negative function of trading volume, the number of shareholders, and the number of markets which list the security. Demsetz tests this theory using a cross-section of 200 securities, randomly selected from the New York Stock Exchange, on two separate trading days in 1965. Except for the markets' effect, the data support the predictions of the liquidity theory.[1]

Bagehot (1971) outlines the second, adversary theory of market maker behavior. According to this theory, the market maker faces two groups of transactors—those who trade for liquidity purposes and those who trade on inside information. The market maker is assumed to profit in trades with the former group and to lose in trades with the latter group. If the market maker can distinguish information traders and anticipate information, he may actively change his spread to reduce his losses to this group.

An important consequences of this theory is that the two groups of transactors face different costs. In this framework, a transactor with significant inside information can face "negative" transaction costs.[2] The theory predicts that the bid-ask spread is a positive function of security risk (since new information is likely to have a larger price impact) and a negative function of volume (since high volume lowers positioning costs and marketability risks). For a sample of 80 stocks listed on the New York Stock Exchange, Barnea and Logue (1975) are not able to reject either hypothesis.

The final theory of dynamic price/inventory adjustment is suggested by Smidt (1971). This theory is similar to the adversary theory in that some transactors possess inside information; for this group, the security may appear at a disequilibrium price. In response, the market maker may adjust his bid-ask spread, or adjust the average price of the security or both. There is not direct test of this theory although there is evidence of the impact of block trading on security prices.[3]

In the foreign exchange market, less interest has been paid the issue of transaction costs.[4] Perhaps this is because historically these costs have been very small and stable relative to those in other financial markets; however, this explanation is not very convincing. Spreads may be small in the currencies of the major industrial countries, but for the developing countries, markets are thin and spreads are larger. Even in developed countries, foreign exchange crises occur and foreign exchange markets close so that the spread is not defined. In addition, foreign exchange markets evolve and develop. Twenty years ago, a market for five-year forward contracts in sterling did not exist. Effectively, the spread was not defined. Today, such a market exists with a measurable spread.

The papers in Aliber (1969) present information on spreads and brokerage fees in various foreign exchange markets. The informal analysis concludes that these costs are smaller in the wider and more active dollar markets.[5]

Fieleke (1975) studies the behavior of bid-ask spreads for eight major currencies (spot and 90-day forward) during the floating periods of 1971. He hypothesizes that the bid-ask spread should be inversely related to volume of trading and competition among banks and directly related to exchange market restrictions and uncertainty about the future changes in exchange rates. Since data on volume is not available and competition is relatively constant over the short run, Fieleke proposes the following equation:[6]

(2.1) $$M_t = b_0 + b_1 ED_t + b_2 |\dot{S}/S|_t + b_3 G_t$$

where M = percentage bid-ask in foreign exchange
 ED = "excess-over-normal" covered interest differential for 90-day term
 $\dot{S}/S$ = percentage change in spot exchange (mid-point)
 G = dummy variable for official government action which "appears likely" to effect market uncertainty.

The data confirm that b_1, b_2, and b_3 are generally positive and significant.[7] Spreads in the foreign exchange market increase when prices are more volatile and when government announcements create an atmosphere of uncertainty.

McCormick (1975) reports data on the bid-ask spread for five currencies (spot and forward) over the period 1970/74. His calculations indicate the spreads in forward markets are typically larger than in spot markets. They also show that these spreads have increased substantially (sometimes by a factor of six) over the 18-quarter period. However, only quarterly average statistics for each currency are reported and there is no indication of the intraquarter variation.

COVERED INTEREST ARBITRAGE

The concept of covered interest arbitrage which leads to the interest rate parity relationship is sometimes associated with Keynes, who stated the relationship in *A Tract on Monetary Reform*.[8]

> Forward quotations for the purchase of the currency of the dearer money market tend to be cheaper than spot quotations by a percentage per month equal to the excess of the interest which can be earned in a month in the dearer market over what can be earned in the cheaper (Keynes 1923, p. 124).

Empirically, however, the parity condition, which we have restated as hypothesis one, is not always satisfied. This finding has been disturbing since it implies that markets are not eficent in policing arbitrage boundary conditions and exploiting profit opportunities. A wide range of explanations has been developed and tested.[9] Surveys of these issues are provided by Stein (1962) and Officer and Willet (1970). Only three alternative explanations are examined here.

Branson (1969) examines the role of transaction costs in arbitrage between U.S. and U.K. Treasury Bills (January 1959–December 1964) and between U.S. and Canadian Treasury Bills (July 1962-December 1964). After eliminating periods of heavy speculation, the mean absolute deviation from interest parity is computed. This statistic is *the cost of arbitrage*. The problem with this methodology is that it assumes that interest parity holds for the selected assets. All observed deviations from parity are presumed to be the result of transaction costs, rather than some other factor. What is needed is another, independent estimate of the cost of arbitrage.

An additional test by Branson is a regression of the form

$$(2.2) \qquad \frac{F - S}{S} = a + b\,(r_d - r_f).$$

Branson's data cannot reject the null hypothesis that $a = 0$ and $b = 1$.[10] However, these statistics are irrelevant for testing hypothesis one. Deviations of $+2\%$ and -2% scattered about the interest parity line could lead to the regression results $a = 0$ and $b = 1$. If the cost of arbitrage were only 1%, the data reject interest parity theory and hypothesis one.

A second explanation for deviations from interest parity is based on the supply elasticity for arbitrage funds. When the supply elasticity is less than infinite, arbitragers will not commit sufficient funds to establish interest parity. This argument is not convincing since an upward sloping supply schedules implies that arbitragers view their activity as risky and that they require extra compensation for supplying more arbitrage funds. This violates the basic assumption that arbitrage is always a risk-free activity. Frenkel (1973) calculates that the supply elasticity would have to be extremely low in order to provide a complete explanation of deviations from interest parity.

A final explanation relying on risk comparability of assets has been investigated by Aliber (1973). For the sample period 1968/70, Aliber calculates deviations from interest parity using two pairs of securities: U.S. and U.K. Treasury Bills, and Euro-dollar and Euro-sterling deposits. The deviations are much smaller and more tightly distributed around zero with the Euro-currency pair. The conclusion is that when the assets are more nearly comparable in terms of risk, the interest parity relation holds.

TIME SERIES BEHAVIOR OF EXCHANGE RATES

Poole (1966) examines the time series properties of Canadian spot exchange rates during the flexible rate period, 1950/62. Using daily data, he finds statistically significant first order serial correlation in exchange rate changes. Higher order serial correlation coefficients are not reported. Poole concludes, however, that the results are not economically significant; that is, one cannot use the knowledge of first-order serial correlation to devise a profitable trading rule after transaction costs. In this sense, the Canadian exchange market appears efficient over the sample period.

Poole (1967) conducts similar tests on nine other time series of flexible exchange rates in the post-World War I period. Statistically significant departures from randomness are found and filter rule strategies tend to make large profits relative to a buy-and-hold strategy.[11] Once again, however, Poole argues that in a world of transaction costs, some serial dependence is consistent with rational speculation.

A fundamental issue raised by Poole's research is the relationship between the random behavior of exchange rates and market efficiency. If the fundamental determinants of exchange rates are serially correlated, then *equilibrium* exchange rates will be serially correlated. Therefore, serial correlation of exchange rates, per se, does not imply market inefficiency.

Upson (1972) examines a weekly time series of 90-day forward sterling rates for the period December 30, 1960 to November 17, 1967. Using spectral analysis, he rejects the hypothesis that first differences of weekly observations follow a random walk. Upson interprets this as an indication of market inefficiency. He suggests that there is periodicity in the market (32, 3.8, and 2.5 week cycles) which could be of assistance in developing forecasts and trading rules.[12]

Upson's analysis can be criticized on two levels. First, during the sample period, spot exchange rates were pegged. Periodic central bank intervention occurred in both spot and forward markets. Given this behavior, we would not expect exchange rate series to be free of cycles.

On a second more fundamental level, it is not clear why the series which Upson examines should follow a random walk, even in a period free of official intervention. Investors set today's forward price for delivery on day $t + 90$ (P_{t+90}) so that it properly anticipates next week's price for an 83 day contract ($P_{t+7,t+90}$) as well as all future prices for delivery on day $t+90$. Weekly revisions in prices ($P_{t,t+90} - P_{t+7,t+90}$) should fluctuate randomly about their expected values—the required rate of return for holding a financial claim of this type.[13] However, Upson examines the series $P_{t,t+90}$, $P_{t+7,t+97}$, $P_{t+14,t+104}$, ...—a series of 90-day contracts that cannot be stored and traded like other financial claims. There is no theory to suggest why this series should move randomly through time.

Giddy and Dufey (1975) use Box-Jenkins time series analysis to analyze spot exchange rate series for Canada, France, and the United Kingdom during two floating rate periods—post-World War I and the early 1970s.[14] Giddy and Dufey report a wide difference in volatility of exchange rate movements across countries. In each sample period, Canada had the least volatile currency and France the most volatile. Giddy and Dufey select the standard deviation of daily percentage changes in the spot rate as a measure of volatility. However, they note that measures of covariance risk would be relevant for portfolio decisions.

Formal time series models indicate wide departures from the random walk model, especially for the post-World War I period. However, Giddy and Dufey do not report a full set of diagnostic statistics for these models, so it is not clear whether the models over-fit or under-fit the data. The departures from random behavior appeared to be less significant in the 1970s than in the 1920s. However, a tendency for nonstationary behavior remains in the 1970s data. This is an important result which suggests why time series models which are estimated during one period may not produce superior forecasts in a subsequent period.

A more recent examination of exchange rate behavior under floating exchange rates is in Dooley and Shafer (1976). The authors examine daily spot exchange rates for nine countries over the period March 1973 to September 1975; they examine three statistics: autocorrelation of daily price changes; runs of consecutive price changes; and profits associated with a filter rule trading system. Formal time series models are not estimated.

The data indicate that sample autocorrelations (at lags one to twenty days) are often significantly different from zero—the value expected under the random walk model. The pattern of autocorrelation varies across currency and so different times series models would be necessary to describe each currency. As noted earlier, this finding by itself does not reject market efficiency.

A second test analyzes the sequence of signs of exchange rate changes. Dooley and Shafer classify exchange rate changes as positive (+) or negative (−). For all sample countries, Dooley and Shafer cannot reject the null hypothesis that day-to-day price changes are independent.

Finally, Dooley and Shafer test a simple trading strategy based on a filter rule. These rules are profitable if turning points in the price series are followed by trends. Random exchange rate behavior rules out trends and profitable trading rules. The empirical results indicate that small (1%, 3%, and 5%) filters yield large profits for several currencies during the sample period. The results reflect the difference in bid and ask exchange prices and the opportunity cost of funds. The authors report a tendency for filter rule profits to decline in later subperiods. However, large profits remain for three of the five currencies, suggesting that the spot exchange market is not efficient in removing profit opportunities that result from using available information (in this case, the past price series). The authors suggest that these inefficiencies may be because the process generating prices is unstable and investors require long periods of time to learn the new process.

A serious problem with the Dooley and Shafer analysis is their assumption about the time path of the spot rate. Any test of market efficiency is *simultaneously* a test of how returns are generated. Dooley and Shafer assume that spot exchange rates follow a martingale process; consequently, the returns from a buy-and-hold strategy should be zero. The *gross* profits from the filter rule strategies which are reported are meant to be the *net, abnormal* profits as well.

This is erroneous if the martingale model is wrong. For example, suppose the Canadian dollar appreciates monotonically from $1.00 to $1.15 over a 12-month period. A 1% filter rule leads to a 14% profit while a buy-and-hold strategy results in a 15% profit. The filter rule strategy profits are large relative to a risk-free return but small relative to the naïve buy-and-hold strategy. Without knowing the process which generates the required rate of return for holding foreign assets which subject the investor to exchange risk, the results of filter rule analysis may be misleading.

FOREIGN EXCHANGE FORECASTING

Structural Models

Although forecasting exchange rates using structural models is not the main interest in this dissertation, two alternative structural models are reviewed.[15] Hodgson (1972) examines the dollar-sterling rate using monthly data from 1919/25. He assumes demand and supply for each currency is primarily associated with trade flows, capital flows, and gold flows. Six equations describe each source of demand or supply for each currency. A seventh equation which equates U.S. demand and U.K. supply of currency clears the system.

The reduced form expression for the exchange rate is a function of between 10 and 25 variables. The model explains approximately 90% of the variation in the level of the spot rate. The value of this model as a forecasting tool is doubtful since it requires forecasts for a large number of exogenous variables. The stability of the model is not tested. In fact, the model is not used to forecast postsample observations. The model provides information on the determinants of spot rates, but it is not clear that estimates of these determinants can be known in advance for forecasting.

Models based on purchasing power parity (PPP) or a monetary theory of exchange rates are also structural models of exchange rate determination. These models have been tested on a wide variety of currencies and time periods.[16] Overall, the data support the view that money, income, and interest rates are fundamental determinants of exchange rates.[17] Once again, it has not been demonstrated that the exogenous variables can be predicted so that the models are useful in forecasting.

Forecasting Based on Interest Rates and Forward Rates

Research in this area has been reported by Moses (1969), Porter (1971), Kaserman (1973), Giddy and Dufey (1975), Kohlhagen (1975), Bilson (1975), and Frenkel (1976).

An early statement of the principle that interest rates on similar risk assets denominated in different currencies should reflect anticipated exchange rate changes was formulated by Irving Fisher (1896). Fisher presented data for the period 1865/95 on Indian debt, some of which was denominated in silver and some of which was denominated in gold. Interest on the silver bonds was paid by draft on India (in rupees) and interest on the gold bonds was paid in gold. Both securities were traded in London. Fisher also presented a matching time series on rupee exchange rates (see Table 2.1). He concluded:

> From 1884 exchange fell much more rapidly than before, and the difference in the two rates of interest rose accordingly, amounting in one year to 1.1%. Since the two bonds were issued by the same government, possess the same degree of security, are quoted side by side in the same market, and are in fact similar in all important respects *except in the standard in which they are expressed,* the results afford substantial proof that the fall of exchange (after it once began) was discounted in advance. Of course investors did not form perfectly definite estimates of the future fall, but the fear of a fall predominated in varying degrees over the hope of a rise (emphasis added) (Fisher 1896, p. 390).

The basic thrust of the analysis is that for markets to clear, investors demand a higher nominal return on assets denominated in a (relatively) depreciating unit of account; investors accept a lower nominal return on assets denominated in a (relatively) appreciating unit of account. Other things equal, exchange rate changes tend to equalize the nominal rates of return across assets that are similar in all respects except currency of denomination.

Table 2.1. Interest Rates and Forecasts of the Rupee Exchange Rate

Year	Interest Rates[a]		Exchange Rates[b]		Percent Error
	Silver	Gold	Actual	Forecast	
1870	4.3	4.0	23.6	—	—
1871	4.1	3.8	23.2	23.53	1.41
1872	3.9	3.7	22.6	23.13	2.05
1873	3.9	3.7	22.4	22.62	.96
1874	3.9	3.8	22.2	22.36	.70
1875	4.0	3.6	21.9	22.18	1.26
1876	4.1	3.7	20.5	21.82	6.03
1877	4.1	3.7	20.9	20.43	−2.34
1878	4.2	3.9	20.2	20.82	2.98
1879	4.4	3.7	19.7	20.15	2.19
1880	4.3	3.6	20.0	19.57	−2.21
1881	4.0	3.4	19.9	19.87	−.17
1882	3.9	3.5	19.5	19.79	1.44
1883	4.1	3.4	19.5	19.42	−.39
1884	4.1	3.3	19.5	19.37	−.68
1885	4.1	3.5	18.5	19.35	4.39
1886	4.1	3.5	17.5	18.39	4.86
1887	4.1	3.4	17.2	17.40	1.14
1888	4.1	3.1	16.5	17.08	3.42
1889	4.1	3.0	16.5	16.34	−.97
1890	3.9	3.1	19.3	16.33	−18.22
1891	3.8	3.1	17.1	19.15	10.71
1892	3.9	3.1	15.3	16.98	9.92
1893	3.9	3.0	15.0	15.18	1.20
1894	3.9	3.0	13.5	14.87	9.21
1895	3.4	2.8	13.4	13.38	−.13

Source: Columns 2, 3, 4 from Fisher (1896, p. 47).
[a] Percent per annum.
[b] Pence per rupee.

Fisher's analysis indicates this equalization is less than complete. He calculates (see Table 2.2) that the interest rate differential forecasts an annual change in the exchange rate of 0.8%, while the actual change is 2.1% over a 20-year period. This deviation, Fisher reasons, might be partially explained by transaction costs (Fisher suggests 0.1%). Furthermore, Fisher notes a slight preference for gold denominated bonds, since gold rates are 0.2%–0.3% less than silver rates, even when the exchange rate is unchanged. Therefore, the bulk of the *ex post* deviations seem attributable to *ex ante* uncertainty.

Alternatively, we might use Fisher's data to construct a yearly forecast of the one-year-ahead spot exchange rate. The forecasts appear in Table

Table 2.2. Fisher's Analysis of Interest Rates and Exchange Rates

	Interest Rate		Appreciation of Exchange Rate	
Period	Silver	Gold	Estimated	Actual
1875/91	4.1	3.5	0.6	1.6
1876/92	4.3	3.6	0.7	1.8
1877/93	4.5	3.6	0.9	2.1
1878/94	4.6	3.8	0.8	2.6
1879/95	4.8	3.9	0.9	2.4
Average	4.5	3.7	0.8	2.1

Source: Fisher (1896, p. 50).

2.1 and the results are summarized in Table 2.3. The forecast errors are 1.55% and standard deviation 5.40%. The implied t-statistic is 1.43, indicating that on average, the forecast errors are not significantly different from zero. While some of the forecast errors exceed the boundary suggested by transaction costs or a preference for holding gold, the forecast errors do not exhibit significant autocorrelation. Given 25 years of data, a case for interest rate differentials as unbiased forecasts of exchange rate changes can be supported.

Moses (1969) applies the Fisherian theory in two more recent samples. From 1931 to 1966, some Canadian government debt was denominated in U.S. dollars (nine bonds) while most was denominated in Canadian dollars (57 bonds). Similarly, between 1958 and 1966 the International Bank for Reconstruction and Development issued debt denominated in U.S. dollars (13 bonds) and Canadian dollars (two bonds). Following Fisher, Moses calculates the expected exchange rate changes implied by the interest rates and compares these to actual exchange rate changes.

Table 2.3. Summary Statistics for Yearly Forecast Errors

Distributional Properties
Mean	1.55%
Standard Deviation	5.40%
T-Statistic	1.43

Time Series Properties
Lag	1	2	3	4	5	6
Autocorrelation	−0.130	−0.246	0.121	−0.336	−0.064	0.171

Standard Error of each coefficient = 0.20
Box-Pierce statistic = 5.95
Expected value of Box-Pierce statistic given random model = 6.0

Moses reports that expected changes in exchange rates do not average to actual changes. Moses rejects the notion that investors systematically form incorrect expectations in favor of the hypothesis that investors hold systematic currency preferences—that is, they accept a smaller return for the privilege of holding debt denominated in the preferred currency. During most of the sample period, the preference is for U.S. dollar denominated debt, except in periods of stress (e.g., the early depression years, 1931/33, and the early war years) when the preference is on Canadian currency.

Porter (1971) analyzes the term structure of Canadian interest rates under several expectations hypotheses to derive a term structure of exchange rate expectations. He formulates a model that uses yield ratios to predict exchange rate movements. The model is tested on Canadian-U.S. data for the period 1953/60.[18]

One of his findings is that the coefficients in the model have the correct sign for the one, two, and three year forecasts, but only the coefficient in the two-year model is statistically significant. For three-month maturities, the coefficient is the wrong sign and significant, higher Canadian rates imply *appreciation* of the Canadian dollar. The best result, for the two-year model, is shown below.

(2.3) $$\frac{S_{t+2}}{S_t} = \underset{(0.09)}{0.026} + \underset{(3.23)}{0.957} \left(\frac{1 + i_2}{1 + i_2^*} \right)^2$$

$R^2 = .32$, d.f. = 22, D-W = 1.07, t-statistics in parentheses.

The coefficient of the interest rate term is nearly one and the constant term is approximately zero. In this case, interest rates produce unbiased forecasts.

In a separate test, Porter analyzes the forecasting ability of the forward rate. His results (2.4) indicate that the three-month forward rate is a very bad predictor of exchange rate *changes*.

(2.4) $$\frac{S_{t+3}}{S_t} = \underset{(1.49)}{0.75} + \underset{(0.49)}{0.25} \frac{F_t}{S_t}$$

$R^2 = 0.01$, d.f. = 30, D-W = 1.63, t-statistics in parentheses.

Kaserman (1973) examines the forecasting performance of 90-day Canadian forward rates during the floating rate period July 1955 to March 1961. Forward rates tend to produce biased forecasts during this period. Moreover, the bias displays a predictable time pattern: underestimates are most common when the spot rate is increasing, overestimates predominate when the spot rate is falling. This pattern is consistent with profit maximization on the part of speculators. Under competitive forward market conditions, if speculators' expectations are perfect, the forecast error ($F_t - E(\tilde{S}_{t+1})$) equals the marginal cost of speculation.[19]

Kaserman does verify (using a technique described in Chapter VII) that the relationship between forecast errors and spot price movements is significant. The absolute value of the forecast bias over the entire period is small and can perhaps be attributed to the stability of the Canadian dollar and transaction costs. A regression for overall bias leads to equation (2.5).

(2.5) $$S_{t+1} = \underset{(0.17)}{0.12} + \underset{(0.17)}{0.88} \ F_t$$

$R^2 = .58$, d.f. $= 20$, D-W $= 1.61$, standard errors in parentheses.

The joint hypothesis that the constant term is 0 and the coefficient 1 cannot be rejected at the 5% level. The point estimate of the coefficient (0.88) is consistent with Kaserman's theory of bias since the Canadian spot rate generally declines over this period and the forward rate often overestimates the fall.

Bilson (1975) and Frenkel (1975) estimate (2.5) for other exchange rates and time periods. Bilson (equation 2.6) examines the Sterling/Deutsch mark rates from January 1971 to November 1975; Frenkel (equation 2.7) selects the Deutsch mark/sterling rates for the period February 1921 to August 1923.

(2.6) $$S_{t+3} = \underset{(.21)}{.27} + \underset{(.03)}{.95} \ F_t$$

$R^2 = .95$, d.f. $= 55$, D-W $= .83$, standard errors in parentheses.

(2.7) $$\log S_t = .46 + 1.09 \log F_{t-1}$$
$$(.24) \quad (.03)$$

$R^2 = .98$, d.f. = 29, D-W = 1.90, standard errors in parentheses.

Bilson's results are suspect since the use of monthly observations on three-month forward rates induces positive serial correlation in the residuals.[20] Frenkel avoids this problem by using monthly observations on one-month forward rates. During Frenkel's sample period, the spot rate increased exponentially. The regression coefficient 1.09 implies consistent underestimation of the future spot rate during this period.

The results of Kaserman, Bilson, and Frenkel do not necessarily conflict with Porter's analysis. The first three authors use the forward rate to predict the *level* of the future spot rate while Porter predicts *changes* in the spot rate. Since the level of the spot rate is highly autocorrelated over time, a high value of R^2 is expected.

Giddy and Dufey (1975) examine both forward rate and interest rate based forecasts for three countries (Canada, United Kingdom, France) over the 1973/74 period. Statistics for bias are not reported but MSE comparisons indicate that interest rate based forecasts dominate the forward rate. In some cases the random walk forecast minimizes MSE. The authors conclude that some mixture of random walk and interest rate forecasts may produce optimal results although they do not calculate this composite forecast.

They also find that in many cases a forecast based on the random walk model is superior to the others they consider. In general, the random walk forecast dominates a full Box-Jenkins time series forecast. In a stationary world this will not be the case since the Box-Jenkins univariate model is selected to minimize the residual error in the sample periods. These results suggest that lagged moving average terms are significant in the sample period but vanish during the postsample prediction period.

NOTES

1. Furthermore, Demsetz estimates that the division of transaction costs between the bid-ask spread and brokerage fees is about 40% and 60% respectively. Therefore, total transaction costs can be estimated by multiplying the bid-ask spread by 2.5. Other evidence

supporting the liquidity theory is in Tanner and Kochin (1971), who investigate the Canadian bond market, and in West and Tinic (1971), who use data from equity markets.

2. The possibility of a "negative trading cost" is suggested in Black and Scholes (1974). An empirical test is in Cuneo and Wanger (1975).

3. See Scholes (1972) and Kraus and Stoll (1972). This again suggests that transactors with inside information could transact at relatively low costs if they can transact at disequilibrium prices.

4. Estimates of the incentive necessary to induce covered arbitrage range from Einzig's (1961) estimate of 0.03–0.10% to Holmes and Schott's (1965) estimate of 0.25% to Keynes's (1923) estimate of 0.50%. These estimates are based on an informed view of the market rather than formal models.

5. Some of the aspects are discussed in Swoboda (1969).

6. In equation (2.1) Fieleke uses *current* changes in the exchange rate as a proxy for unanticipated future changes.

7. For our purposes, the constant term b_0 is of particular interest since it is a proxy for the minimum bid-ask spread given normal trading volume, a fixed degree of competition among foreign exchange traders, and relatively "quiet" market conditions. Estimates of b_0 are similar to those obtained by triangular arbitrage methods. See Chapter III.

8. An earlier, though less precise, statement can be found in Goschen (1864). See Chap. IV, n. 6.

9. Most of these explanations were anticipated in the explicit and implicit assumptions made by Keynes and other early writers.

10. Given the situation, the correct test is of the joint hypothesis that $a = 0$ and $b = 1$ simultaneously. Stoll (1968) tested the interest parity relation in a similar regression framework.

11. In reporting the profits from a filter rule strategy no risk measure is reported. It must be assumed that the filter rule strategy is no more risky than the buy-and-hold strategy.

12. This periodicity is similar to the three-week trading rule which led to the highest returns in Grubel (1966).

13. The formal proof of this price behavior is in Samuelson (1965). Currency futures contracts for delivery on fixed dates are traded on the International Monetary Market in Chicago.

14. The sample period begins on January 1, 1971 for Canada; March 19, 1973 for France; and June 23, 1972 for the U.K. Each sample ends on October 18, 1974.

15. Recently, commercial foreign exchange advisory services have made attempts to model the foreign exchange market. One firm that publicizes some of its methodology and results is Predex Corporation (1975). Predex uses the following general specification:

$$S_{ij} = f(CB_{i,t-n}; CB_{j,t-n}; \frac{(MS/CP \cdot IP)_i}{(MS/CP \cdot IP)_j})$$

where S_{ij} = spot rate between currencies i and j
$CB_{i,t-n}$ = cumulative trade balance of country i over last n periods.
MS = money supply
CP = consumer price index
IP = industrial production index

The cumulative balance terms are intended to be a proxy for the outstanding debt or credit not adequately represented by a single balance of payments figure. The third term measures the relative demand for real money balances.

Predex tests different empirical specifications for each of the 14 currencies it forecasts. Empirical models are revised periodically. The models project a quarterly average exchange rate. Predex has been in operation too short a time to warrant a formal analysis of their forecasting accuracy. Some preliminary tests indicate that they forecast about as accurately as the market.

16. For a survey of this literature see Officer (1976) and Magee (1976).

17. Bilson (1976) has tested a model with three factors—money, income, and interest rates. In a sample of 33 countries over 20 years, the models explain 97% of the variation in exchange rates.

18. Porter calls his analysis exploratory and suggests the results be interpreted cautiously.

19. This relationship is described in Tsiang (1959).

20. A technique for dealing with this problem is developed and tested in Bilson and Levich (1976).

Chapter III

Estimates of Transaction Costs in International Money Markets

PURPOSE

This chapter presents alternative estimates of the cost of transacting in the international money market. Estimates of these costs are incorporated in testing the three hypotheses advanced in Chapter I. With respect to hypotheses one and three, efficiency requires that unusual profits, inclusive of transaction costs, are eliminated. With respect to hypothesis two, transaction costs may lead to apparent forecasting errors even when investors formulate accurate estimates of the future spot rate. Two major groups of transactions are relevant for this analysis: foreign exchange and security market transactions.

This chapter presents evidence that transaction costs have been highly variable across currencies and over time. In the case of estimating foreign exchange transaction costs, a new method based on triangular arbitrage is outlined. The approach is a useful supplement to an analysis of bid-ask prices. Furthermore, the analysis is consistent with the view that sample periods can be defined by the discount or premium in the forward market rather than the formal, institutional arrangement of the foreign exchange market.

ESTIMATING CURRENCY TRANSACTION COSTS

The Bid-Ask Spread Approach

Theory and Methodology. In Chapter II, three models of market maker behavior and the determinants of the bid-ask spread were outlined. Both the adversary theory and the dynamic price adjustment theory predict: 1) transactors with inside information may face transaction costs smaller than the bid-ask spread; and 2) the spread is directly related to security risk and marketability risk. While both these theories may operate in the foreign exchange market, the current state of theory and data do not permit a direct test.

Specifically, an adequate, short run model of foreign exchange pricing is not available. Measuring the impact of informed trades on market prices relative to a theoretical standard is therefore ruled out. Furthermore, there is no adequate model of foreign exchange risk measurement and data on the volume of foreign exchange transactions are not available. Therefore, it is difficult to measure the impact of asset risk and marketability risk on the bid-ask spread.

Consequently, the cost of transacting is defined as the cost of liquidity services for a transactor without inside information who faces equilibrium prices. Given competitive market conditions, the bid-ask spread measures the reward that market makers must obtain for standing ready

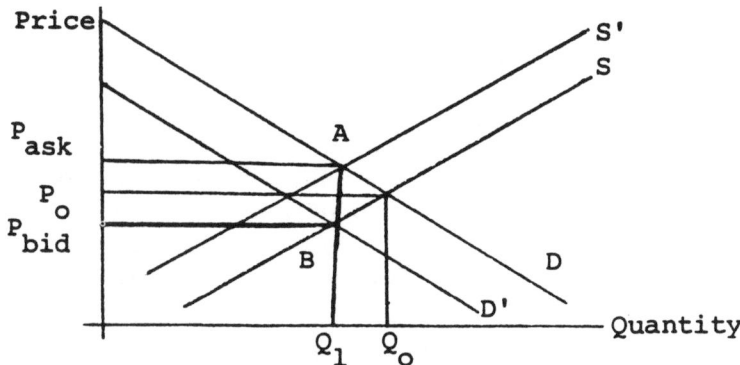

Figure 3.1.
Market Clearing Prices with Transaction Costs

to buy and sell on *immediate* demand.[1] Thus the bid-ask spread corresponds to the cost of two transactions (Demsetz 1968). Figure 3.1 illustrates this point.

In the traditional case, curves S and D describe the schedules of those who want to sell immediately and those who want to buy immediately. At equilibrium, the quantity Q_o is traded at price P_o.

If buy orders and sell orders do not arrive simultaneously in the market, then an immediate trade is denied to one party in the transaction. In this case, a market maker may enter to reduce the search cost and opportunity costs for the waiting party. Curves S' and D' describe the schedules of a market maker who stands always ready to sell (at S') and always ready to buy (at D'). Trades now take place between those who have an immediate demand and the market maker (intersection at A) and also between those who have an immediate supply and the market maker (intersection at B). The percentage bid-ask spread measures the cost of immediately buying and then selling. An estimate of the cost of one transaction is therefore[2]

(3.1) $$t = 1/2 \ (P_{ask} - P_{bid})/P_{ask}$$

Empirical Results. Lack of data for the entire sample period prevents a complete analysis of bid-ask spreads. However, there are enough data to provide an indication of the magnitude of these spreads. Table 3.1 summarizes these data.[3] We rely on two previously reported studies, private correspondence, and a new analysis based on data reported in the International Monetary Market (IMM) Newsletter.[4]

The private correspondence from the Federal Reserve Bank of New York intends to represent two "normal" trading days (August 21, 1963 and April 2, 1970) widely separated in time and one "hectic" day (October 15, 1972). Fieleke (1971) reports the average bid-ask spread in each of 18 months. Table 3.1 summarizes these 18 observations per currency. Because Fieleke reports a monthly average, the extreme high and low spreads are averaged. Therefore, the summary measure in Table 3.1 underestimates the maximum value of the spread and overestimates the minimum value of the spread that was quoted in any given month.

McCormick (1975) reports the average bid-ask spread in each of 18 quarters. Once again, because McCormick reports a quarterly average,

Table 3.1. Bid-Ask Spread in Foreign Exchange Markets (in percent)

Source	Date	N		£		DM		$C	
				Spot	Forward	Spot	Forward	Spot	Forward
Federal Reserve Bank of New York[a]	8/21/63	1		.0107	.0107	.0199	.0199	.0325	.0325
	4/2/70	1		.0125	.0250	.0183	.0367	.0215	.0429
	10/15/72	1		.0214	.0430	.0320	.0367	.0295	.0393
Fieleke (1971)	1/70–6/71	18	Max	.0104	.0337	.0530	.1056	.0467	.0958
			Mean	.0081	.0209	.0129	.0356	.0274	.0511
			Min	.0046	.0136	.0045	.0177	.0215	.0397
McCormick (1975)	1/70–6/74	18	Max	.0684	.1210	.1026	.1734	.0339	.0607
			Mean	.0243	.0484	.0400	.0869	.0281	.0511
			Min	.0069	.0171	.0078	.0242	.0222	.0431
International Monetary Market	6/72–5/75	72	Max	—	.1830	—	.4082	—	.3715
			Mean	—	.0715	—	.1831	—	.1729
			Min	—	.0192	—	.0477	—	.0761

[a]Private correspondence.

he underestimates the maximum spread and overestimates the minimum spread quoted in any quarter.

The IMM reports daily bid-ask prices on 90-day forward exchange. Our sampling technique is to select two observations per month in the 36 months from June 1972 to May 1975. Since the data are not averaged, the maximum and minimum percentage spread is a result that actually occurred during the sample period.

The data in Table 3.4 suggests several comparisons. First, spreads in forward markets are typically larger than spreads in spot markets. In this sample of data, it appears that forward spreads may be larger by a factor of two. Since the volume of transactions is generally greater in the spot market and forward prices are generally more volatile than spot prices, the data are consistent with the several theories of rational market maker behavior.[5]

Second, the spreads appear to be increasing over time. In the forward market, the pound sterling (£) spread in 1975 may be five to seven times the value for 1963. For forward Deutsch marks (DM) the increase may be from four to nine times; for forward Canadian dollars ($C), the increase may be as high as four times. These general trends coincide with the movement from a pegged to a floating exchange rate system. While these increases are substantial, the bid-ask spreads themselves are small relative to spreads in other financial markets. For example, McCormick's sample indicates average spreads of .0308% and .0621% in the spot and forward market respectively. The average spot spread is roughly the same as recent spreads in the U.S. Treasury Bill market and Euro-dollar deposit market. However, both spot and forward spreads are significantly smaller than spreads for Euro-sterling or for stocks listed on the New York Stock Exchange.[6]

Finally, Table 3.4 indicates that bid-ask spreads vary across currencies. On average, the spreads appear smallest for sterling. This is expected since the sterling-U.S. dollar market is the largest sector of the foreign exchange market. In the 1960s and early 1970s spreads in the Deutsch mark were smaller than in the Canadian dollar. In the middle 1970s this relationship appears to have been reversed. This may be the result of an increase in the relative volatility of the Deutsch mark, but there are no data to confirm this hypothesis.

In general, the data suggest that the bid-ask spread is highly variable across maturities, time periods, and currencies. It follows that, in empirical research, estimates of foreign exchange transaction costs should be specific to the sample currency, maturity, and time period.

The Triangular Market Approach

Theory and Methodology. The essence of triangular arbitrage is to keep cross-exchange rates consistent. Accordingly, in the absence of transaction costs, consistency of equilibrium requires that:

$$(3.2) \qquad (\$/£)_\tau = (\$/\$C)_\tau \cdot (\$C/£)_\tau$$

where the left side of (3.2) indicates the price of one pound sterling in terms of U.S. dollars, and the right side indicates the product of the price of one Canadian dollar in terms of U.S. dollars and the price of one pound sterling in terms of Canadian dollars. The subscript τ indicates that these prices are for foreign exchange delivered at the same maturity τ.

In the presence of transaction costs, (3.2) must be revised to include an error term, U'_τ.[7]

$$(3.3) \qquad (\$/£)_\tau = (\$/\$C)_\tau \, (\$C/£)_\tau + U'_\tau$$

Solving for the percentage deviation from triangular parity, we get:

$$(3.4) \qquad U_\tau = U'_\tau/(\$/£)_\tau = \frac{(\$/£)_\tau - (\$/\$C)_\tau \, (\$C/£)_\tau}{(\$/£)_\tau}$$

The purpose of this section is to investigate the relationship between U_τ and the cost of transacting. The following table of prices is useful. The bid-ask spread in each market is 1%, therefore the cost per transaction is 0.5%.

In a competitive market, the prices in Table 3.2 are constrained so that no profitable arbitrage opportunities exist. The effective constraint on

Table 3.2. Sample Data in Triangular Arbitrage

Row	Market	Bid Price		Midpoint		Ask Price	
1	$ /£	1.99	(B$_1$)	2.00	(M$_1$)	2.01	(A$_1$)
2	$ /$C	0.995	(B$_2$)	1.00	(M$_2$)	1.005	(A$_2$)
3	$C/£	1.99	(B$_3$)	2.00	(M$_3$)	2.01	(A$_3$)

price movements is easily illustrated. Suppose an investor holds U.S. dollars and wishes to hold sterling. He may purchase sterling directly or indirectly through the Canadian dollar market.[8] The price in each case is given by

$$\text{Direct:} \quad \text{price} = \$2.01/\pounds = A_1$$

$$\text{Indirect:} \quad \text{price} = \frac{\$1.005}{\$C} \cdot \frac{\$C\ 2.01}{\pounds} = \$2.02005/\pounds$$

$$= A_2 \cdot A_3$$

As soon as the direct price, A_1, reaches \$2.02005 there will be an incentive for the other prices, A_2 and A_3, to rise. Therefore, \$2.02005 is the maximum value of A_1 (call it $A_{1,\max}$) given A_2 and A_3. Using midpoint prices, the maximum value U_τ is 0.005.

Now consider an investor who holds sterling and wishes to hold U.S. dollars. He may transact directly or indirectly at prices given by

$$\text{Direct:} \quad \text{price} = \$1.99/\pounds = B_1$$

$$\text{Indirect:} \quad \text{price} = \frac{\$C\ 1.99}{\pounds} \cdot \frac{\$0.995}{\$C} = \$1.98005/\pounds$$

$$= B_2 \cdot B_3$$

If the direct price, B_1, fell below \$1.98005 investors would sell sterling through the indirect market, since they would receive more U.S. dollars in return. Therefore \$1.98005 is the minimum value of B_1 (call it $B_{1,\min}$) given B_2 and B_3. Using midpoint prices, the minimum value of U_τ is -0.005.

When the cost of transacting is equal across currencies, the value of U_τ, calculated using midpoint prices, can range between -0.005 and 0.005. Therefore, the maximum absolute value of U_τ corresponds to the cost of one transaction in the foreign exchange market. This estimate is interpreted to encompass the total cost associated with a transaction. Thus it includes elements like brokerage fees, time cost, search cost, subscription costs, and all other components that comprise the cost of being informed.

In principle, the suggested procedure could be criticized on the grounds that it presumes that arbitrage in currencies is efficient and therefore that the upper limit of the deviations from the equality implied by triangular arbitrage measures the cost of transaction and nothing else. In practice, however, it seems that if there is a market for which this presumption is justified, it is the market for foreign exchange.[9]

Taking the cost of transactions in the market for foreign exchange as the upper limit of the discrepancy from triangular arbitrage assumes that the structure of the cost remains stable throughout the period under examination. It is only under this assumption that we can interpret smaller deviations from triangular arbitrage as being within a neutral band such that the cost of transaction exceeds arbitrage profits. Although it is unlikely that the cost structure remained rigidly stable since the early 1960s, it is equally unlikely that it underwent fundamental changes from week to week or from month to month. It is necessary therefore to identify periods during which market conditions were approximately homogenous. In identifying such periods we follow the suggestion of Leamer and Stern (1972) and inspect the ratio of the forward to the spot exchange rates for various currencies. A forward rate lying outside the support limits may indicate (under a regime of pegged exchange rates) speculative pressures reflecting lack of confidence in the government's ability to maintain the peg. When the exchange rate is flexible, there is no obligation to maintain a specific rate; in this case periods may be classified according to the degree of volatility of the ratio of the forward to the spot exchange rate.

Empirical Results. To use the triangular market approach, we first must identify periods that appear homogenous. Figure 3.2 shows the ratio of the 90-day forward to the spot exchange rates for two pairs of currencies: the DM/$ and the $/£ rates.[10] The series suggest several periods: 1962/67—the quiet peg period; 1968/69—the turbulent peg; and 1973/75—the managed float. We chose not to analyze the period 1970/72 which marks the breakdown of the pegged rate system and the transition toward the current regime.

The various peaks and troughs in Figure 3.2 correspond to the major international financial crises.[11] The sterling devaluation of November 1967 ends the quiet peg period. The turbulent peg period closes at the end of 1969 after the Deutsch mark revaluation. The Deutsch mark revaluation coincides with a precipitous decline in the sterling discount (vis-à-vis the dollar) and a decline in the discount on other currencies

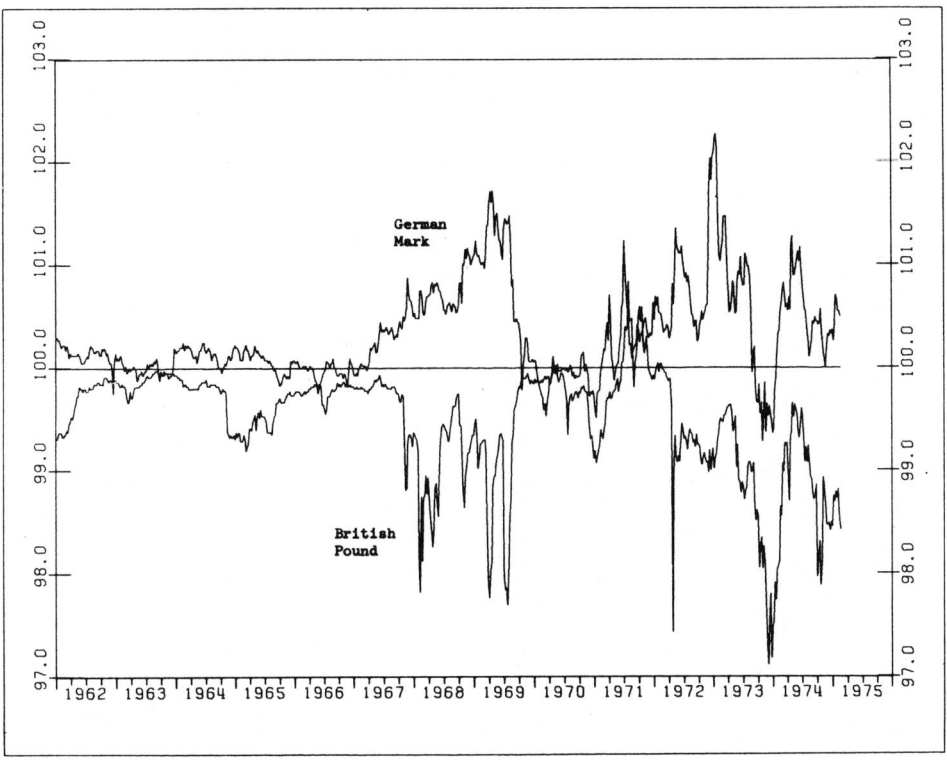

Figure 3.2.
Weekly Observations of the Ratio of 90-Day Forward to Spot Exchange Rates

(vis-à-vis the dollar). The managed float period begins with the second U.S. dollar devaluation in March 1973.

To further explore the homogeneity of the periods, the deviations from triangular arbitrage (U_r) are examined. Time series graphs and summary statistics indicate that these deviations differ markedly among periods; however, their structure is relatively stable within each period. While no formal tests for stationarity are performed, within each period the deviations appear to have an affinity for a mean value with a constant variance. Accordingly, we conclude that there are basically three periods for which we need to estimate the cost of transactions in the market for foreign exchange.[12]

To estimate transaction costs the series of weekly observations on the spot and the 90-day forward exchange rates are analyzed.[13] Using these observations, a series of weekly percentage deviations from triangular arbitrage (U_r) is constructed for the spot and forward markets. The upper limits of each series of deviations correspond to t_S and t_F respectively, which represent the cost of transacting in the spot and forward markets on any day within the period. To allow for errors in measurement and other data inaccuracies, we take a more conservative measure. Our estimates of t_S and t_F for the various periods are the percentage deviation which bounds 95% of the weekly deviations from triangular arbitrage.

In expression (3.2) we assume that triangular arbitrage occurs through the Canadian dollar; however, other currencies could be used as intermediaries. Given competitive conditions, we expect that the cost of transacting should tend to equalize across leading vehicle currencies. To allow for possible differences in transaction costs, deviations are also computed with the Deutsch mark as the intermediate currency.

The estimates of the cost of transactions are summarized in Table 3.3.[14] The estimates show little variation with respect to the choice of an intermediate currency within each period.

Estimates of t_F are larger than estimates of t_S. This is consistent with bid-ask spread data. In Table 3.1, forward spreads twice as large as spot spreads are common. However, using triangular arbitrage estimates, t_F is never more than 57% greater than t_S.

Table 3.3. Estimates of the Percentage Cost of Transactions in the Market for Foreign Exchange (Spot and 90-Day Forward)

Period	Arbitrage Between	Intermediate Currency	t_S	t_F	$t_S + t_F$
January 1962 to	$U.S. and £	DM	0.051	0.076	0.127
November 1967	$U.S. and £	$C	0.058	0.068	0.126
N=307					
January 1968 to	$U.S. and £	DM	0.102	0.160	0.262
December 1969	$U.S. and £	$C	0.085	0.112	0.197
N=103					
July 1973 to	$U.S. and £	DM	0.523	0.507	1.030
May 1975	$U.S. and £	$C	0.438	0.442	0.880
N=57					

Table 3.4. Estimates of the Percentage Cost of Transactions in the Markets for 90-Day Securities

Period	U.S. Treasury Bills t	Euro $ Rate t (external)	Euro £ Rate t* (external)
January 1962 to November 1967	0.0095	N.A.	N.A.
January 1968 to December 1969	0.0132	0.0381	0.1172
July 1973 to May 1975	0.0299	0.0381	0.1175

Table 3.3 also illustrates a period-to-period increase in transaction costs. Depending on the intermediate currency and on the maturity of the contract, the cost of transactions during the managed float period is between six and ten times higher than the corresponding cost during the quiet peg period. These increases are similar to those calculated using bid-ask spreads. The increases are also consistent with a theory that links increasing uncertainty (about the path of exchange rates, private financial institutions and government's role in the foreign exchange market) with increasing transaction costs.[15]

Finally, the estimates of t_S and t_F using the triangular arbitrage method are compared with the estimates based on bid-ask spreads reported in Table 3.1.[16] Estimates of t_S and t_F from triangular arbitrage are greater than the corresponding estimates based on bid-ask spreads, which is not surprising since the triangular method takes into account the search costs and opportunity costs involved in transacting. These costs must be covered to earn an unusual profit in *risk-free* triangular arbitrage. The triangular arbitrage estimate, which corresponds more to a *total* measure of foreign exchange market transaction costs, is therefore more appropriate when testing for unusual profits in *risk-free* covered interest arbitrage.

ESTIMATING SECURITY TRANSACTION COSTS

Theory and Methodology

Demsetz (1968) uses the bid-ask spread and brokerage fee as the basis for estimating the cost of transacting securities. Under competitive conditions the bid-ask spread is the compensation charged by dealers for

34 / *The International Money Market*

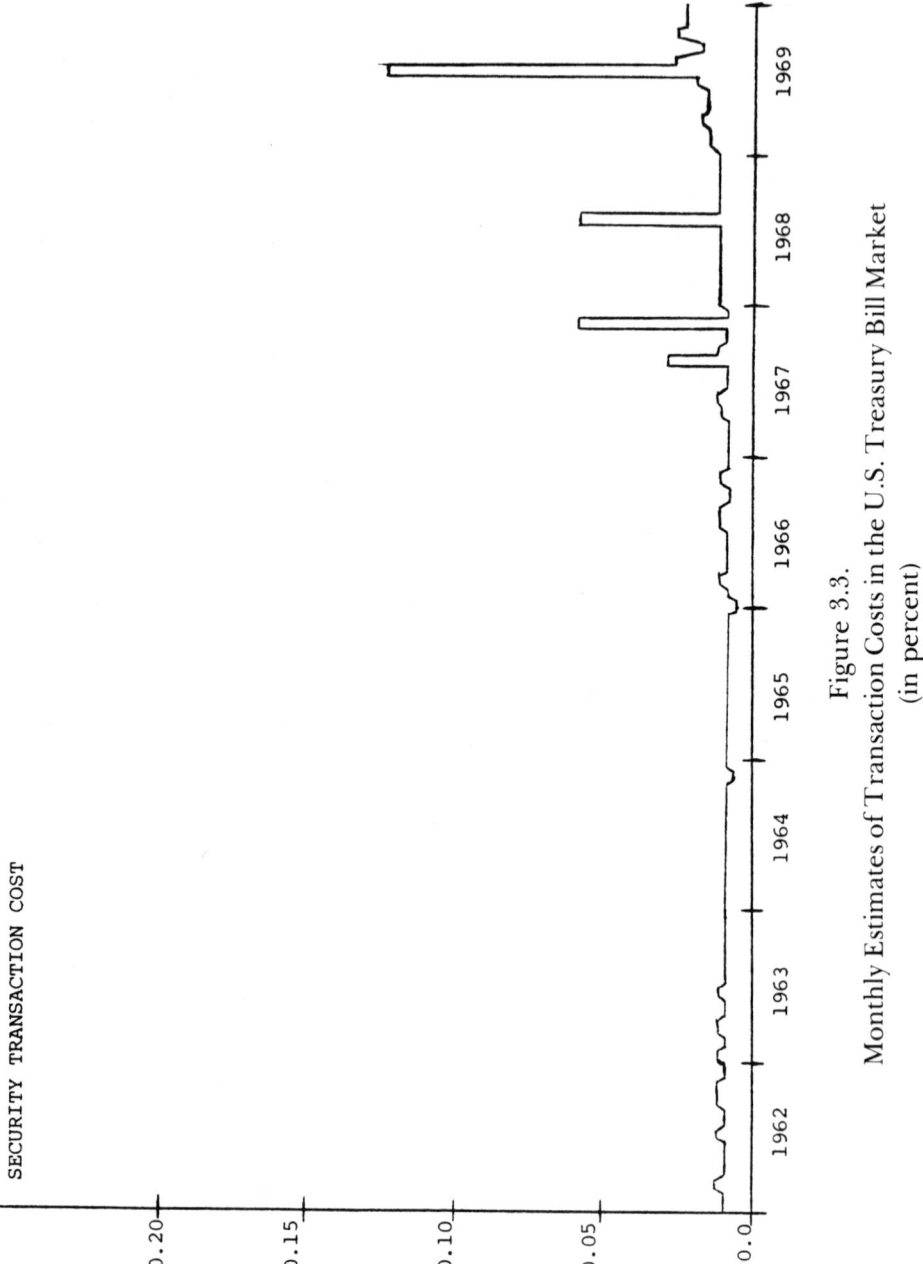

Figure 3.3.
Monthly Estimates of Transaction Costs in the U.S. Treasury Bill Market
(in percent)

standing ready to buy and sell on *immediate* demand. Other components like brokerage fees must be added to the bid-ask spread in order to compute the total cost of transactions. Demsetz estimates that total costs are about 2.5 times the bid-ask spread. Since the bid-ask spread corresponds to the cost of two transactions, our estimate of the cost of a *single* transaction is 1.25 times the bid-ask spread. Periods in which the bid-ask spread appears stationary are to be identified. A central value (such as the mode) can be used to represent transaction costs for the entire period.

Empirical Results

Transaction costs are estimated in three security markets—the U.S. Treasury Bill market and the external currency market for dollar and sterling deposits for the 90-day maturity. Figures 3.3 and 3.4 plot the time series of the cost of transactions in the various securities. The results are summarized in Table 3.4.

In the 1962/67 period, the bid-ask spread for monthly observations on 90-day U.S. Treasury Bills has modal value .0076%, and thus the modal value of *total* transaction costs (for a *single* transaction) is .0095%.[17] The cost of transactions in the U.S. Treasury Bills increases across periods while the cost in the Euro-dollar market remains stable.[18] There is not a uniform source of information on the spreads in the Euro-currency markets for the first period and thus estimates are reported only for the latter two periods. The cost in the thinnest market—the Euro-sterling market—exceeds the corresponding cost in the other markets by a factor of three.

CONCLUSIONS

The evidence in this chapter suggests that transaction costs in foreign exchange markets have been highly variable across currencies and over time. In the U.S. security markets, transaction costs appear to have increased sharply, although they are still smaller than in the Euro-sterling market. These results are consistent with hypotheses that have been rigorously tested elsewhere. Transaction costs are greater during uncertain times, in longer maturity instruments and in markets where the trading volume is relatively small. A new estimation technique based on

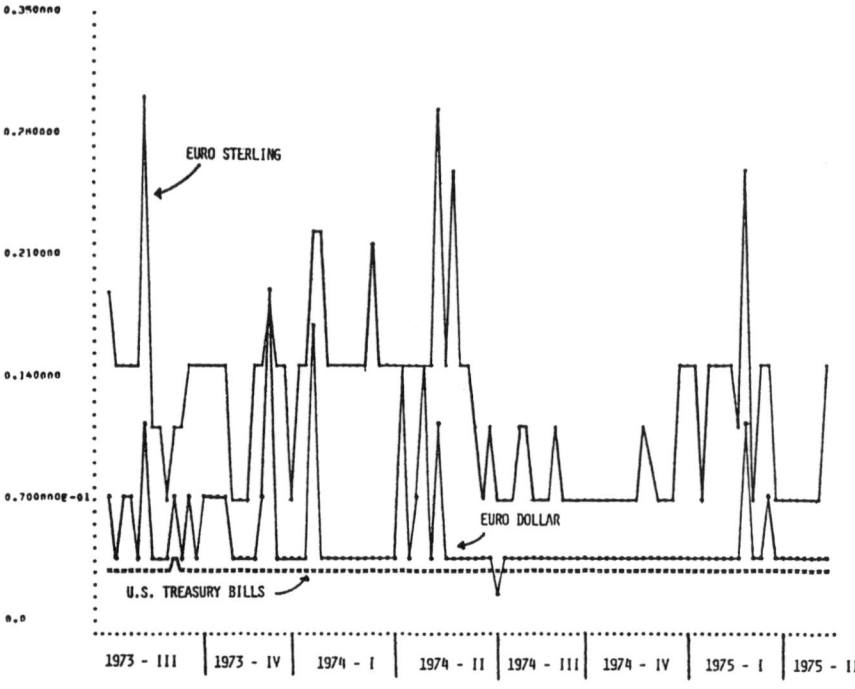

Figure 3.4.
Weekly Estimates of Transaction Costs in the 90-Day U.S. Treasury Bill Market and in the Euro-Currency Market (in percent)

triangular arbitrage was tested and yielded results consistent with a bid-ask spread analysis and our expectations.

In connection with the estimation of transaction costs using triangular arbitrage, numerous time series were checked for stationarity over the sample period. The years 1968/69 stand out as a turbulent period. This effect is mirrored in the U.S. Treasury Bill market. These findings support the view that sample periods can be defined by the level of the premium or discount in the forward market rather than by the institutional arrangement of the foreign exchange market.

NOTES
1. In the New York foreign exchange market, a market maker would be a foreign exchange dealer in a large commercial bank. These banks hold inventories to profit from price changes and to supply foreign exchange to their commercial customers. We do not

use the term *specialist* which is often associated with monopolistic market makers on the New York Stock Exchange or the term *broker* which denotes the individual who matches foreign exchange orders between large New York commercial banks. This terminology will vary in other foreign exchange markets. See Holmes and Schott (1965), Aliber (1969), and Wells (1976).

2. The spread underestimates the *total* cost of transacting since it ignores administrative costs and the costs of being informed. A transactor with inside information may be able to trade at a disequilibrium price and reduce his positioning cost below the quoted bid-ask spread.

3. All of the spreads are based on quotations in the New York interbank market. Spreads available to retail customers would be larger. Demsetz (1968) estimates that total costs are about 2.5 times the bid-ask spread. Since the spread corresponds to the cost of two transactions, our estimate of a single transaction is 1.25 times the bid-ask spread.

4. In addition to these sources, *International Financial Statistics* 1950–67 reports end-of-month bid and ask prices for spot sterling. Invariably, the spread reported is 1/8 cent or .044%. Fieleke (1975) analyzes bid-ask spreads and reports time series graphs of monthly averages for 1971. He does not report summary statistics on the magnitude of these spreads.

5. The IMM also reports bid and ask prices on one, three, six, and twelve month forward contracts. An analysis of this data suggests that the bid-ask spread increases with the maturity of the forward contract.

6. See Table 3.4; spreads for stocks listed on the New York Stock Exchange are estimated to be nearly 1%. The total cost of transacting, including brokerage fees, search costs, and information costs, may be closer to 5%. See Cuneo and Wagner (1975).

7. Morgenstern (1959) examines deviations from triangular parity using a similar framework. However, he suggests that transaction costs alone would not account for the deviations

> What are the reasons for . . . deviations from a *true zero*—this being the difference between the two rates where no profit can be made by interchanging the three currencies involved? Certainly not variations in costs, risk factors, and the like. The only plausible interpretation aside from the rejection of the data as inaccurate . . . is that the demand and supply of the currencies could not be absolutely equated as between the three centers. In other words, . . . (excess) demand or supply remained which had to be settled by securities, gold, and even other commodities" (p. 235, emphasis in original).

8. Morgenstern (1959, p. 223) names the two rates the "arbitrage" rate and the "derived" rate.

9. This assumption is consistent with discussions of arbitrage in foreign exchange markets presented by Ricardo (1811, pp. 9–10), Cournot (1838, Chap. III) and Walras (1870, Lesson 34).

10. Similar statistics and graphs were constructed for the seven other currencies and three other forward maturities in the sample. The two series illustrated in Figure 3.2 are representative of the entire sample.

11. Stokes (1972) develops a more comprehensive Crisis Index which leads to a similar classification.

12. A graph of bid-ask spreads in the U.S. Treasury Bill market also indicated a difference between the 1962/67 period and the 1968/69 period (see Figure 3.3).

13. The theory previously outlined indicates that we should use midpoint prices quoted

at the same instant in time. While our data differ from this standard, they should not lead to a biased estimate. See Appendix, pages 171–73.

14. For empirical tests, we select July 1973 as the beginning of the managed float period. By this date, the floating rate regime had been in place for about three months. Since high transaction costs (McCormick 1975) and market inefficiencies (Dooley and Shafer 1976) have been associated with this early floating period, our estimates of t_S and t_F are conservative.

15. The failure of the Herstatt bank provides an example of uncertainty associated with a private financial institution.

> "The Bundesbank's closing of a large German bank due to foreign exchange losses was received with nervous uncertainty in all exchange markets.... Starting next month, all German banks will be required to report their foreign currency positions up to the month's and in one month, three months, and over three months categories... By weekend, most exchanges settled back to a thin but restrained trading with unusually wide trade margins." *Harris Bank Weekly Review*, June 28, 1974.

16. Recall that our estimate of the total cost of a single transaction is 1.25 times the bid-ask spread.

17. The bid price and the ask price (expressed as a percentage of par) were computed according to 1) bid price = 100 − (bid yield × days to maturity)/360; 2) ask price = 100 − (ask yield × days to maturity)/360 and the percentage spread is (ask price − bid price)/ask price. The data on the bid yield and ask yield are from *Salomon Brothers Monthly Bond Report*. It should be noted that since 90-day Treasury Bills are not issued on every day, for each observation date, we have computed the ask-bid spread on the treasury bill whose maturity was closest to 90 days. The range of maturities accepted was between 87 and 93 days.

The distribution of the spreads around the modal values of the spread is extremely tight; in fact, in 52 of the 71 months under investigation, the spreads are between .0072% and .0078%.

18. The estimates of the transaction costs on 90-day Euro-dollar securities are almost identical with those provided by Heagy (1970) who reports the (annualized) cost for securities of various maturities.

Chapter IV

The Efficiency of Short-Term Covered Arbitrage Flows

PURPOSE

This chapter presents a test of hypothesis one—that unusual profit opportunities in covered interest arbitrage are quickly eliminated. A fundamental property of an efficient market is that risk-free profit opportunities do not exist. Logic requires that we test this hypothesis first before testing hypotheses that involve uncertain future variables or risky profit opportunities.

There are two methodological contributions in this chapter. First, transaction costs are explicitly introduced into the interest parity model. This enables us to compute a summary statistic (namely the percentage of observations within an equilibrium band) that has meaning in an efficient market context. Second, we stress that arbitrage is a one-period model, consequently, the data which are typically reported must be standardized to fit the model.

The empirical evidence is consistent with four general conclusions. First, securities issued in the Euro-currency market appear to be more nearly comparable in terms of risk than those issued in domestic markets. Second, transaction costs tend to increase as the arbitrage period lengthens. Third, sample periods can be defined by the level of speculation rather than institutional arrangements. Fourth, we cannot reject hypothesis one; most profit opportunities in covered interest arbitrage are quickly eliminated.

TRANSACTION COSTS AND INTEREST RATE PARITY

The early theory of the forward exchange rate emphasizes the role of covered interest arbitrage in determining the link between the forward premium on foreign exchange and the domestic and foreign rates of interest (Keynes 1923). The interest parity theory maintains that the equilibrium forward premium on foreign exchange is

$$(4.1) \qquad \frac{F - S}{S} = \frac{r_d - r_f}{1 + r_f}$$

where F and S are, respectively, the forward and spot exchange rates, and where r_d and r_f are the domestic and foreign rates of interest on securities that are identical in all respects except for the currency of denomination. Equation (4.1) describes parity line pp in Figure 4.1. When equation (4.1) is satisfied there are no unexploited profit opportunities from covered interest arbitrage.

Equation (4.1) is a stable equilibrium since all points not satisfying (4.1) set up economic forces that result in a return to parity. For example, at point A we expect an outflow of covered arbitrage funds from the domestic to the foreign market.[1] Table 4.1 summarizes the four transactions in a covered outflow and the four factors contributing to the adjustment process. The equilibrium value of the forward premium, $p \equiv (F-S)/S$ will be set so that $A_1 < p_A < A_2$. In a similar fashion, at point B we expect an inflow of covered arbitrage funds from the foreign to the domestic market. The equilibrium value of the forward premium, p, will be set so that $B_2 < p_B < B_1$. Therefore, in the absence of transaction costs, all disequilibrium points should be forced unambiguously to parity line pp.

Transaction costs in securities and foreign exchange markets imply the existence of a neutral band—around the interest parity line—within which no additional arbitrage is profitable.[2] Thus, points not on the traditional interest parity line may still be considered "equilibrium" points since within this band transaction costs exceed arbitrage profits.

Consider again an outflow of covered arbitrage funds explicitly including these transactions costs.[3] The cost (C) associated with a capital outflow of the amount X is the foregone earnings on the holdings of domestic securities:

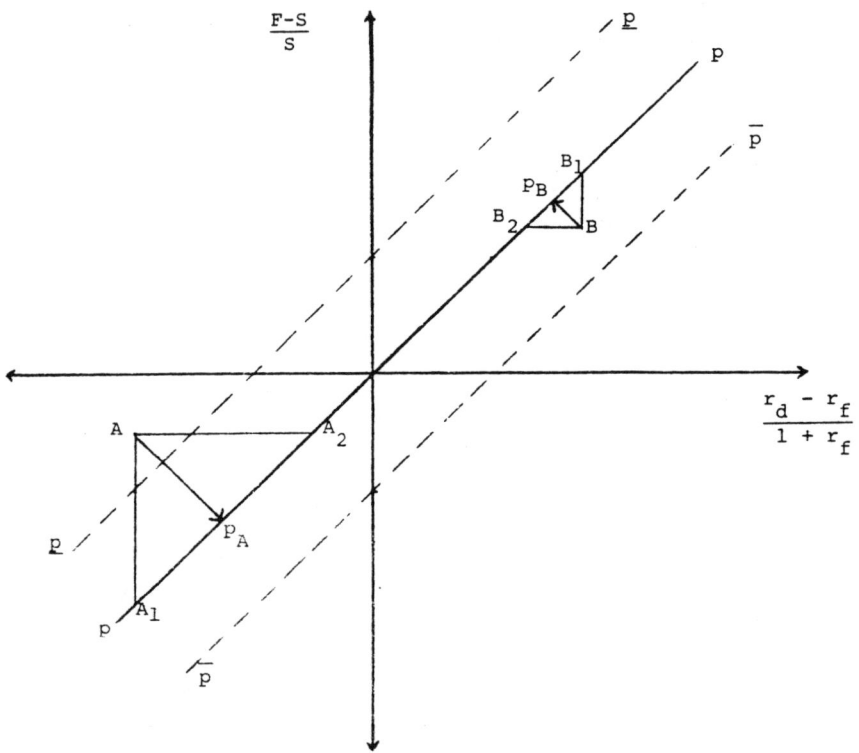

Figure 4.1.
Interest Parity and the Neutral Band

(4.2) $$C = X(1 + r_d).$$

The revenue (R) derived from a covered investment of these funds in comparable securities abroad is:

(4.3) $$R = X\Omega(1 + r_f)F/S$$

where

$$\Omega = (1 - t)(1 - t_S)(1 - t^*)(1 - t_F).$$

Equating the marginal cost (dC/dX) with the marginal revenue (dR/

Table 4.1. Summary of Transactions in Covered Arbitrage Outflow

Transaction	Partial Adjustment	Transaction Cost
Sale of domestic securities	$r_d \uparrow$	t
Purchase of foreign currency (spot)	$S \uparrow$	t_S
Purchase of foreign securities	$r_f \downarrow$	t^*
Sale of foreign currency (forward)	$F \downarrow$	t_F

dX) yields the *lower* limit on p for which marginal *outflow* of arbitrage funds is profitable:

$$(4.4) \qquad \underline{p} = \frac{(1 + r_d) - \Omega (1 + r_f)}{\Omega (1 + r_f)} .$$

This formulation of transaction costs assumes that there are no lumpy costs independent of the quantity transacted, and that the initial position of arbitragers is in securities rather than in cash. Since, however, at each point of time some fraction of the existing stock of securities matures, some arbitragers may initially hold cash. In this case their transaction costs are lower. Consequently, to have a more conservative estimate of the cost of transactions, we replace Ω in equation (4.4) and equation (4.7) below by Ω' where $\Omega' = \Omega / (1 - t^2)$.

Consider again an inflow of covered arbitrage funds from the foriegn to the domestic market. Including transaction costs, the cost (foregone earnings) and revenue of the operation are, respectively,

$$(4.5) \qquad C = X (1 + r_f)$$

and

$$(4.6) \qquad R = X\Omega (1 + r_d)S/F.$$

Equating marginal cost with marginal revenue [from (4.5) and (4.6), respectively] yields the *upper* limit on p for which marginal *inflow* of arbitrage funds is profitable:

$$(4.7) \qquad \bar{p} = \frac{\Omega (1 + r_d) - (1 + r_f)}{1 + r_f} .$$

Conditions (4.4) and (4.7) define a neutral band in which marginal covered arbitrage flows are not profitable. The limits of this neutral band are illustrated in Figure 4.1.[4]

(4.8) $$\bar{p} \leq p \leq \underline{p}.$$

For the special case in which all transaction costs are zero, condition (4.8) reduces to equation (4.1) as $\bar{p} = p = \underline{p}$, and the neutral band includes only the traditional interest parity line. Whenever any of the costs of transaction are positive, $\bar{p} < \underline{p}$.

Given our estimates of t, t^*, t_S, and t_F we can apply (4.8) to test the interest parity equilibrium condition. If market forces are efficient in locating and exploiting riskless arbitrage opportunities, then a large fraction of sample observations should be bounded by the neutral band. This statistic—the percentage of observations bounded by the neutral band—allows us to make a direct inference about the efficiency of markets. When the percentage of observations bounded is low, we will reject hypothesis one.

DATA CONSIDERATIONS AND INTEREST RATE PARITY

Transforming the Data to Fit the Model

Ideally, we would like to have the data that an international investor actually faces—a set of bid-ask prices quoted at the same instant for a set of securities, and for spot exchange and forward exchange. Our situation differs from this ideal. Our sources of data are described in detail in the Appendix, but two factors should be discussed at this time: 1) Treasury Bill rates are quoted using the bankers discount method which understates the true holding period yield,[5] and 2) all security rates and forward rates are expressed as a percentage *per annum,* which effectively multiplies the deviations from interest parity by four.

The second issue is very important given our model. Arbitrage represents a one-period investment. The rational investor compares the expected after-tax profits from the arbitrage contract (in our case, with a life of 90 days) with the relevant transaction costs. As a purely arithmetic matter, when the premium and interest rates in 90-day arbitrage are compounded over arbitrarily long (or short) periods, deviations from interest parity can be made to be arbitrarily large (or small), leaving the impression of illusory profit opportunities.[6] Moreover, since our estimates of the costs of transactions are for 90-day covered arbitrage, applying these estimates to the annualized data raises the question of the dependence of the costs of transactions on the maturity of the arbitraged assets. Since our estimates of the costs are specific to 90-day maturity contracts, it is important to associate them with contracts of this length only. Consequently, to pay adherence to the 90-day, one-period model, the annualized data have been converted back into their 90-day counterparts by dividing the published forward premia and interest rates by four. The following analysis is based on the transformed data.

Asset Selection and Interest Rate Parity

In testing market efficiency and interest rate parity, a basic question is: Which pair of securities should be used? To be consistent with our one-period model, the securities should have comparable risk properties and maturities that match the forward exchange contract. Traditionally, when arbitrage flows between the U.S. and U.K. were considered, the securities were the 90-day U.S. and U.K. Treasury Bills. Aliber (1973) argues that the traditional pair of securities does not always satisfy the comparability criterion since Treasury Bills are issued in financial centers that may differ in political risk. Instead, he argues, one should go to an external market and compare the rates of interest on, for example, a (U.S.) dollar-denominated security and a (U.K.) sterling-denominated security. Since these securities are issued in an external center, they are more nearly comparable.

To examine this proposition, two pairs of securities are used: the traditional pair, U.S. and U.K. 90-day Treasury Bills; and the external pair, Euro-market rates on 90-day securities denominated in U.S. dollars and U.K. pounds.

Empirical Results

Using the various estimates of transaction costs in foreign exchange (t_S and t_F) and the modal estimates of the cost of transactions in securities (t and t*) the neutral band around the interest parity line was computed. In the absence of information on the bid-ask spreads in the U.K. and Canadian Treasury Bill markets, we assume that they are equal to the spread on U.S. Treasury Bills, that is, t=t*, which may introduce a downward bias in the estimate of these costs. Since no estimates of transaction costs in Euro-dollar and Euro-sterling deposits are available for the period 1962/67, we again assume that they are equal to the spread on U.S. Treasury Bills. This also may result in a conservative estimate of transaction costs.

Table 4.2 reports the fraction of the observations bound within the neutral band in each period, both for the traditional as well as the external pairs of securities. In computing the neutral band, arbitragers are assumed to start from two alternative initial positions: first, where the initial position is in securities, the cost corresponds to Ω; and second, where the initial position is in cash, the cost corresponds to Ω'.

Table 4.2 suggests several comparisons. First, the percentage of observations bound when the arbitrage is between securities traded in the external market is consistently greater than for the traditional pair of securities. Second, when arbitragers begin with cash (Ω') rather than securities (Ω), the neutral band is narrower and fewer observations are bound. As a practical matter, the difference between the two cases (Ω and Ω') appears small. Third, the fraction of observations bounded in arbitrage between U.S. dollars and U.K. sterling and between U.S. dollars and Canadian dollars appears similar, except in the turbulent peg period.

Finally, Table 4.2 allows us to analyze the results across periods. The data suggest that transaction costs play a very similar and significant role

Table 4.2. Transaction Costs and Neutral Band for 90-Day Covered Arbitrage

Period	Arbitrage Between Securities Denominated in	t_S and t_F Estimated as	Observations Bounded Within Neutral Band (%)			
			Traditional Pair		External Pair	
			Ω	Ω'	Ω	Ω'
January 1962 to	$U.S. and £	DM	87.0	82.4	99.7	99.3
November 1967	$U.S. and £	$C	87.0	82.1	99.7	99.3
	$U.S. and $C	$C	87.6	82.1	N.A.	N.A.
January 1968 to	$U.S. and £	DM	36.9	35.0	97.1	87.4
December 1969	$U.S. and £	$C	33.0	30.1	94.2	69.9
	$U.S. and $C	$C	67.0	63.1	N.A.	N.A.
July 1973 to	$U.S. and £	DM	89.7	87.6	100.0	99.0
May 1975	$U.S. and £	$C	84.5	81.4	99.0	99.0
	$U.S. and $C	$C	99.0	99.0	100.0	100.0

during the quiet peg (1962/67) and the managed float (1973/74) periods. In both of these periods, transaction costs account for a similar fraction of deviations from interest rate parity; even though transaction costs estimates differ by a factor of from six to ten, for these two periods.

During these two periods the role played by transaction costs in accounting for deviations from interest rate parity was almost invariant with respect to the arbitraged assets. The observation that similar fractions of the deviations from parity are explained by transaction costs supports the conclusion that, in spite of the large differences in the estimated costs, there has been no fundamental structural change concerning the relative role of transaction costs, despite the institutional changes in the exchange rate regime.

During the turbulent peg period (1968/69), transaction costs account for a much smaller proportion of the deviations from parity. Moreover, the fraction of the deviations that is explained by transaction costs differs between the pairs of the arbitraged assets. For traditional assets in U.S. dollar-U.K. sterling arbitrage, the neutral band contains two-thirds of the cases; in U.S. dollar-Canadian dollar arbitrage, only one-third of the cases are bound. It thus seems that unlike the periods 1962/67 and 1973/75, the traditional pair of securities was not comparable during the period 1968/69. Many elements of incomparability apparently are removed when arbitrage is within the Euro-currency market.

Overall, the results indicate that a large fraction of the deviations from interest rate parity can be explained by transaction costs—especially in the quiet peg and managed float periods. This evidence, along with evidence from Chapter III, suggests that it may be constructive to classify periods by the extent of turbulence or speculative pressures in the forward market rather than by the formal arrangement in the foreign exchange markets (e.g., pegged or flexible rate systems).

Transaction costs do not provide a complete explanation for deviations from interest parity. In the following section, an additional explanation is examined.

ACCOUNTING FOR THE RESIDUAL—THE ROLE OF TIMING[7]

The timing of transactions suggests a possible explanation for the residual profit opportunities. If there is a time interval between the receipt of information signaling arbitrage profit opportunities and the actual execution of the (four) arbitrage transactions, investors face the risk that quoted prices may change. In this case, covered arbitrage is not risk-free.[8] The fact that *ex post* calculations indicate the existence of profit opportunities does not imply that an investor could have devised an *ex ante* trading rule to capture these profits.

Investors err when they fail to exploit such profit opportunities. If the market is efficient, errors of this type should not occur. Therefore, the analysis should verify two points: that the reported prices correspond to actual transaction prices; and that the information conveyed *ex post* was available *ex ante*.

The first point pertains to the data base. Typically the data reported (e.g., in the *Federal Reserve Bulletin*) is "consensus" data; that is, the source has sampled various market makers, in various locations, perhaps, at various points in time.[9] Therefore, it cannot be inferred that investors actually transacted and therefore made profits at these reported prices.

The second point raises the issue of a possible lag between the receipt of information signaling arbitrage profit opportunities and the actual execution of the arbitrage transactions. When lags exist, quoted prices may change to eliminate profit opportunities. In this case, profit opportunities may be illusory in the sense that (1) arbitragers view the situation as a risky investment opportunity, or (2) that arbitragers could not act quickly enough to exploit the situation.

To examine the consequences of a possible lag, a simple trading rule is formulated and tested. Assume investors receive information at period t. Whenever they calculate a profit opportunity (after allowing for transaction costs), arbitrage transactions are executed at period t + 1 (at the prices prevailing at t+1). Table 4.3 summarizes the results of this trading rule for the alternative measures of the cost of transactions and for the alternative assumptions concerning the initial positions of arbitragers. If investors are able to transact at quoted prices in period t, there would be N profit opportunities—the N points outside the neutral band. The implied mean percentage profit is indicated in the corresponding entry with a t-statistic in parentheses below the mean. For example, during 1962/67 the mean percentage profit would have been about 0.05%, while during 1973/75 it would have been about 0.2%. However, when actual transactions are delayed until t+1, the mean percentage profit is

Table 4.3. Mean Percentage Profits of a Simple Trading Rule (Traditional Pair)

				t		t+1	
	t_S and t_F	N		Mean Profit		Mean Profit	
Period	Estimated as	Ω	Ω'	Ω	Ω'	Ω	Ω'
January 1962 to	DM	40	54	0.055	0.058	0.038	0.045
November 1967				(7.2)	(8.4)	(3.7)	(5.4)
	$C	40	55	0.056	0.058	0.039	0.044
				(7.3)	(8.4)	(3.8)	(5.4)
	$C	38	55	0.058	0.058	0.046	0.041
				(7.8)	(8.7)	(3.8)	(4.2)
January 1968 to	DM	65	67	0.577	0.585	0.540	0.550
December 1969				(9.6)	(9.8)	(8.3)	(8.6)
	$C	69	72	0.606	0.607	0.572	0.586
				(10.2)	(10.4)	(9.1)	(9.4)
	$C	34	38	0.107	0.120	0.086	0.102
				(6.8)	(7.9)	(4.1)	(5.2)
July 1973 to	DM	10	12	0.261	0.272	0.076	0.097
May 1975				(4.3)	(4.6)	(0.8)	(1.1)
	$C	15	18	0.304	0.306	0.115	0.187
				(5.1)	(5.3)	(1.2)	(2.0)
January 1968 to	DM	3	13	0.310	0.154	−0.319	−0.210
December 1969				(4.1)	(3.2)	(6.4)	(2.7)
(External Pair)	$C	6	31	0.193	0.104	−0.357	−0.055
				(2.2)	(3.9)	(3.08)	(1.5)

Note: t-statistic in parentheses.

reduced to about 0.04% during 1962/67 and to about zero during 1973/75.

The period 1968/69 again is an exception. During that period the number of apparent profit opportunities as well as the mean rate of profit is high, and the simple trading rule still leaves relatively high and statistically significant profits. However, as argued before, during that period the traditional pairs of securities do not seem to be comparable and thus, they do not seem to be appropriate for the analysis of covered interest arbitrage. Indeed, when the same computation is applied to the external pair of securities (see the last panel of Table 4.3) the positive and significant mean percentage profit implied if transactions could be executed at t, result in significant losses under the simple trading rule.

The final result indicates that market forces act to eliminate arbitrage profit opportunities in the external markets. However, a conclusive test of the trading rule requires much more refined data than used in the present computation. Ideally, the difference between t and t+1 should approximate the reaction time of arbitragers. This would require observations on consecutive transactions or, at least, daily data. Since the results of Table 4.3 are based on weekly data, they should be viewed only as illustrative.

CONCLUSIONS

This chapter presented a test of hypothesis one. Transaction costs were explicitly introduced into the interest parity model. The proper test of market efficiency is to check that a large fraction of observations is within a neutral band around the equilibrium line. If arbitragers require a time interval to adjust to new information, then observations may exist temporarily outside the neutral band.

The major empirical conclusions are that transaction costs appear to account for many of the observed deviations from interest parity. Even though transaction costs have increased, these costs play a similar quantitative role in accounting for deviations from parity during the quiet peg (1962/67) and managed float (1973/75) periods. The turbulent peg period (1968/69) is an exception. The data suggest that after adjusting the reported data to fit the one-period model, allowing for transaction costs, and ensuring that the arbitraged assets are comparable, there are few unexploited opportunities for profit. In external markets, when profit opportunities do appear, they are quickly bid away. Overall, the evidence supports the view that the international capital market is efficient in that there are few unexploited opportunities for risk-free profit in covered interest arbitrage. Therefore, we cannot reject hypothesis one.

COVERED INTEREST ARBITRAGE IN THE PERIOD 1967/75

In this section we test several hypotheses concerning covered interest arbitrage. The formulation (4.1) in Chapter IV refers to *the* domestic currency and foreign currency interest rates—r_d and r_f. In practice, there are numerous interest rates and therefore numerous interest rate parity conditions.

Table 4.4. Frequency Distribution for Deviations from Interest Rate Parity and Other Summary Statistics: Weekly Observations 1967/75

BIN	CASE 1	CASE 2	CASE 3	CASE 4	CASE 5	CASE 6	CASE 7	CASE 8	CASE 9	CASE 10
X< −5.00	0.00	0.00	0.00	0.00	0.00	0.00	0.00	0.00	0.00	0.00
−5.00 <X< −4.00	0.00	0.00	0.00	0.00	0.00	0.00	0.00	0.00	0.00	0.00
−4.00 <X< −3.00	0.00	0.00	0.00	0.00	0.00	0.00	0.00	0.00	0.00	0.72
−3.00 <X< −2.00	0.00	0.00	0.00	0.00	0.00	0.24	0.00	0.00	0.00	0.00
−2.00 <X< −1.75	0.00	0.00	0.00	0.00	0.00	0.94	0.00	0.00	0.24	0.00
−1.75 <X< −1.50	0.00	0.00	0.00	0.00	0.00	0.94	0.00	0.00	0.00	0.00
−1.50 <X< −1.25	0.00	0.00	0.00	0.00	0.00	2.82	0.00	0.00	0.00	0.00
−1.25 <X< −1.00	0.00	0.00	0.00	0.47	0.00	2.59	0.00	0.00	0.00	2.90
−1.00 <X< −0.75	0.00	0.00	0.00	0.70	0.71	5.18	0.00	0.24	0.24	3.62
−0.75 <X< −0.50	0.70	0.00	0.47	3.29	0.71	7.76	0.00	0.48	1.94	17.39
−0.50 <X< −0.25	12.33	0.47	5.63	6.57	5.71	13.88	1.67	2.38	13.32	34.78
−0.25 <X< 0.00	38.60	95.07	81.46	74.88	77.86	28.94	80.48	76.25	69.49	28.99
0.00 <X< 0.25	33.26	4.23	11.97	12.21	13.57	26.82	17.62	20.43	14.29	8.70
0.25 <X< 0.50	11.86	0.00	0.47	1.64	0.71	6.82	0.00	0.00	0.24	2.90
0.50 <X< 0.75	2.56	0.23	0.00	0.23	0.00	2.82	0.24	0.24	0.24	0.00

	Case 1	Case 2	Case 3	Case 4	Case 5	Case 6	Case 7	Case 8	Case 9	Case 10
0.75 <X< 1.00	0.70	0.00	0.00	0.00	0.71	0.24	0.00	0.00	0.00	0.00
1.00 <X< 1.25	0.00	0.00	0.00	0.00	0.00	0.00	0.00	0.00	0.00	0.00
1.25 <X< 1.50	0.00	0.00	0.00	0.00	0.00	0.00	0.00	0.00	0.00	0.00
1.50 <X< 1.75	0.00	0.00	0.00	0.00	0.00	0.00	0.00	0.00	0.00	0.00
1.75 <X< 2.00	0.00	0.00	0.00	0.00	0.00	0.00	0.00	0.00	0.00	0.00
2.00 <X< 3.00	0.00	0.00	0.00	0.00	0.00	0.00	0.00	0.00	0.00	0.00
3.00 <X< 4.00	0.00	0.00	0.00	0.00	0.00	0.00	0.00	0.00	0.00	0.00
4.00 <X< 5.00	0.00	0.00	0.00	0.00	0.00	0.00	0.00	0.00	0.00	0.00
5.00 <X	0.00	0.00	0.00	0.00	0.00	0.00	0.00	0.00	0.00	0.00
MINIMUM	−0.65	−0.28	−0.73	−1.24	−0.75	−2.11	−0.44	−0.99	−1.87	−3.12
MEDIAN	−0.01	−0.03	−0.05	−0.07	−0.09	−0.11	−0.02	−0.03	−0.09	−0.29
MAXIMUM	0.86	0.71	0.38	0.57	0.87	0.87	0.69	0.66	0.75	0.44
NOBS	430.00	426.00	426.00	426.00	140.00	425.00	420.00	421.00	413.00	138.00

Case 1: Canada, 3-month Treasury Bill rate.
Case 2: Canada, 1-month Euro-currency deposit rate.
Case 3: Canada, 3-month Euro-currency deposit rate.
Case 4: Canada, 6-month Euro-currency deposit rate.
Case 5: Canada, 12-month Euro-currency deposit rate.
Case 6: United Kingdom, 3-month Treasury Bill rate.
Case 7: United Kingdom, 1-month Euro-currency deposit rate.
Case 8: United Kingdom, 3-month Euro-currency deposit rate.
Case 9: United Kingdom, 6-month Euro-currency deposit rate.
Case 10: United Kingdom, 12-month Euro-currency deposit rate.

continued

Table 4.4. continued

BIN	CASE 11	CASE 12	CASE 13	CASE 14	CASE 15	CASE 16	CASE 17	CASE 18	CASE 19	CASE 20
X< -5.00	0.00	0.00	0.00	0.00	0.00	0.00	0.00	0.00	0.00	0.00
-5.00 <X< -4.00	0.00	0.00	0.00	0.27	0.00	0.00	0.00	0.00	0.00	0.00
-4.00 <X< -3.00	0.00	0.00	0.25	0.27	2.96	0.00	0.00	0.00	0.00	0.00
-3.00 <X< -2.00	0.72	0.00	0.00	1.91	11.11	0.00	0.00	0.00	0.56	0.72
-2.00 <X< -1.75	0.48	0.25	0.25	0.82	4.44	0.00	0.00	0.00	0.28	0.00
-1.75 <X< -1.50	0.72	0.00	0.75	1.09	10.37	0.00	0.00	0.00	0.28	2.16
-1.50 <X< -1.25	1.21	0.00	1.00	2.18	6.67	0.00	0.00	0.26	1.11	5.76
-1.25 <X< -1.00	1.69	0.00	1.25	2.45	5.93	0.54	0.00	0.79	1.39	2.88
-1.00 <X< -0.75	1.69	1.75	1.50	2.72	1.48	0.00	0.27	1.06	4.18	12.95
-0.75 <X< -0.50	1.45	2.24	4.50	4.90	2.96	0.00	0.27	2.11	7.80	13.67
-0.50 <X< -0.25	4.35	5.74	6.25	10.63	5.93	0.00	5.57	10.55	15.32	29.50
-0.25 <X< 0.00	12.80	74.06	53.00	43.05	11.11	7.57	87.80	75.46	59.33	27.34
0.00 <X< 0.25	24.15	12.72	25.25	18.26	13.33	22.16	4.77	7.39	6.96	4.32
0.25 <X< 0.50	26.57	1.75	2.50	6.54	9.63	34.05	0.53	0.79	1.11	0.72
0.50 <X< 0.75	16.67	0.75	1.50	1.63	4.44	24.86	0.53	0.26	0.28	0.00
0.75 <X< 1.00	3.62	0.25	1.00	1.63	6.67	1.08	0.00	0.00	0.00	0.00
1.00 <X< 1.25	1.45	0.25	0.75	0.82	1.48	0.54	0.00	0.53	0.28	0.00

	1.25 <X< 1.50	1.50 <X< 1.75	1.75 <X< 2.00	2.00 <X< 3.00	3.00 <X< 4.00	4.00 <X< 5.00	5.00 <X	MINIMUM	MEDIAN	MAXIMUM	NOBS
Case 11	1.21	0.48	0.48	0.24	0.00	0.00	0.00	-2.86	0.25	2.57	414.00
Case 12	0.25	0.00	0.00	0.00	0.00	0.00	0.00	-1.94	-0.05	1.28	401.00
Case 13	0.00	0.25	0.00	0.00	0.00	0.00	0.00	-3.18	-0.05	1.74	400.00
Case 14	0.54	0.27	0.00	0.00	0.00	0.00	0.00	-4.00	-0.10	1.51	367.00
Case 15	0.74	0.74	0.00	0.00	0.00	0.00	0.00	-3.67	-0.30	1.53	135.00
Case 16	0.54	4.32	0.54	3.24	0.54	0.00	0.00	-1.01	0.42	3.21	185.00
Case 17	0.00	0.27	0.00	0.00	0.00	0.00	0.00	-0.82	-0.06	1.52	377.00
Case 18	0.53	0.00	0.26	0.00	0.00	0.00	0.00	-1.47	-0.08	1.97	379.00
Case 19	0.28	0.56	0.00	0.28	0.00	0.00	0.00	-2.73	-0.13	2.07	359.00
Case 20	0.00	0.00	0.00	0.00	0.00	0.00	0.00	-2.14	-0.38	0.34	139.00

Case 11: Belgium, 3-month Treasury Bill rate.
Case 12: Belgium, 1-month Euro-currency deposit rate.
Case 13: Belgium, 3-month Euro-currency deposit rate.
Case 14: Belgium, 6-month Euro-currency deposit rate.
Case 15: Belgium, 12-month Euro-currency deposit rate.
Case 16: France, 3-month Treasury Bill rate.
Case 17: France, 1-month Euro-currency deposit rate.
Case 18: France, 3-month Euro-currency deposit rate.
Case 19: France, 6-month Euro-currency deposit rate.
Case 20: France, 12-month Euro-currency deposit rate.

continued

Table 4.4. continued

BIN	CASE 21	CASE 22	CASE 23	CASE 24	CASE 25	CASE 26	CASE 27	CASE 28	CASE 29	CASE 30
X< −5.00	0.00	0.00	0.00	0.00	0.00	0.00	0.00	0.00	0.00	0.93
−5.00 <X< −4.00	0.00	0.00	0.00	0.00	0.00	1.19	0.00	0.00	0.28	0.93
−4.00 <X< −3.00	0.00	0.00	0.00	0.00	0.00	7.51	0.00	0.00	0.00	5.56
−3.00 <X< −2.00	0.00	0.00	0.00	0.00	0.71	11.46	0.00	0.53	1.13	20.37
−2.00 <X< −1.75	0.00	0.00	0.00	0.00	0.00	1.19	0.00	0.00	1.41	6.48
−1.75 <X< −1.50	0.00	0.00	0.00	0.00	0.00	6.72	0.00	0.00	1.69	6.48
−1.50 <X< −1.25	0.00	0.00	0.24	0.00	0.00	5.14	0.00	0.00	3.39	4.63
−1.25 <X< −1.00	0.71	0.00	0.00	0.00	0.00	6.72	0.27	2.67	4.24	10.19
−1.00 <X< −0.75	1.18	0.00	0.00	0.00	0.00	7.51	2.67	4.81	5.93	17.59
−0.75 <X< −0.50	5.67	0.24	0.95	1.18	2.14	2.37	3.48	7.49	13.84	11.11
−0.50 <X< −0.25	17.26	81.32	69.74	1.65	10.71	7.51	9.36	18.45	26.55	4.63
−0.25 <X< 0.00	26.95	17.73	29.08	58.87	43.57	4.35	79.41	60.70	36.44	8.33
0.00 <X< 0.25	19.62	0.47	0.00	34.52	35.71	6.72	4.28	5.08	4.52	0.93
0.25 <X< 0.50	13.24	0.00	0.00	3.07	6.43	6.72	0.27	0.00	0.00	0.00
0.50 <X< 0.75	9.46	0.24	0.00	0.71	0.71	12.25	0.27	0.27	0.28	0.93
0.75 <X< 1.00	3.07	0.00	0.00	0.00	0.00	8.70	0.00	0.00	0.00	0.93
1.00 <X< 1.25	0.71	0.00	0.00	0.00	0.00	3.56	0.00	0.00	0.00	0.00
1.25 <X< 1.50		0.00	0.00	0.00	0.00	0.40	0.00	0.00	0.28	0.00

		Case 21	Case 22	Case 23	Case 24	Case 25	Case 26	Case 27	Case 28	Case 29	Case 30
1.50 <X<	1.75	0.71	0.00	0.00	0.00	0.00	0.00	0.00	0.00	0.00	0.00
1.75 <X<	2.00	1.47	0.00	0.00	0.00	0.00	0.00	0.00	0.00	0.00	0.00
2.00 <X<	3.00	0.00	0.00	0.00	0.00	0.00	0.00	0.00	0.00	0.00	0.00
3.00 <X<	4.00	0.00	0.00	0.00	0.00	0.00	0.00	0.00	0.00	0.00	0.00
4.00 <X<	5.00	0.00	0.00	0.00	0.00	0.00	0.00	0.00	0.00	0.00	0.00
5.00 <X		0.00	0.00	0.00	0.00	0.00	0.00	0.00	0.00	0.00	0.00
MINIMUM		−0.83	−1.14	−0.26	−0.75	−2.31	−4.39	−1.03	−2.33	−4.16	−8.20
MEDIAN		0.22	−0.02	−0.02	−0.02	−0.05	−0.48	−0.10	−0.17	−0.31	−1.09
MAXIMUM		1.93	0.22	0.79	0.60	0.58	1.45	0.59	0.66	1.36	0.94
NOBS		423.00	423.00	423.00	423.00	140.00	253.00	374.00	374.00	354.00	108.00

Case 21: Germany, 3-month Treasury Bill rate.
Case 22: Germany, 1-month Euro-currency deposit rate.
Case 23: Germany, 3-month Euro-currency deposit rate.
Case 24: Germany, 6-month Euro-currency deposit rate.
Case 25: Germany, 12-month Euro-currency deposit rate.
Case 26: Italy, 3-month Treasury Bill rate.
Case 27: Italy, 1-month Euro-currency deposit rate.
Case 28: Italy, 3-month Euro-currency deposit rate.
Case 29: Italy, 6-month Euro-currency deposit rate.
Case 30: Italy, 12-month Euro-currency deposit rate.

continued

Table 4.4. continued

BIN	CASE 31	CASE 32	CASE 33	CASE 34	CASE 35	CASE 36	CASE 37	CASE 38	CASE 39	CASE 40
X< −5.00	0.00	0.00	0.00	0.00	0.00	0.00	0.00	0.00	0.00	2.56
−5.00 <X< −4.00	0.00	0.00	0.00	0.00	0.00	0.00	0.00	0.00	0.00	2.81
−4.00 <X< −3.00	0.00	0.00	0.00	0.00	0.00	0.00	0.00	0.00	0.00	3.58
−3.00 <X< −2.00	0.00	0.00	0.00	0.00	0.00	0.00	0.00	0.00	0.00	8.70
−2.00 <X< −1.75	0.00	0.00	0.00	0.00	0.00	0.00	0.00	0.00	0.00	4.60
−1.75 <X< −1.50	0.00	0.00	0.00	0.00	0.71	0.00	0.00	0.00	0.00	4.86
−1.50 <X< −1.25	0.00	0.00	0.00	0.00	0.00	15.15	0.00	0.00	0.00	5.37
−1.25 <X< −1.00	0.00	0.00	0.00	0.00	0.00	21.21	0.00	0.00	0.00	3.58
−1.00 <X< −0.75	0.00	0.00	0.00	0.26	2.86	15.15	0.00	0.00	0.00	4.60
−0.75 <X< −0.50	0.59	0.00	0.00	0.53	2.86	21.21	0.00	0.00	0.24	5.88
−0.50 <X< −0.25	5.60	0.47	2.37	2.91	21.43	27.27	0.71	0.94	3.76	8.18
−0.25 <X< 0.00	13.57	91.23	82.23	72.49	50.00	0.00	89.41	73.88	63.76	18.16
0.00 <X< 0.25	42.77	7.58	15.17	22.22	17.86	0.00	9.41	24.71	30.59	17.14
0.25 <X< 0.50	16.22	0.24	0.00	1.32	2.86	0.00	0.00	0.24	0.94	2.81
0.50 <X< 0.75	8.85	0.24	0.24	0.26	0.71	0.00	0.47	0.00	0.47	1.79
0.75 <X< 1.00	5.90	0.24	0.00	0.00	0.71	0.00	0.00	0.00	0.00	1.28
1.00 <X< 1.25	4.42	0.00	0.00	0.00	0.00	0.00	0.00	0.00	0.00	0.51

	Case 31	Case 32	Case 33	Case 34	Case 35	Case 36	Case 37	Case 38	Case 39	Case 40
1.25 <X< 1.50	1.77	0.00	0.00	0.00	0.00	0.00	0.00	0.00	0.00	0.26
1.50 <X< 1.75	0.29	0.00	0.00	0.00	0.00	0.00	0.00	0.00	0.00	0.77
1.75 <X< 2.00	0.00	0.00	0.00	0.00	0.00	0.00	0.00	0.00	0.00	0.51
2.00 <X< 3.00	0.00	0.00	0.00	0.00	0.00	0.00	0.00	0.24	0.00	1.28
3.00 <X< 4.00	0.00	0.00	0.00	0.00	0.00	0.00	0.00	0.00	0.24	0.00
4.00 <X< 5.00	0.00	0.00	0.00	0.00	0.00	0.00	0.00	0.00	0.00	0.51
5.00 <X	0.00	0.00	0.00	0.00	0.00	0.00	0.00	0.00	0.00	0.26
MINIMUM	−0.55	−0.39	−0.47	−0.82	−1.61	−1.11	−0.29	−0.44	−0.71	−6.74
MEDIAN	0.17	−0.03	−0.04	−0.04	−0.13	−0.52	−0.03	−0.02	−0.03	−0.40
MAXIMUM	1.57	0.82	0.55	0.50	0.78	0.00	0.66	2.05	3.31	6.96
NOBS	339.00	422.00	422.00	378.00	140.00	33.00	425.00	425.00	425.00	391.00

Case 31: Netherlands, 3-month Treasury Bill rate.
Case 32: Netherlands, 1-month Euro-currency rate.
Case 33: Netherlands, 3-month Euro-currency rate.
Case 34: Netherlands, 6-month Euro-currency rate.
Case 35: Netherlands, 12-month Euro-currency rate.
Case 36: Switzerland, 3-month Treasury Bill rate.
Case 37: Switzerland, 1-month Euro-currency rate.
Case 38: Switzerland, 3-month Euro-currency rate.
Case 39: Switzerland, 6-month Euro-currency rate.
Case 40: Switzerland, 12-month Euro-currency rate.

continued

Table 4.4. continued

BIN	CASE 41	CASE 42	CASE 43	CASE 44	CASE 45	CASE 46	CASE 47	CASE 48	CASE 49	CASE 50
X< −5.00	0.00	0.00	0.00	0.00	0.00	0.00	0.00	0.00	0.00	0.00
−5.00 <X< −4.00	0.00	0.00	0.00	0.00	0.00	0.00	0.00	0.00	0.00	0.00
−4.00 <X< −3.00	0.00	0.00	0.00	0.00	0.00	0.00	0.00	0.00	0.00	0.00
−3.00 <X< −2.00	0.00	0.00	0.00	0.00	0.00	0.00	0.00	0.00	1.18	3.39
−2.00 <X< −1.75	0.00	0.00	0.00	0.00	0.00	0.00	0.00	0.00	1.65	1.45
−1.75 <X< −1.50	0.00	0.00	0.00	0.00	0.00	0.00	1.65	1.42	1.65	1.21
−1.50 <X< −1.25	0.00	0.00	0.00	0.23	0.24	0.47	0.71	0.94	0.94	1.69
−1.25 <X< −1.00	0.00	0.00	0.00	0.00	0.00	0.71	1.89	1.18	2.83	3.15
−1.00 <X< −0.75	0.00	0.00	0.00	0.00	0.00	2.84	3.55	2.36	4.01	1.45
−0.75 <X< −0.50	0.00	0.00	0.00	0.23	3.35	6.38	9.69	4.95	2.59	2.42
−0.50 <X< −0.25	0.00	0.00	0.23	2.57	6.22	35.93	28.84	6.37	4.95	4.12
−0.25 <X< 0.00	34.11	23.72	17.52	15.19	15.31	52.25	45.63	22.17	10.38	6.30
0.00 <X< 0.25	65.89	71.86	65.19	42.29	33.73	1.42	7.09	41.04	18.16	12.11
0.25 <X< 0.50	0.00	4.42	12.38	32.71	27.99	0.00	0.95	16.75	29.95	19.37
0.50 <X< 0.75	0.00	0.00	2.57	5.61	10.29	0.00	0.00	1.65	16.04	22.03
0.75 <X< 1.00	0.00	0.00	1.87	0.93	1.91	0.00	0.00	0.94	4.01	12.35
1.00 <X< 1.25	0.00	0.00	0.23	0.00	0.48	0.00	0.00	0.00	0.71	5.33
1.25 <X< 1.50	0.00	0.00	0.00	0.00	0.24	0.00	0.00	0.24	0.71	1.45
1.50 <X< 1.75	0.00	0.00	0.00	0.23	0.00	0.00	0.00	0.00	0.00	0.24

		Case 41	Case 42	Case 43	Case 44	Case 45	Case 46	Case 47	Case 48	Case 49	Case 50
1.75 <X<	2.00	0.00	0.00	0.00	0.24	0.00	0.00	0.00	0.00	0.00	1.21
2.00 <X<	3.00	0.00	0.00	0.00	0.00	0.00	0.00	0.00	0.00	0.00	0.48
3.00 <X<	4.00	0.00	0.00	0.00	0.00	0.00	0.00	0.00	0.24	0.00	0.00
4.00 <X<	5.00	0.00	0.00	0.00	0.00	0.00	0.00	0.00	0.00	0.00	0.00
5.00 <X		0.00	0.00	0.00	0.00	0.00	0.00	0.00	0.00	0.00	0.24
MINIMUM		−0.18	−0.25	−0.28	−1.47	−1.42	−1.10	−1.42	−1.67	−2.39	−2.82
MEDIAN		0.02	0.05	0.10	0.20	0.20	0.01	0.02	0.07	0.27	0.43
MAXIMUM		0.20	0.49	1.02	1.53	1.89	0.47	0.68	1.45	3.72	6.27
NOBS		428.00	430.00	428.00	428.00	418.00	423.00	423.00	424.00	424.00	413.00

Case 41: Canada prime finance, 30 days.
Case 42: Canada prime finance, 60 days.
Case 43: Canada prime finance, 90 days.
Case 44: Canada prime finance, 180 days.
Case 45: Canada prime finance, 270 days.
Case 46: United Kingdom hire purchase, 30 days.
Case 47: United Kingdom hire purchase, 60 days.
Case 48: United Kingdom hire purchase, 90 days.
Case 49: United Kingdom hire purchase, 180 days.
Case 50: United Kingdom hire purchase, 270 days.

Several interest rates—Treasury Bill rates, a term structure of external currency deposit rates and a term structure of commercial paper rates—for several countries are reported in the Harris Bank *Weekly Review*. Estimates of the percentage deviation (D) from interest rate parity are calculated

$$D = \frac{F - S}{S} - \frac{r_d - r_f}{1 + r_f}.$$

The deviations are calculated for all sample countries using a maximum of 430 weekly observations for the sample period January 3, 1967 to May 9, 1975. Missing observations are excluded.

The results are reported in Table 4.4. For each case, a frequency distribution for D is displayed. Cases are classified according to currency, maturity, and financial instrument. Each case presumes that the covered arbitrage is against a similar U.S. dollar financial instrument of the same maturity. For example, Case 1 is 3-month Canadian dollar Treasury Bills arbitraged against 3-month U.S. dollar Treasury Bills. There are 430 weekly observations and 12.33% of the deviations (D) are between −0.50% and −0.25%. In Case 49, 180-day U.K. Hire Purchase is arbitraged against 180-day U.S. commercial paper. There are 424 weekly observations and 16.04% of the deviations (D) are between 0.50% and 0.75%.

Analysis

Since we use three factors—currency, maturity, and financial instrument—to classify each case, the analysis compares results across each factor, while holding the other two factors constant. Three summary tables are constructed which report the percentage of observations bounded by a 0.25% neutral band—that is, deviations less than 0.25% and greater than −0.25%.

Table 4.5 reports on country comparisons for three separate maturity-financial instrument combinations. There is clearly a wide variation across countries. In the 12-month external deposit comparison, the difference between Canada and Italy is nearly a factor of ten. The percentage of points bounded by this .25% band is consistent with the hypothesis that transaction costs and other factors which contribute to deviations from interest parity vary considerably across countries.

Table 4.5. Country Comparisons—Percentage of Deviations from Interest Parity Within ± .25%

	3-Month Treasury Bills		12-Month External Deposit		180 Day Commercial Paper	
Country	Case No.[a]	P[b]	Case No.	P	Case No.	P
Canada	1	71.86	5	91.41	44	57.48
United Kingdom	6	55.76	10	37.69	49	28.54
Belgium	11	36.95	15	24.43	—	—
France	16	29.73	20	31.66	—	—
Germany	21	44.21	25	79.28	—	—
Italy	26	11.07	30	9.26	—	—
Netherlands	31	56.37	35	67.86	—	—
Switzerland	36	27.27	40	35.30	—	—

[a] See Table 4.4.
[b] Percentage of deviations within ± .25%.

Tables 4.4 and 4.6 are useful for analyzing the effect of maturity. In Table 4.4 consider cases 2-5, 7-10, 12-15, 17-20, 22-25, 27-30, 32-35, 37-40, 41-45, and 46-50 as groups of similar assets with increasing term to maturity. The deviations always increase with maturity, suggesting that transaction costs are higher in longer maturity forward markets and security markets.

However, the effect of maturity does not seem to be similar across countries. Table 4.6 illustrates that for 3-month external Canadian deposits, 93.43% of the observations are within our sample neutral band. At

Table 4.6. Maturity Comparisons—Percentage of Deviations from Interest Parity Within ± .25%

	3-Month External Deposit		12-Month External Deposit		Difference
Country	Case No.[a]	P[b]	Case No.	P	$P_3 - P_{12}$
Canada	3	93.43	5	91.41	2.02
United Kingdom	8	96.68	10	37.69	58.99
Belgium	13	78.25	15	24.43	53.82
France	18	82.85	20	31.66	51.19
Germany	23	98.82	25	79.28	19.54
Italy	28	65.78	30	9.26	56.52
Netherlands	33	97.40	35	67.86	29.66
Switzerland	38	78.59	40	35.30	33.29

[a] See Table 4.4.
[b] Percentage of deviations within ± .25%.

Table 4.7. Instrument Comparisons—Percentage of Deviations from Interest Parity Within ± .25%

	Canada				United Kingdom			
	3-Month		6-Month		3-Month		6-Month	
Instrument	Case No.[a]	P[b]	Case No.	P	Case No.	P	Case No.	P
Treasury Bill	1	71.86	—	—	6	55.76	—	—
External Deposit	3	93.43	4	87.09	8	96.68	9	83.78
Commercial Paper	43	82.71	44	57.48	48	63.21	49	

[a] See Table 4.4.
[b] Percentage of deviations within ± .25%.

the 12-month maturity, this percentage drops to 91.41%, a difference of 2.02 percentage points. At the other extreme, the drop for U.K. external deposits is 58.99%. An interpretation is that Canadian forward markets and external markets are much deeper in the range from three months to one year than the markets in U.K., Belgium, France, and Italy. Transaction costs may be significantly greater in these markets or arbitrage activities may be less.

Table 4.7 summarizes the deviations for two countries and three financial instruments. In both Canada and the U.K. the rankings are similar. The deviations from interest parity are smallest for external deposit rates, followed by commercial paper and then Treasury Bills. The results suggest that external deposits are more similar in terms of risk than Treasury Bills. We do not have direct information on transaction costs in commercial paper markets, however, international arbitrage appears to be more complete in this market than in Treasury Bills. The final column in Table 4.7 reports on the effect of maturity. At the 6-month maturity, the decrease in observations bounded is much greater for commercial paper than for external deposits. Since forward exchange transaction costs are the same, our interpretation is that transaction costs increase more in commercial paper markets than in external deposit markets.

NOTES

1. The example also applies to an outflow of covered arbitrage funds denominated in the domestic currency to funds denominated in a foreign currency. All transactions can

take place in a third country (e.g., an external center) so no funds need cross a political border.

2. We define transaction costs as the cost of liquidity services. This is the relevant cost for an investor without inside information who faces equilibrium prices.

3. Income taxes could also be analyzed in this framework. If a domestic investor faces a marginal income tax rate $t_{d,y}$ which is applicable to both foreign and domestic investments, we revise equations (4.2) and (4.3) so that $C' = C(1 - t_{d,y})$ and $R' = R(1 - t_{d,y})$. Introducing taxes does not effect the results.

If, however, the forward exchange gains are subject to capital gains tax ($t_{d,k}$) while the interest income is taxed at the ordinary income tax rate and $t_{d,k} < t_{d,y}$, the slope of the interest parity line changes. Equation (4.1) becomes:

$$\frac{F-S}{S} = \frac{r_d - r_f}{1 - r_f} \cdot \frac{(1 - t_{d,y})}{(1 - t_{d,k})}.$$

For example, if $t_{d,k} = 30\%$ and $t_{d,y} = 48\%$, ignoring transaction costs, the new parity line has a slope of .74 rather than 1.0. For more on these issues, see Levi (1977).

4. Since (4.4) and (4.7) are not homogeneous of degree zero in the interest rates, the width and shape of the band will depend on particular values of r_d and r_f. In this respect the graph is only a heuristic device.

5. The bankers discount formula is $i = (100-P) 360/D$ where i is the bankers discount yield, P the bond price as a percentage of par and D the number of days to maturity. For example, a 360-day bond priced at 95 would result in a 5% bankers discount yield. The holding period yield is $(100-95)/95 \doteq 5.26\%$.

Equation (4.1) is not homogeneous of degree zero with respect to the method of calculating yields, therefore, a bias is introduced. As an empirical matter, however, the difference between the two methods of interest rate calculation becomes significant only for high interest rates.

6. Similar issues were dealt with by Viscount Goschen in his attempt to reconcile what seemed to be unexploited profit opportunities:

> It may well be inquired—How is it possible that, in spite of the rapid flow of capital from one country to another to fill up any gaps that may have been left, such a difference in the rates of interest can exist between two countries as has occasionally been witnessed for some time in the case of England and the Continent?... This is a mystery which has puzzled many.... It is a question, however, which can be solved with the greatest ease.... It must not be forgotten that—the interest being taken at a percentage calculated per annum, and the probable profit having, when an operation in three-month bills is contemplated, to be divided by four, whereas, the percentage of expense has to be wholly borne by the one transaction—a very slight expense becomes a great impediment. If the cost is only 1/2 percent, there must be a profit of 2 percent per annum in the rate of interest, or 1/2 percent on three months, before any advantage commences: and thus, supposing that Paris capitalists calculate that they may send their gold over to England for 1/2 percent expense, and chance their being so favoured by the exchanges as to be able to draw it back without any cost at all, there must nevertheless be an excess of more than 2 percent in the London rate of interest over that in Paris, before the operation of sending gold over from France, merely for the sake of higher interest, will pay (Goschen 1864, pp. 139-143).

7. If the elasticities of demand and supply in the securities and the foreign exchange market are less than infinite, the neutral band will widen and will therefore account for a larger percentage of the deviations from interest parity. The exact formulae are developed

in Frenkel and Levich (1975). Given the cost of transactions and assuming all the elasticities are equal, the estimated values of the elasticities needed to account for all of the deviations from the interest parity line are very high, reaching many hundreds in all cases. These high values are not inconceivable given the highly competitive organization of the markets in question.

8. An additional source of risk, default on forward contracts, is assumed not to exist.

9. The Harris Bank *Weekly Review* is less subject to these problems. This source reports closing prices from Harris Bank quotation sheets.

Chapter V

Approaches to Forecasting Foreign Exchanges Rates—Theory

PURPOSE

The purpose of Chapter V is to develop a set of alternative forecasts for testing hypothesis two. There are three broad classes of models which could be used to forecast exchange rates—structural models, arbitrage models, and pure forecasting models. Our emphasis is on the last two classes.[1]

Several forecasting models are presented that use the market prices of financial claims as inputs. If these prices reflect information concerning future exchange rates, then the models should produce accurate and consistent forecasts.

Transaction costs and risk premia are analyzed since these factors may lead to forecasting errors. Systematic currency preferences and systematic premia for bearing exchange risk are also analyzed since these factors may lead to a forecasting bias. The chapter concludes with a discussion of several methodological issues, including the appropriate way to analyze forecasting performance.

ARBITRAGE AND SPECULATION MODELS

Interest Rate Based Forecasts

Some Algebra of Uncovered Interest Arbitrage. In this section, the basic Fisherian relationship between interest rates and exchange rates is developed. To begin, assume a world of perfect certainty and no transaction costs. An investor with the option of placing X units of domestic currency in a domestic asset or an equivalent amount of foreign currency in a foreign asset is indifferent when (5.1) holds.

$$(5.1) \qquad X(1 + r_{d,n})^n = \frac{X}{S_t}(1 + r_{f,n})^n S_{t+n}$$

where $r_{i,n}$ = n period return in currency i
S_j = spot exchange rate (domestic/foreign) at time j.

For the simple, one-period model, (5.1) can be rearranged to yield

$$(5.2) \qquad \dot{S} \equiv \frac{S_{t+1} - S_t}{S_t} = \frac{r_{d,1} - r_{f,1}}{1 + r_{f,1}}$$

We will denote (5.2) as the exact one-period Fisher Open effect (FO).[2] In other words, the discounted interest rate differential exactly equals the anticipated percentage change in the spot rate. Figure 5.1 displays this relationship.[3]

At time t, all values are known except S_{t+1}. The implied market forecast of S_{t+1} is

$$(5.3) \qquad \hat{S}_{t+1} = S_t \left(\frac{1 + r_d}{1 + r_f}\right).$$

Given a term structure of interest rates the implied market forecast of the term structure of exchange rates is

$$(5.4) \qquad \hat{S}_{t+n} = S_t \left(\frac{1 + r_{d,n}}{1 + r_{f,n}}\right)^n.$$

Equation (5.4) represents a simplification; to forecast the future spot rate we need only two inputs—the interest rates in both currencies. The cost is that we no longer see how underlying economic variables affect the exchange rate. Implicitly, we are acting as though equation (5.4) is the reduced form equation for the spot rate in a correctly specified

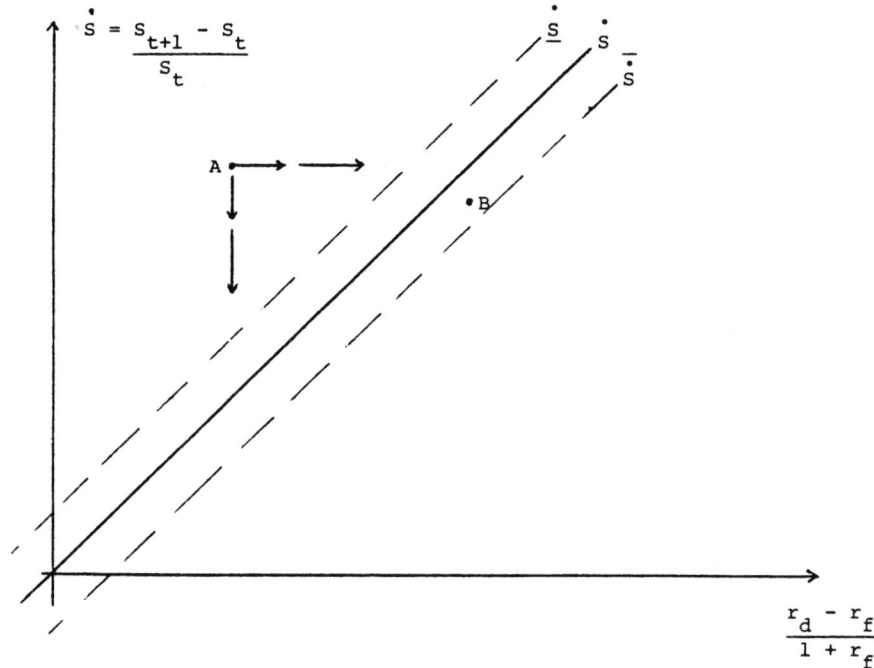

Figure 5.1.
The Fisher Open Effect

structural model. In effect, we rely on markets to be efficient processors of information.

The Effect of Transaction Costs. In this section we relax the assumption that transaction costs are zero. Positive transaction costs lead to a neutral band—around the parity line (5.2)—within which uncovered interest arbitrage is not profitable. Thus, points not on this parity line will lead to errors when we use (5.4) to forecast future spot exchange rates.

The formal analysis is analogous to the treatment of covered interest arbitrage in Chapter IV. In this case, a future spot transaction (at the price S_{t+1} and transaction cost t_S) replaces a forward transaction (at the price F_t and transaction cost t_F).

Equation (5.5) indicates the *lower* limit on $\dot{S}$ for which a marginal outflow of uncovered arbitrage funds is profitable.[4]

(5.5) $$\underline{\dot{S}} = \frac{(1 + r_d) - v(1 + r_f)}{v(1 + r_f)}$$

where

$$v = (1-t)(1-t_S)(1-t^*)(1-t_S)$$

The exchange rate forecast associated with this lower limit is

(5.6) $$\underline{\hat{S}}_{t+1} = \frac{S_t}{v} \frac{(1 + r_d)}{(1 + r_f)}.$$

Equation (5.7) indicates the *upper* limit on $\dot{S}$ for which marginal *inflow* of uncovered arbitrage funds is profitable:

(5.7) $$\overline{\dot{S}} = \frac{v(1 + r_d) - (1 + r_f)}{(1 + r_f)}.$$

The exchange rate forecast associated with this upper limit is

(5.8) $$\overline{\hat{S}}_{t+1} = vS_t \frac{(1 + r_d)}{(1 + r_f)}.$$

Conditions (5.5) and (5.7) define a neutral band in which marginal uncovered arbitrage flows are not profitable. The limits of this neutral band are illustrated in Figure 4.2:

(5.9) $$\overline{\dot{S}} \leq \dot{S} \leq \underline{\dot{S}}$$

Similarly, (5.6) and (5.8) define a neutral band on exchange rate forecasts:

(5.9') $$\overline{\hat{S}}_{t+1} \leq \hat{S}_{t+1} \leq \underline{\hat{S}}_{t+1}.$$

Given estimates of t, t*, and t_S we can apply (5.9) and (5.9') to test market efficiency and the accuracy of exchange rate forecasts (hypothesis two). The data in Chapter III suggest that t = 0.03%, t* = 0.1%, and t_S = 0.5% are reasonable estimates of these costs in the managed float period. In this case, v = 0.9887. Condition (5.9') suggests that a point forecast of S_{t+1} may be too high or too low by as much as 1.13%.

If market forces are efficient in assessing information about the future spot exchange rate, than a large fraction of sample observations should be bounded by the neutral band (5.9). In this case, we will not reject hypothesis two. However, if the fraction of observations bounded is low, there are two alternative conclusions. First, it may be that market participants are inefficient in processing exchange rate expectations. Second, it may be that (5.4) is not the correct reduced form model of exchange rates which market participants use to set prices. This conundrum is common to any data which reject market efficiency and empirically, there is no technique for distinguishing the correct conclusion.

Sources of Forecasting Bias.[5] In this section, we relax the assumption of perfect certainty. In this case, the future spot rate is a random variable, $\tilde{S}_{t+1}$. Equation (5.2) becomes

(5.10) $$\frac{r_d - r_f}{1 + r_f} = \tilde{\tilde{S}} + u$$

where $$\tilde{\tilde{S}} = (\tilde{S}_{t+1} - S_t)/S_t.$$

If over time the average value of the residual, u, is not zero, then FO is a biased relationship. Exchange rate forecasts implied by FO will also reflect a bias.

Transaction costs could suggest a bias if the sample observations are not scattered randomly about the parity line. However, the size of the bias will be less than half the width of the neutral band implied by transaction costs. Aliber (1975) suggests two explanations—political risk and currency preference—for a bias in excess of transaction costs. Political risk resulting from assets being issued by or traded in different political areas was outlined in Chapter IV.

The currency preference argument is that there may be a convenience or other nonpecuniary yield associated with a currency. For example, a London importer (who is risk averse) may hold dollar balances to lessen exposure to exchange risk and to reduce transaction costs from trading in and out of sterling. A U.S. investor may hold Swiss franc assets to benefit from anonymity in the Swiss banking system. In both examples, the nominal interest rate does not adequately measure the desirability of these assets for investors.

In (5.10), u < 0 implies a preference for assets denominated in domestic currency. Holders of domestic currency denominated assets accept a lower rate of return than is implied by exchange rate changes. Similarly u > 0 implies a foreign currency preference.

Neither the political risk nor the currency preference arguments are in conflict with Fisher's original thesis or with market efficiency. If assets are dissimilar in terms of political risk or if there are significant non-pecuniary returns not reflected in market prices, then exchange rate forecasts based on FO need not be unbiased.

The Contribution of Portfolio Theory. Portfolio models suggest an alternative explanation for the error term (u) in equation (5.10). An investor who deals in uncovered interest arbitrage is exposed to exchange risk since $\tilde{S}_{t+1}$ is uncertain. The term (u) represents a premium for bearing an exchange risk which is non-diversifiable. The model developed by Solnik (1973) assumes that exchange risk is priced independently of equity market risk.[6] Solnik's formal expression for the interest differential is

$$(5.11) \qquad R_i - R_n = \dot{S}_i + \frac{\phi_{iw}}{\phi_w^2} R_w$$

where R_i = risk free asset of country i,

$$R_w = \sum_{i=1}^{n} w_i (R_i + \dot{S}_{ij}), \text{ any } j$$

and ϕ_{iw} = covariance of exchange rate i with other n-1 countries.

The interest rate differential between two countries is equal to the expected change in the exchange rate plus a term depending on exchange risk covariances. If the exchange risk covariance term is non-zero, a naive Fisherian approach will produce biased forecasts.

Forward Exchange Rate Based Forecasts

Equivalence to Interest Rate Based Forecasts. In the absence of transaction costs and uncertainty, both Fisher Open and interest rate parity hold exactly. As a result, the current forward rate (F_t) and the future spot rate (S_{t+1}) are equal. It follows that the forward rate will have similar properties to a forecast based on FO. Under more general conditions, the current forward rate can be used as a forecast:[7] $\hat{S}_{t+1} = F_t$. The remainder of this section explores the properties of the forward rate as a predictor of the future spot rate.

The Effect of Transaction Costs. In this section, the assumption of zero transaction costs is relaxed. Table 5.1 summarizes the transactions necessary to speculate on an increase in the price of foreign exchange.

Table 5.1. Summary of Transactions in a Speculative Purchase of Forward Exchange

Transaction	Price	Transaction Cost
Sale of domestic securities	r_d	t
Purchase foreign currency forward	F_t	t_F
Receive interest on margin account	r_m	t_m
Sell foreign currency in future	S_{t+1}	t_S

The scenario for the speculator is first to sell an amount, X, of domestic securities. The amount X is deposited in a margin account which earns a return, r_m. The margin account finances the purchase of X/F_t forward contracts at price F_t. When the contracts mature the foreign exchange is sold in the spot market as price S_{t+1}.

The cost (C) associated with the investment of the amount X is the foregone earnings on the holdings of domestic securities:

(5.12) $$C = X(1 + r_d).$$

The revenue from the investment is

(5.13) $$R = Xw(1 + r_m)S_{t+1}/F_t$$

where $$w = (1-t)(1-t_F)(1-t_m)(1-t_S).$$

Equating marginal cost with marginal revenue yields the *lower* limit on π ($\pi \equiv (S_{t+1} - F_t)/F_t$) for which this speculation is profitable:

(5.14) $$\underline{\pi} = \frac{(1 + r_d) - w(1 + r_m)}{w(1 + r_m)}.$$

The exchange rate forecast associated with this lower limit is

$$(5.15) \quad \hat{\underline{S}}_{t+1} = \frac{F_t(1+r_d)}{w(1+r_m)}.$$

To speculate on a decrease in the price of foreign exchange, the investor reverses the previous set of transactions. Equation (5.16) indicates the *upper* limit on π for which this speculation is profitable:

$$(5.16) \quad \bar{\pi} = \frac{w(1+r_m) - (1+r_f)}{(1+r_f)}.$$

The exchange rate forecast associated with this upper limit is

$$(5.17) \quad \bar{\hat{S}}_{t+1} = wF_t \frac{(1+r_m)}{(1+r_f)}.$$

Conditions (5.14) and (5.16) define a neutral band in which speculative flows are not profitable. The limits of this neutral band are given by

$$(5.18) \quad \bar{\pi} \leq \pi \leq \underline{\pi}.$$

Similarly, (5.15) and (5.17) define a neutral band on exchange rate forecasts.

$$(5.19) \quad \bar{\hat{S}}_{t+1} \leq \hat{S}_{t+1} \leq \hat{\underline{S}}_{t+1}.$$

For the special case in which all transaction costs are zero and investors are paid the opportunity cost on their margin deposits, the forward rate will be an exact forecast of the future spot rate.

Sources of Forecasting Bias. A fundamental case for forward rate bias is inherent in the so-called Modern Theory of forward exchange.[8] The Modern Theory hypothesizes that the observed forward rate, F_t, is determined jointly by speculators who demand forward contracts and arbitragers who supply them.[9] Assuming that demand and supply functions are linear (with slope $-B$ and A, respectively); the observed forward rate is a weighted average of the interest parity forward rate F_t^* and the expected future spot rate,[10]

(5.20) $$F_t = \frac{A}{A+B} F_t^* + \frac{B}{A+B} E(\tilde{S}_{t+1}).$$

As long as arbitragers play some role in the forward market and speculative demand is not infinitely elastic, $F_t \neq E(\tilde{S}_{t+1})$.[11] This situation is illustrated in Figure 5.3. Given supply (S) and demand (D) curves, we anticipate the forecast error U. Note also that speculators expect foreign currency to appreciate (they hold a long position) and the forward rate, F_t, *underestimates* the expected appreciation.[12]

Portfolio theory also suggests a possible forward rate bias. Combining Solnik's model of uncovered interest arbitrage (5.11) and the interest parity relationship implies that

(5.21) $$F_t = S_{t+1} + S_t \left(\frac{\phi_{iw}}{\phi_w^2} \right) R_w.$$

The forward rate equals the future spot rate plus a factor which is proportional to the exchange risk covariance for currency (i) in portfolio of the (n−1) other currencies in the world. The forward rate will equal the future spot rate only if the covariance term is zero.[13]

Transaction Costs and the Time Pattern of Forecast Errors. The previous sections have concluded, in part, that the forward rate will tend to underestimate the future spot rate when the spot rate is rising; the forward will tend to overestimate the future spot rate when the spot rate is falling. In this section we expand on this hypothesis.

Assume a two country world with the spot rate (midpoint), S = $2.00/£ and the one-period forward rate (midpoint), F = $2.00£. Assume transaction costs are $0.01 per transaction. This leads to bid-ask prices of $1.99 and $2.01 (respectively) in both markets. An equilibrium has been maintained at these prices for many periods until time t = 0. Assume also that speculators have perfect foresight and they will act to exploit any expected profit greater than some critical level, $P_c = \$.01$.

A speculator who expects sterling to appreciate compares his expected profit S(t+1,bid) − F(t,ask) with P_c. He buys forward sterling when expected profits exceed P_c. A speculator who expects sterling to depreciate compares his expected profit F(t,bid)−S(t+1,ask) with P_c. He sells forward sterling when expected profits exceed P_c.

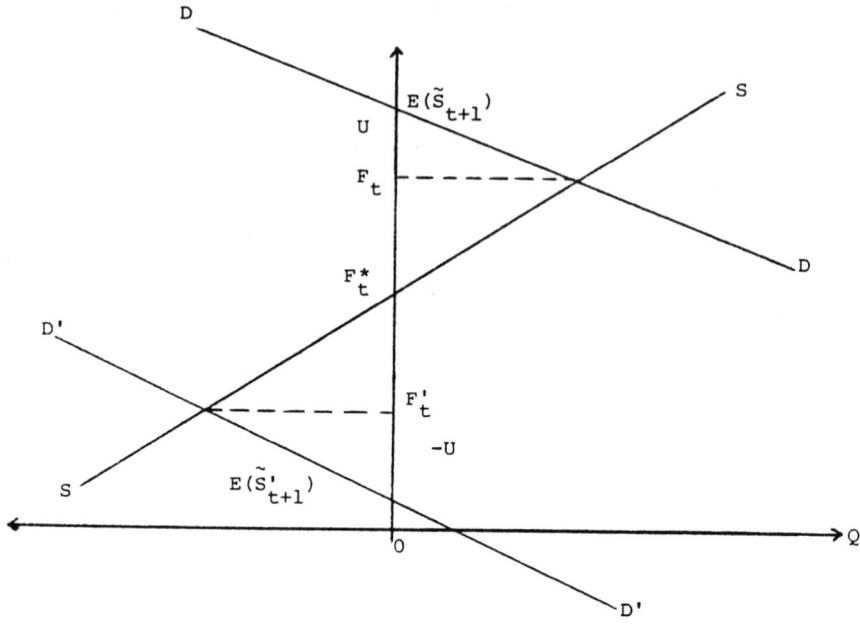

Figure 5.3.
Equilibrium in the Forward Market

Suppose the time series of spot rates (bid and ask) given in Table 5.2 is known with certainty. Figure 5.3 traces the results of profit maximizing speculation. Since the forward rate is lagged one period the forecast error is the vertical difference between the spot rate curve and the forward rate curve.[14]

The time pattern of overestimation and underestimation agrees with the hypothesized behavior. Because transaction costs are positive, underestimates can exist when the spot rate is falling (periods 7 and 8) and overestimates are possible while the spot rate is rising (period 13).

The time pattern of forecast errors depends critically on two assumptions. First, the cut-off level, P_c, must be positive. Brokerage fees and other administrative costs contribute positively to P_c. However, P_c may also reflect a payment to investors for bearing exchange risk. Positive covariance risk will tend to increase P_c (and the forecasting bias) while negative covariance risk will tend to decrease P_c. We therefore assume

Table 5.2. A Time Series of Spot and Forward Exchange Rates to Simulate the Time Pattern of Forecast Bias

Period	Spot (t) Bid	Ask	Forward (t−1) Bid	Ask
0	$1.99	2.01	1.99	2.01
1	2.01	2.03	1.99	2.01
2	2.03	2.05	2.00	2.02
3	2.05	2.07	2.02	2.04
4	2.05	2.07	2.02	2.04
5	2.05	2.07	2.02	2.04
6	2.05	2.07	2.02	2.04
7	2.03	2.05	2.02	2.04
8	2.01	2.03	2.02	2.04
9	1.99	2.01	2.02	2.04
10	1.97	1.99	2.00	2.02
11	1.95	1.97	1.98	2.00
12	1.93	1.95	1.96	1.98
13	1.95	1.97	1.96	1.98
14	1.97	1.99	1.96	1.98
15	1.99	2.01	1.96	1.98
16	2.01	2.03	1.98	2.00
17	2.03	2.05	2.00	2.02
18	2.05	2.07	2.02	2.04
19	2.05	2.07	2.02	2.04
20	2.05	2.07	2.02	2.04

that any negative covariance risk effects do not dominate and that P_c remains positive.

The second assumption is that bid and ask prices in forward markets are effected only by speculators and not by market makers in forward exchange. For example, in Table 5.2., the spot rate rises in period 1 yet market makers do not change the bid and asked prices of forward exchange in period 0. Implicitly, this assumes that market makers do not seek profit opportunities during the one-period horizon. Their primary concern is in very short run changes in the value of their inventories.

PURE FORECASTING MODELS

A pure forecasting model is defined as a model which forecasts in apparent abstraction from typical economic behavioral relationships.[15] For example, knowledge that sun spot activity and stock market activity are

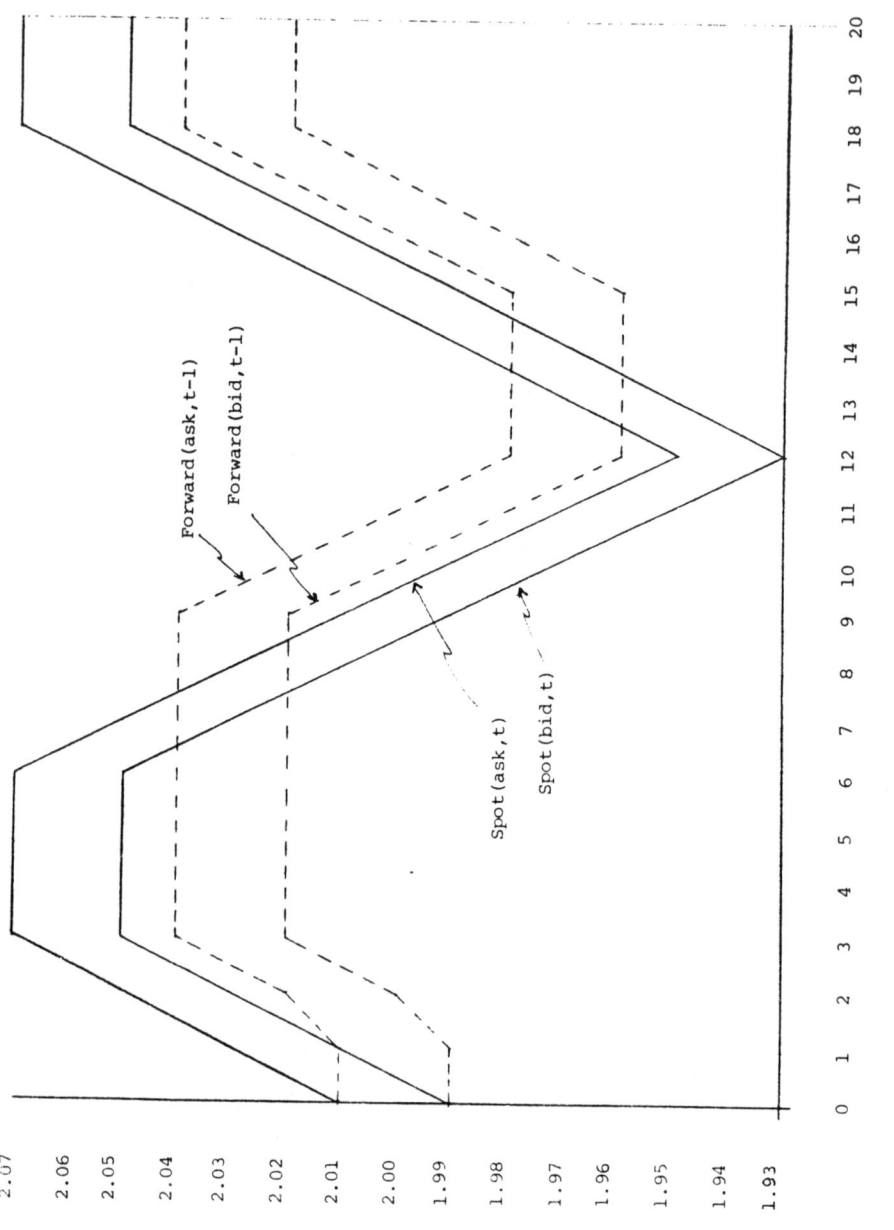

Figure 5.4.
A Time Series of Spot and Forward Exchange Rates to Simulate the Time Pattern of Forecast Bias

correlated may be helpful for forecasting although the economic relationships are not known.

Time Series Analysis

A general statistical approach for analyzing time series data is the multiple input transfer function model, which is a general expression for the Multiple Rational Distributed Lag (MRDL) model.[16] In the MRDL model, random shocks (a_t) and observed exogenous variables (X_{it}) are transformed by a series of linear filters into values of endogenous variables, Y_t:

(5.22) $$Y_t = \gamma_0 + \sum_{i=1}^{m} \frac{W_i(B)}{D_i(B)} X_{it} + \frac{\theta(B)}{\phi(B)} a_t$$

where $E(U_t) = 0$

and $E(a_t a_{t'}) = \begin{cases} \sigma^2, & t = t' \\ 0, & t \neq t' \end{cases}$

The terms $W_i(B)$, $D_i(B)$, $\theta(B)$, and $\phi(B)$ are the linear filters—p_{th} order polynomials in the backshift operator, B, so that;

(5.23) $$W_i(B)X_{it} = (W_{i0}B^0 - W_{i1}B^1 - \ldots - W_{ip}B^p)X_{it}$$
$$= W_{i0}X_{it} - W_{i1}X_{i,t-1} - \ldots - W_{ip}X_{i,t-p}.$$

Our main interest is in univariate time series analysis. When the only input to the system is "white noise," equation (5.22) reduces to the univariate Auto Regressive Moving Average (ARMA) process.

(5.24) $$Y_t = \frac{\theta(B)}{\phi(B)} a_t + \gamma_0.$$

Box and Jenkins (1970) analyze the ARMA model in great detail. They also describe detailed techniques for model identification and estimation. Nelson (1973) develops computer routines for estimating ARMA models and shows the applicability of the model to economic forecasting. The estimation routines are a function only of the time series (Y_t) and abstract from any knowledge of economic structure. This approach which relies on historical prices only, may seem very naive since again there is no way to incorporate structural information into a forecast. However, the efficient market hypothesis suggests that prices reflect available information, and knowledge of economic structure is part of this information set. When prices reflect all information, an ARMA model forecast reflects the complete information set.

Composite Forecasting

Muth (1961) uses the term *rational expectations* to describe a rational economic agent who forms expectations that depend "specifically on the structure of the relevant system describing the economy." Given the structure of the system and a time series of historical values, adding other variables does not increase forecasting accuracy.[17] If all models are correctly specified, they would lead to the same, correct forecasts.

In practice, our n forecasting models are likely to produce n different forecasts. This may reflect transaction costs, information costs, model misspecification, data errors, etc. The observed variety of forecasts may also reflect that international markets are not completely integrated and therefore the information content of data need not be uniform.

A rational economic agent constructs forecasts which exploit all information that has a marginal cost less than its marginal return. A way to make this goal operational is to construct a composite forecast, $\hat{S}$, using the n individual forecasts:

$$\hat{S} = f(\hat{S}_1, \hat{S}_2, ..., \hat{S}_n).$$

If the forecast errors from these models are less than perfectly correlated then a single forecast that is some weighted average of the individual forecasts should reduce the Mean Squared forecasting Error (MSE).

One way to select the weights is by regression analysis,[18]

$$\hat{S} = A_1\hat{S}_1 + A_2\hat{S}_2 + ... + A_n\hat{S}_n$$

where $\hat{S}_i$, $i = 1,...,n$ are forecasts from individual models and $\hat{S}$ is the composite forecast. Here again, the weights (the regression coefficients A_i, $i = 1,...,n$) tell us nothing about exchange rate determination or how to adapt to new structural information. The weights may help answer the following important question: Is there a single model which consistently and accurately reflects available information? If so, only one coefficient will have a nonzero value. If not, then we can conclude that each model is not properly specified to reflect available information. It may be of further interest to inquire why some models, or markets, reflect information better than others.

THREE ISSUES IN METHODOLOGY

On Selecting a Time Series for Analysis

In a financial market dominated by well-informed, rational, profit-maximizing investors, we expect unusual profits earned in one period to be uncorrelated with unusual profits earned in all previous periods. If this condition were not met, investors could use this information to increase their profits. Therefore, the null hypothesis is that observed prices should fluctuate randomly about their expected value.

If a restrictive assumption is made about the process generating the expected rate of return or the expected equilibrium value of prices, it will be possible to test the null hypothesis. One assumption is that investors require a constant rate of return.[19] In this case, observed prices will follow a random walk of the form

$$(5.25) \qquad \ln(P_t/P_{t-1}) = \theta_0 + a_t$$

where a_t is a random shock and θ_0 is the constant required rate of return or "drift" parameter.

The purpose of this section is to consider a set of time series of international financial variables and to examine which series we expect to follow a random walk process, assuming that the required rate of return is constant. Consider the following 5 series:

(a) $F_{t,90}$; $F_{t+1,90}$; $F_{t+2,90}$; ...

(b) $F_{t,90}$; $F_{t+1,89}$; $F_{t+2,88}$; ... $F_{t+89,1}$; $F_{t+90,0}$

(c) $Z_t = \dfrac{S_{t+90} - F_{t,90}}{F_{t,90}}$; $Z_{t+90} = \dfrac{S_{t+180} - F_{t+90,90}}{F_{t+90,90}}$;

$Z_{t+180} = \dfrac{S_{t+270} - F_{t+180,90}}{F_{t+180,90}}$ ...

(d) $S_t; S_{t+1}; S_{t+2}; \ldots$

(e) $Z_t = \dfrac{S_{t+1}(1 + i_t^*)}{S_t} - 1; \quad Z_{t+1} = \dfrac{S_{t+2}(1 + i_{t+1}^*)}{S_{t+1}} - 1;$

$Z_{t+2} = \dfrac{S_{t+3}(1 + i_{t+2}^*)}{S_{t+2}} - 1 \ldots$

where S_t = Spot rate at time t
$F_{t,d}$ = Forward rate at time t for maturity d days
Z_t = Rate of return on a speculative position taken at time t
i_t^* = One day interest rate on foreign currency at time t.

Series (a) is the set of daily prices on the 90-day forward rate. This series does not provide information on the rate of return from some feasible investment opportunity. Investors cannot police the behavior of this time series since 90-day contracts cannot be stored and traded like other financial claims.

If an investor purchases a 90-day forward contract today at price $F_{t,90}$, and sells it tomorrow, he sells at price $F_{t+1,89}$, since tomorrow the asset will be an 89-day contract. This activity is described by series (b). Investors can calculate a rate of return from this investment and therefore, series (b) should follow a random walk.[20]

Forward speculation is another investment opportunity. If an investor buys a 90-day forward contract and closes it out at the future spot rate, his profit will be $(S_{t+90} - F_{t,90})/F_{t,90}$. The series of these rates of return (series (c)) should follow a random process. Note that the series is composed of nonoverlapping 90-day periods. If the investment periods are overlapping, the rates of return will be highly autocorrelated. Therefore, there are only four independent revisions of the 90-day forward rate in every calendar year.

Now consider a daily series (d) of spot prices $S_t, S_{t+1}, S_{t+2}, \ldots$. One can invest in foreign exchange at the price S_t and sell the next at S_{t+1} so the investment is "feasible." If this percentage change equals the total rate of return, we expect the series of changes to be random. However, since there is an opportunity cost to holding currency *qua* currency, a spot speculator will invest the foreign exchange at the overnight rate i_t^*. Therefore, $[S_{t+1}(1+i_t^*)]/S_t - 1$ is the actual 1-day rate of return and this process, series (e), should follow a random walk.[21]

The conclusion of this section is that tests of market efficiency should concentrate on series (b), (c), and (e). Under the restrictive assumption of a constant required rate of return, the returns in these series should fluctuate randomly. Analysis of series (a) and (d) may be useful for descriptive purposes, but they provide no direct information on market efficiency.

On Analyzing the Performance of Forecasting Models

A standard criterion for selecting a forecasting model is to select that model which minimizes the mean square error (MSE) (Nelson 1973). This criterion assumes that forecasters have quadratic utility functions and therefore the loss from incorrect forecasts increases with the square of the forecasting error. Minimizing MSE maximizes the utility of the forecast.

Given a quadratic loss function, the investor's problem is to select a forecast, $\hat{S}$, that minimizes his expected losses.

$$(5.26) \quad \min_{\hat{S}} E(\text{Loss}) = K\, E(\hat{S} - S)^2 \; \alpha \sigma^2(\hat{S}) + (S - E(\hat{S}))^2$$

The first term, $\sigma^2(\hat{S})$, is the variance of the estimator, and the second term, $(S - E(\hat{S}))^2$, is the square of the bias. If the forecast is unbiased, then $E(\hat{S}) = S$, but this need not result in a minimum MSE forecast. Figure 5.5 illustrates a case where a biased forecast, $\hat{S}_1$, has a lower MSE than an unbiased forecast, $\hat{S}_2$.

Given that the bias of S_1 is known, a new forecast

$$\hat{\hat{S}}_1 = \hat{S}_1 - \text{Bias}(\hat{S}_1)$$

can be computed. Since $E(\hat{\hat{S}}_1) = S$ the MSE of the new forecast will take the minimum value, $\sigma^2(\hat{S}_1)$.[22]

The preceding analysis is fairly standard for the problem of forecasting paint sales, attendance at a football game or GNP. The essence of this methodology has been applied to the foreign exchange market by Kohlhagen (1975) who analyzes the bias of the forward rate as a forecast of the future spot rate and by Giddy and Dufey (1975) who evaluate forecasting models on an MSE criterion. However, for some models of foreign exchange forecasting the standard criteria will be irrelevant. The

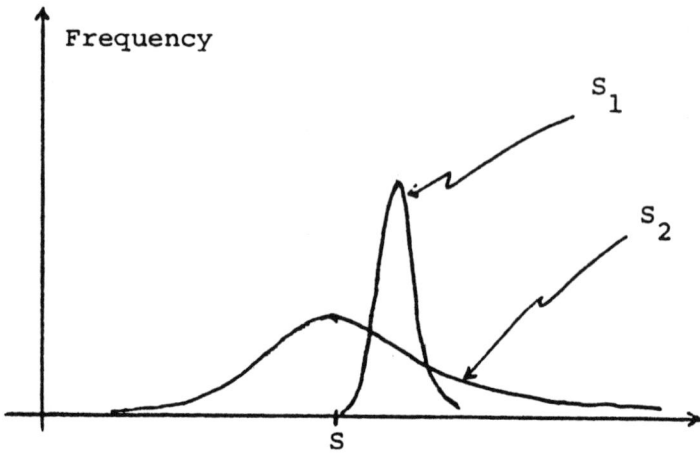

Figure 5.5.
Frequency Distribution of a Biased Forecast and an Unbiased Forecast

models developed earlier in this chapter fall into this category. These forecast rules lead to a neutral band—(5.9) and (5.19)—that should bound the future exchange rate.

Given these models, if the band width were 1.0%, then persistent 0.5% forecast errors would not be disturbing in the sense that they represent a market inefficiency. Knowledge of these serially correlated, nonzero errors cannot lead to a profit opportunity through uncovered arbitrage or forward speculation.[23]

In any sample period the MSE may appear greater than that necessary for profitable speculation perhaps because of the domination of a few large outliers in the sample. This analysis suggests that the forecast errors resulting from the equations based on speculative behavior should be examined analogously to the treatment of interest rate parity deviations in Chapter IV. A meaningful statistic is the percentage of time periods for which sample observations are bounded by the neutral band.

Quoted Yields, Realized Yields, and Risk

Markets tend to pay a risk premium for risk that cannot be diversified away. Otherwise risk-averse investors would not hold risky assets. The essence of a risky asset is that its rate of return is variable. Alternatively, its realized rate of return will differ from its "quoted" or "promised" rate of return.

In the case of a debt security, the realized yield must be less than or equal to the promised yield. For example, a $1 million portfolio of C-rated bonds may *promise* a return of 16%. But investors may expect a return, and in fact realize a return of only 14% if one-eighth of the firms go bankrupt. The 2% deviation between promised return and realized return is a function of the market's estimate of the bankruptcy rate (Van Horne 1970, Chap. V). The relevance of this in the present study is that we use quoted forward rates and Euro-currency rates and assume that the conditions of all contracts are met. This ignores investors who transacted with the Herstatt Bank and the Franklin National Bank and realized rates of return different from quoted rates. It also ignores investors who invested in Swiss banks in 1974 and then experienced retroactive foreign exchange taxes and regulations. Quoted return and realized return diverge.[24] The methodology therefore assumes that international banks honor their contracts. It also assumes that the sovereign does not intervene so as to change the quoted rate of return. The methodology ignores that part of the quoted return which is a compensation for business or political risks.

NOTES

1. Any structural model of an open economy could be used to forecast the spot exchange rate (S). When the reduced form model summarizes all the sources of supply and demand it will be useful for several purposes. First, it estimates $\bar{S}$, the long run equilibrium value of the spot rate. We expect the observed value, S, to move toward $\bar{S}$. Second, the model indicates how $\bar{S}$ changes given unanticipated changes in exogenous variables. It therefore suggests how the market should react to new information. Third, if forecasts of the future exogenous variables are available, then the model can generate conditional forecasts of $\bar{S}$.

The monetary theory of exchange rates suggests a simple structural model that could be adapted for forecasting purposes (see Bilson 1976).

2. The Fisher Closed effect (FC) deals with a closed economy. It states that nominal interest rates reflect a real rate plus anticipated price inflation.

3. The Fisher Open effect (FO) is similar to interest rate parity except that S_{t+1} replaces F_t. The adjustment to equilibrium is strictly analogous to the process described in Table 4.1.

4. Once again, this formulation assumes that all variables (r_d, r_f, S_{t+1}, S_t) and parameters (t, t^*, t_S) do not vary with X.

5. In statistical terminology, an estimator ($\hat{X}$) is biased if the expected value of the estimator does not equal the population mean: $E(\hat{X}) \neq \mu_X$. Alternatively, a prediction or a forecast ($\hat{Y}$) is biased if the forecast errors ($e = \hat{Y} - Y$) have a nonzero mean. We adopt the latter definition (see Theil 1971, Chap. III).

6. Porter (1971) and Kouri (1976) have also formulated portfolio models that demonstrate the possibility of a forecasting bias. For more on the Solnik model, see Chap. VIII.

7. One need not rely on Fisher Open and interest parity to claim that the forward rate will reflect investor expectations. For example, Working (1961) argued that "Futures prices tend to be highly reliable estimates of what should be expected on the basis of contemporarily available information. . . ." By contrast, Fieleke (1975) mentions several foreign exchange traders who were "unanimous and unequivocal in rejecting" the forward rate as a reliable predicator of the future spot rate.

8. Another case for forward rate bias relies on Jensen's inequality. Siegel (1972), Roper (1975), and McCulloch (1975) have shown that the forward rate must be a biased estimator of the price of at least one currency (foreign or domestic). This result is based on the statistical relation $E(X) < [E(1/x)]^{-1}$. To illustrate, let the spot price at time t of dollars in terms of sterling be c_t. The sterling price in terms of dollars is e_t, and clearly $c_t e_t = 1$ and $e_t = 1/c_t$. Therefore, $E(c_t) < [E(1/c_t)]^{-1} = [E(e_t)]^{-1}$. As a numerical example, if c_t will equal 1/2 or 1 with equal probability, then $E(c_t) = 3/4$. It follows that e_t will equal 2 or 1 with equal probability, so that $E(e_t) = 3/2$ and $[E(e_t)]^{-1} = 2/3 < 3/4 = E(c_t)$. We claim that there is no forward rate, $c_{t,f}$, which simultaneously equals 3/4 and 2/3. Therefore, $c_{t,f}$ must be a biased estimator of the future spot price of at least one currency.

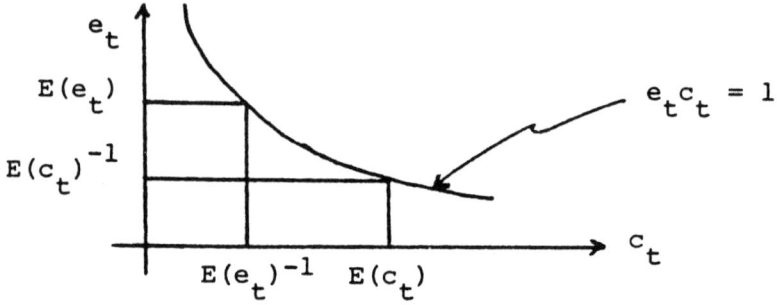

Figure 5.2.
Jensen's Inequality and Forecasting Bias

McCulloch suggests that in empirical work, the bias introduced from looking at only one side (c_t) of the market will be very small.

9. The distinction between arbitragers and speculators is conceptual. Depending on his preference for bearing risk, an investor can include any mix of arbitrage and speculative investments in his portfolio.

10. Using regression analysis to estimate the coefficients in (5.20) for Canada, Stoll (1968) found that interest parity considerations (the coefficient of F_t^*) were most important although speculators did play a statistically significant role. Contrary to the Modern Theory, Aliber (1973) suggests that the forward rate is most always near the interest parity level because in the external currency market the supply of arbitrage funds is very highly elastic.

11. In empirical work, we will compare F_t with S_{t+1}. This tests a joint hypothesis. First that the forward rate reflects expectations: $F_t = E(\hat{S}_{t+1})$; and second, that expectations are

realized $E(\tilde{S}_{t+1}) = S_{t+1}$. If we find that $F_t \neq S_{t+1}$ we cannot determine whether this is because 1) the forward rate does not reflect expectations and/or 2) investors' expectations were not realized.

12. Note, however, that if speculative demand shifts to D', the observed forward rate is F'_t and the anticipated forecast error is $-U$. Speculators hold a short position in foreign currency; they expect the spot rate to depreciate and forward rate, F'_t, *overestimates* the expected depreciation. Therefore, it may be difficult to measure the forward rate bias suggested by the Modern Theory.

13. An alternative portfolio approach is to consider a foreign currency forward contract as an example of a gamble where there is no cash flow at the time one enters the contract. The payout, $\tilde{S}_{t+1} - F_t$, represents a pure gamble.

Levich (1976c) shows that the equilibrium condition for such a gamble is

$$E(\tilde{S}_{t+1}) - F_t = \beta [E(\tilde{R}_M) - R_f]$$

where

$$\beta = \mathrm{Cov}[(\tilde{S} - F), \tilde{R}_M]/\sigma^2(\tilde{R}_M)$$

The forward rate will be an unbiased forecast of the future spot rate only if the coefficient $\beta = 0$.

14. Since forecast errors tend to increase in proportion with the forecasting horizon and in our example transaction costs are a large component of forecasting error, we could conclude the transaction costs in forward markets will rise in proportion to contract maturity.

15. Some writers do not emphasize a distinction between structural models and forecasting models. Following the scientific method, economists will revise economic theory (i.e., structural models) as new information (e.g., superior forecasting models) becomes available. Structural models become indistinguishable from forecasting models. See Klein (1971, p. 12).

16. The term rational does not imply a particular decision-making process. It refers to the fact that any infinite distributed lag function $V(L)X_t = \sum_{i=0}^{\infty} V_i X_{t-i}$ can be approximated by a rational function of two polynomials in the lag operator, $V(L) = W(L)/D(L)$.

17. Nelson (1975) shows that Muth's illustration of rational expectations was "perhaps an unfortunate choice." Since the rational expectation was equivalent to a pure statistical extrapolation, there was no gain from knowledge of structure. In the more general case, however, Nelson concludes that knowledge of economic structure should improve forecasts.

18. Nelson (1972) used this approach to compare the prediction performance of the FRB-MIT-PENN model with an ARIMA model. The results suggest that the ARIMA could be used to significantly reduce the forecast errors in the FMP model.

19. Other possible assumptions are that returns are generated by a market model, a specific two-parameter portfolio model, or some other variable return generating process. In these cases, the simple random walk model of prices need not be observed (see Fama 1970, 1976).

20. The prices of currency futures traded on the International Monetary Market are an example of series (b).

21. By this reasoning, intraday changes in exchange rates should be random since the opportunity cost of money approaches zero. For example, if there is no market for "five-minute money," the series of spot rates in (d) should be random for observations every five minutes.

22. In practice, one should adjust for bias only if the bias is stationary. *Ex post*, bias may be observed and removing bias in the sample period data will always reduce MSE. However, if bias is not stationary, adjusting for bias in postsample data may increase MSE. The same problem applies to any model which is "tailored" to fit the sample data but poorly describes postsample observations because of structural changes.

23. This knowledge may be important when a point estimate of the expected future spot rate is used as an input for a balance of payments model or corporate cash management model.

24. The Herstatt/Franklin cases are not a good example of "political" risk but of business risk. The market value of all Herstatt (and Franklin) liabilities (regardless of currency of denomination) were affected. Similarly, if the Bank of England makes an unexpected announcement, this may effect the market value of U.K. liabilities regardless of country of issue or currency of denomination. For example, U.K. liabilities denominated in U.S. dollars and issued in an external market would be effected by this announcement. In these examples, the risk is associated with the issuer of the liabilities. They do not fit a more typical scenario of political risk such as when a political decision (e.g., to change exchange controls, taxes, or other barriers to the international flow of capital) affects the market which is geographically coincident with the sovereign's territory of political power. However, these examples do illustrate the kind of measurement problem described in the text.

Chapter VI

Time Series Behavior of Spot and Forward Exchange Rates

PURPOSE

This chapter presents statistical evidence that describes the movement of spot and forward exchange rates during the period 1967/75. One objective of this chapter is to describe the behavior of spot rates, since this is the variable we wish to forecast. A second objective is to identify stationary periods. If stationary periods exist, then time series analysis will be applicable as a modeling and forecasting technique.

At the end of the chapter two additional hypotheses using time series analysis are examined. The first section is the time series of exchange rates of a longer period, 1962/75. The data indicate that time series models for the periods 1962/67 and 1973/75 are more like each other than they are like time series models for another period 1968/69. This indicates that the process generating exchange rates is more similar during two periods with different exchange rate systems than during two periods with the same exchange rate system but different levels of speculative activity.

The 1950/62 Canadian float is examined in the second section. A time series analysis indicates that the Canadian spot rate did not follow a random walk over most of the sample period and that the deviations from random behavior are greatest during the initial and final episodes of this period.

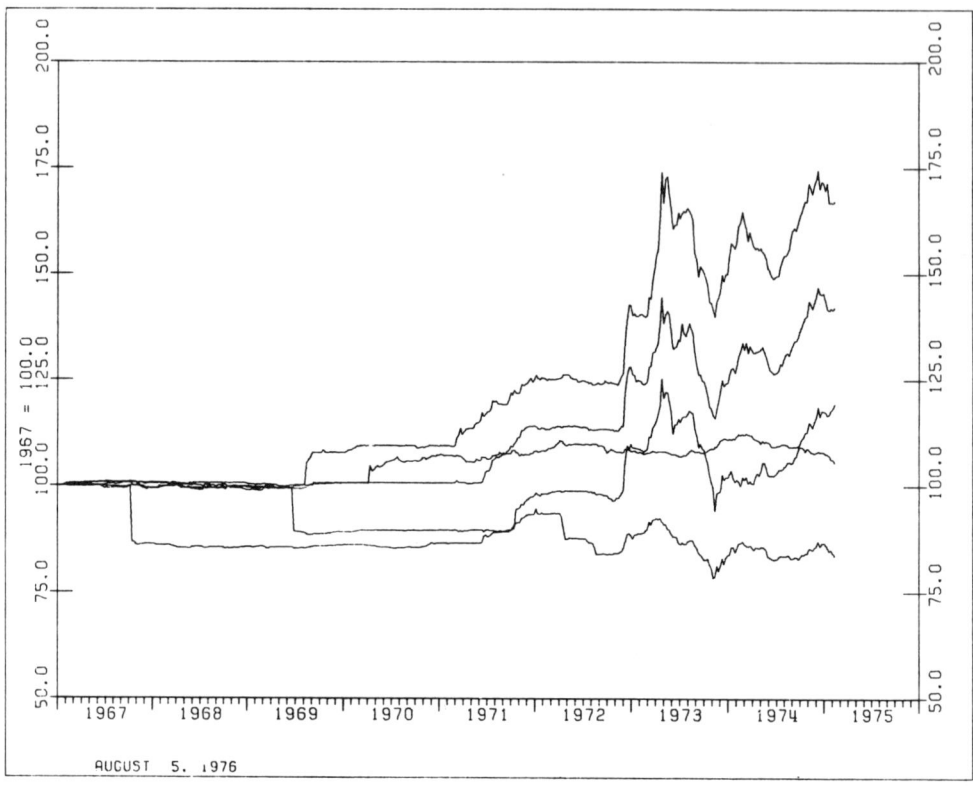

Figure 6.1.
Weekly Spot Exchange Rates—Canada (C), England (E), Belgium (B), France (F), Germany (G)

DESCRIPTIVE STATISTICS OF THE SPOT EXCHANGE RATES

In the period January 1967 to May 1975, the spot exchange rates display a wide range of behavior. The time series of spot rates for the nine sample countries is shown in Figures 6.1 and 6.2. The original spot rates, $S_{i,t}$, have been transformed so that the first observation for each transformed series, $S'_{i,1}$, equals 100. The transformation is defined by

(6.1) $\qquad S'_{i,t} = 100 \cdot S_{i,t}/S_{i,1}$ for $i = 1, \ldots, 9$ countries

and $t = 1, \ldots, 430$ weeks.

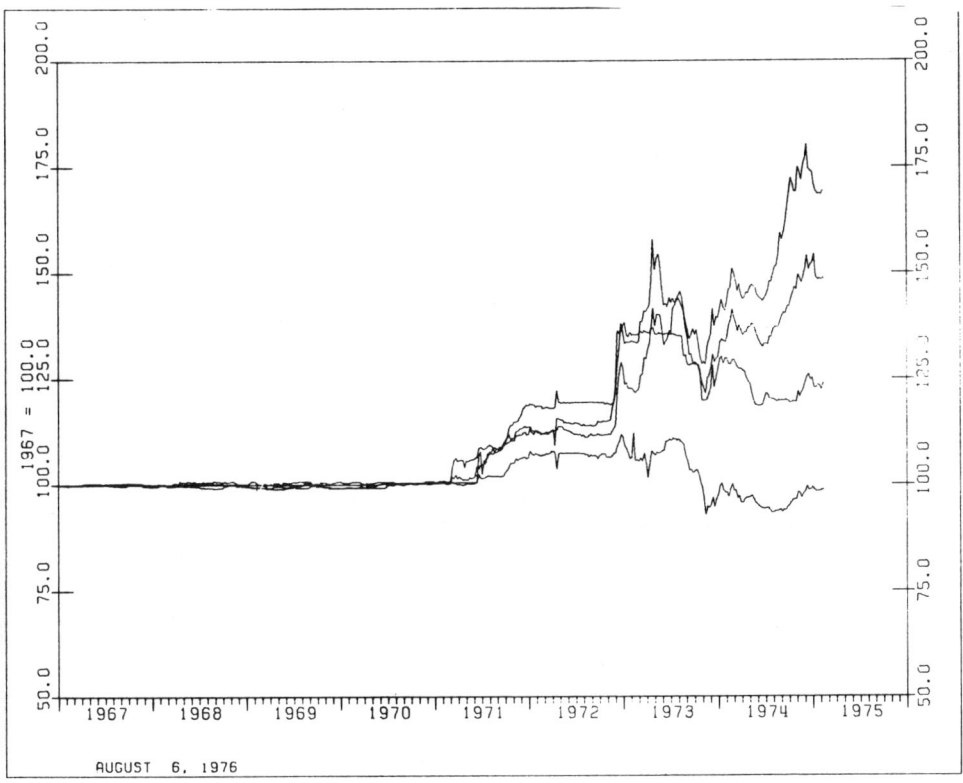

Figure 6.2.
Weekly Spot Exchange Rates—Italy (I), Netherlands (N), Switzerland (S), Japan (J)

The transformation enables us to identify major events in each series and to compare these events and movements across currencies.

Table 6.1 reports the minimum, maximum, and ending values for each series. All of the currencies except sterling and the lira appreciated relative to the dollar. Sterling depreciated by about 17% while the lira was nearly unchanged. Of the appreciating currencies, the Swiss franc was strongest, rising by about 70%, followed by the German mark. Most of this increase occurred over the last four years.[1]

After 1973, several currencies display similar price movements vis-à-vis the U.S. dollar. These currencies—the Deutsch mark, Belgian franc, Dutch guilder, and French franc—participated in the joint float of

Table 6.1. Minimum, Maximum, and Ending Values of Transformed Spot Rates

Country	Minimum Date	Minimum Value	Maximum Date	Maximum Value	Ending Value
Canada	1/19/68	99.12	5/24/74	112.50	105.05
United Kingdom	1/18/74	78.53	4/14/67	100.36	82.61
Belgium	11/22/68	99.13	2/28/75	146.93	143.12
France	10/10/69	88.52	7/6/73	125.43	120.23
Germany	4/11/69	98.87	2/28/75	174.52	168.15
Italy	1/25/74	92.93	4/19/73	112.21	99.50
Netherlands	5/29/69	98.97	3/28/75	154.34	150.19
Switzerland	2/23/68	99.54	2/28/75	180.25	171.93
Japan[a]	7/17/70	99.67	3/16/73	137.91	123.06

[a] Data for Japan begin on 6/19/70.

European currencies, the "snake in the tunnel."[2] If Figures 6.1 and 6.2 are reconstructed using the German mark as the numeraire currency, the price stability of the other joint float currencies vis-à-vis the German mark would be much more apparent.[3]

A major conclusion from Figures 6.1 and 6.2 is that the spot exchange rate series are not stationary over the sample period.[4] In a stationary series, the moments of the distribution (i.e., the mean, variance, and higher moments, if they exist) are constant over time. Given a stationary time series, a picture of one segment appears much like a picture of any other segment. Stationarity is a strong assumption that greatly simplifies estimation. With stationarity, all sample observations can be used to estimate the constant parameters of the time series process.

The series in Figures 6.1 and 6.2 are not stationary because the moments of the spot rate distribution are changing. During pegged rate periods, the spot rate tends to a mean value (the central rate) with a very small variance. During floating periods, the central value of the exchange rate wanders away from its previous value and the variance increases. During transitional periods, the central value changes precipitously as does the variance estimate. To measure the stationarity of $S'_{i,t}$, the sample period is divided into the major periods of pegged and floating exchange rates. The dates for these periods are reported in Table 6.2. The mean and standard error of $S'_{i,t}$ are reported in Table 6.3. The data indicate that for each currency, the mean of S'_i is changing over time. Except for the United Kingdom, France, and Germany (countries which changed the central rate during Peg I) the standard error of

Table 6.2. Ending Dates for Sample Periods Peg I, Float I, Peg II[a]

Country	Peg I	Float I	Peg II
Canada	6/1/70	—	—
United Kingdom	8/15/71	12/21/71	6/23/72
Belgium	8/15/71	12/21/71	3/19/73
France	8/15/71	12/21/71	3/19/73
Germany	5/9/71	12/21/71	3/19/73
Italy	8/15/71	12/21/71	2/13/73
Netherlands	5/9/71	12/21/71	3/19/73
Switzerland	8/15/71	12/21/71	1/23/73
Japan	8/15/71	12/21/71	2/13/73

[a] Data for Peg I begins on 1/3/67 for all countries except Japan which begins at 9/1/70. The Float II period extends until 5/9/75 for all countries.

Table 6.3. Summary Statistics for Standardized Spot Rates ($S_{i,t}$)

Country	Statistic	Peg I	Float I	Peg II	Float II
Canada	Mean	100.318	108.217	N.A.	N.A.
	S.E.	0.380	1.730	N.A.	N.A.
	Nobs	173	257	0	0
United Kingdom	Mean	88.325	89.240	93.144	85.830
	S.E.	5.319	0.170	0.922	2.734
	Nobs	236	18	27	149
Belgium	Mean	100.435	106.865	114.659	132.251
	S.E.	0.532	2.094	3.494	7.233
	Nobs	236	18	65	111
France	Mean	95.316	89.631	98.856	109.296
	S.E.	5.326	0.183	3.088	6.955
	Nobs	236	18	65	111
Germany	Mean	103.232	117.195	125.994	157.444
	S.E.	4.570	3.011	4.282	9.473
	Nobs	222	32	65	111
Italy	Mean	99.969	102.224	107.015	100.907
	S.E.	0.407	0.667	0.741	5.832
	Nobs	236	18	60	116
Netherlands	Mean	99.897	105.018	113.502	136.692
	S.E.	0.448	3.175	3.723	8.202
	Nobs	222	32	65	111
Switzerland	Mean	100.706	109.236	113.440	147.483
	S.E.	1.356	1.001	1.497	13.772
	Nobs	236	18	58	119
Japan	Mean	100.250	107.984	118.502	127.199
	S.E.	0.163	2.357	1.498	6.415
	Nobs	61	18	60	116

the mean has increased substantially—typically by a factor of ten. This does not suggest stationary behavior.

It is unlikely that a single time series will adequately model each series. Therefore, time series analysis must concentrate on subperiods that appear stationary.

The weekly percentage change in the spot rate is calculated to examine further the stationarity of these series:

(6.2) $\quad X_{i,t} = 100 \cdot (S_{i,t} - S_{i,t-1})/S_{i,t-1}, \quad i = 1, \ldots 9 \text{ countries}$

$$t = 2, \ldots 430 \text{ weeks}.$$

These series are displayed in Figures 6.3–6.11. Summary statistics for $X_{i,t}$ are reported in Table 6.4.[5] For each series, the largest values of $X_{i,t}$ usually mark a transition from one pegged value to another or from a pegged rate system to a floating rate system. The exception is a few large shocks associated with the Middle East oil crisis (Belgium, 1973; France, 1974; Italy, 1974; Japan, 1974).

Overall, during pegged rate periods the series are not stationary, and additional differencing of the data or log transformations do not result in stationarity. While the large rate changes could be excluded and the remaining data modelled as a stationary process, this is no solution to the forecasting question. Time series models are not appropriate for forecasting in pegged rate periods.

The stationarity of $X_{i,t}$ can be examined further with the statistics in Table 6.4. For the Canadian dollar, the mean percentage change is essentially constant and equal to zero. However, the standard error of this change is about three times as large as under pegged rates. A similar pattern is observed in the other currencies. For every currency (except the French franc during Float I) the standard error of $X_{i,t}$ increases under floating rates relative to pegged rates, by a factor of 6 for the Swiss franc and 13 for the lira.

The analysis of the $X_{i,t}$ provides further evidence of nonstationary behavior over the complete sample period. However, during the Float II period, the $X_{i,t}$ for Canada, England, Netherlands, and Switzerland fall within a relatively constant band. For the other five countries, the weekly percentage changes are declining. Nevertheless, if we assume that a

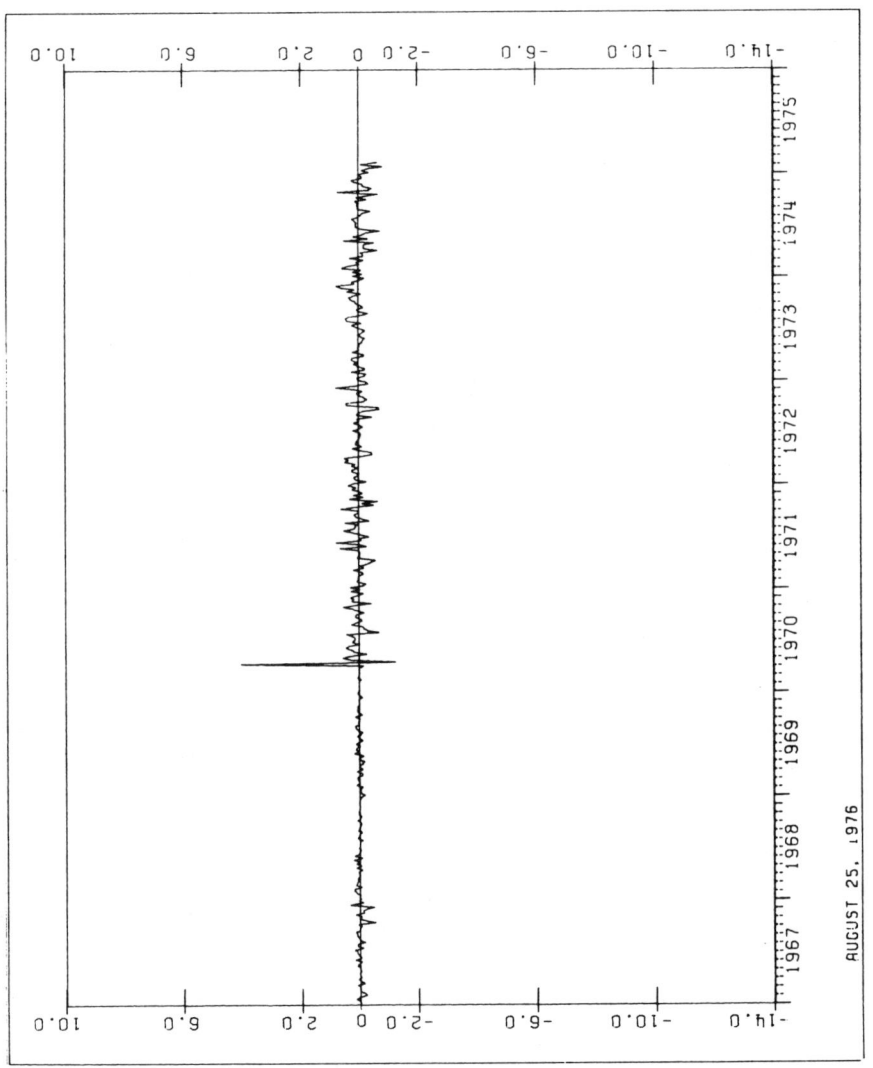

Figure 6.3.
Weekly Percentage Change in Spot Rate—Canada

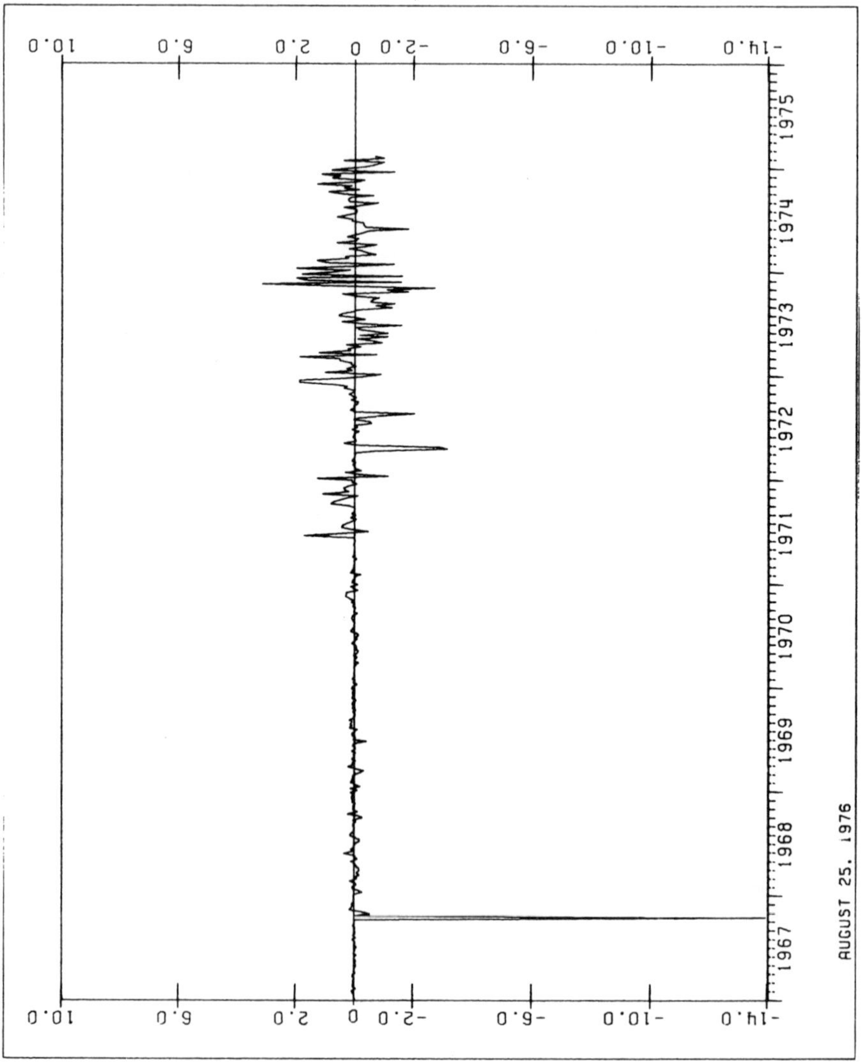

94 / *The International Money Market*

Figure 6.4.
Weekly Percentage Change in Spot Rate—England

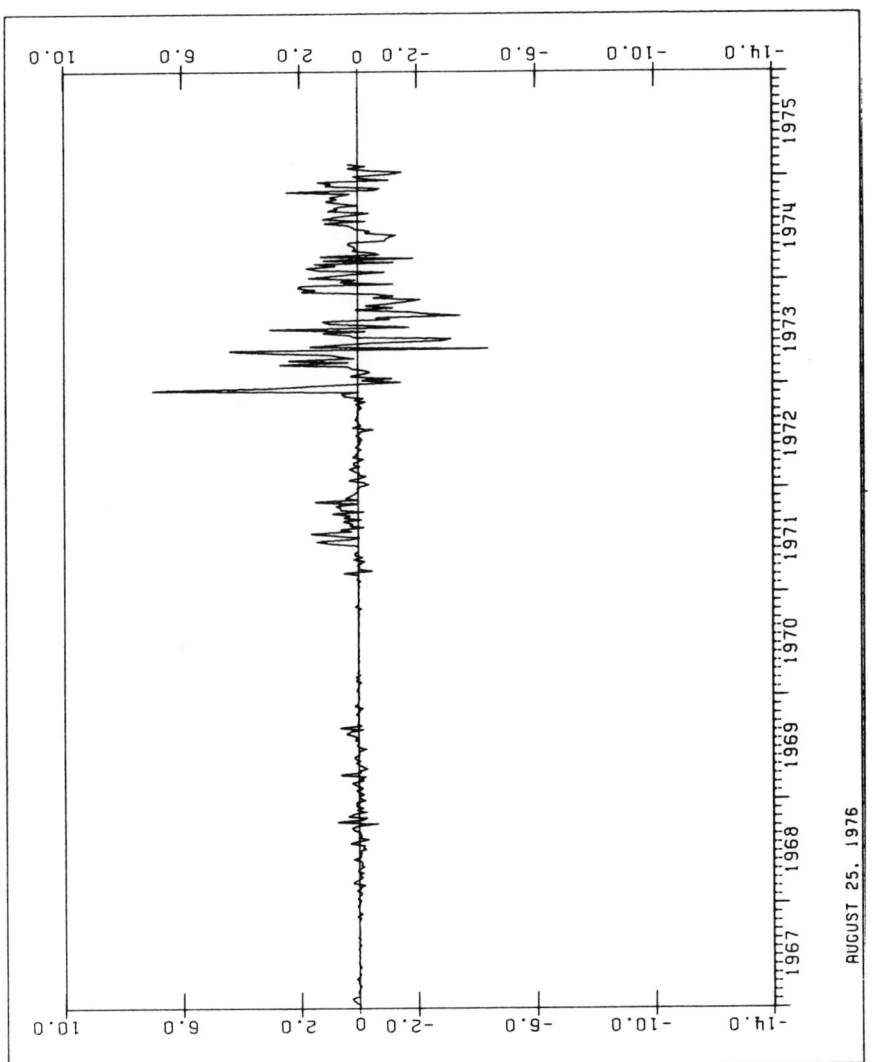

Figure 6.5.
Weekly Percentage Change in Spot Rate—Belgium

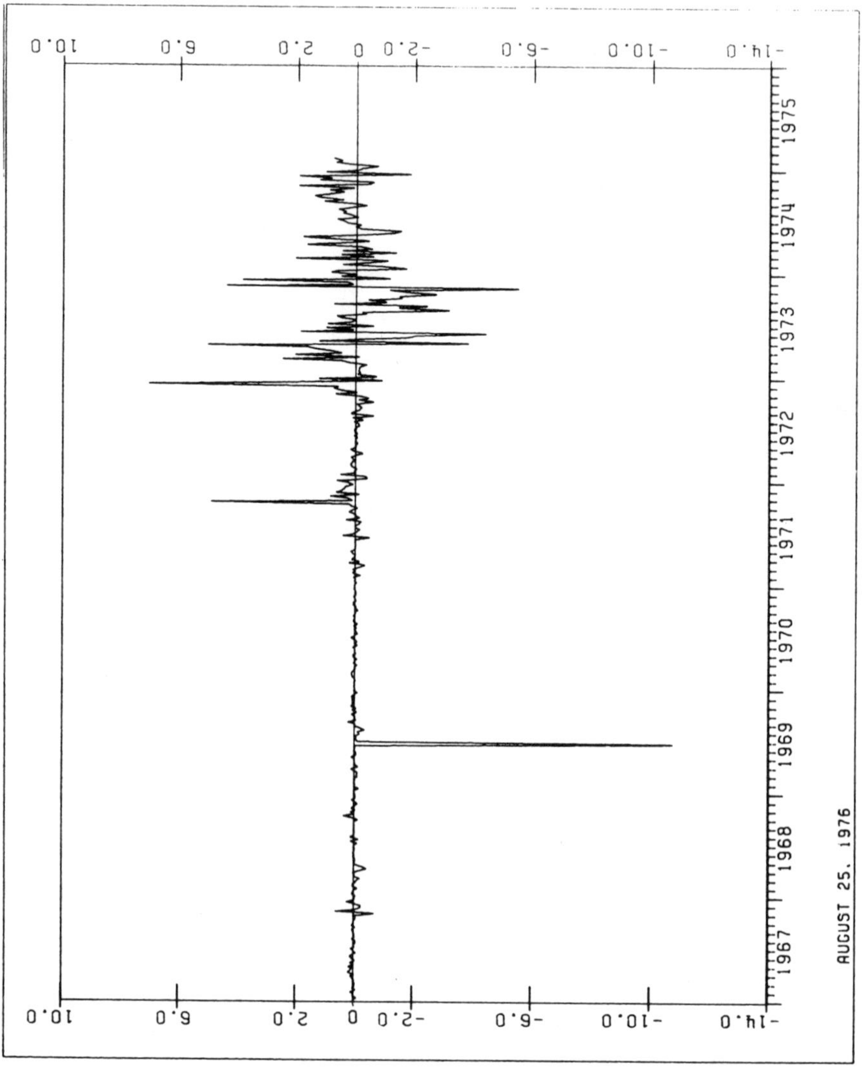

96 / *The International Money Market*

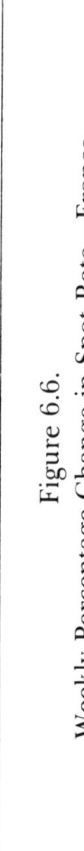

Figure 6.6.
Weekly Percentage Change in Spot Rate—France

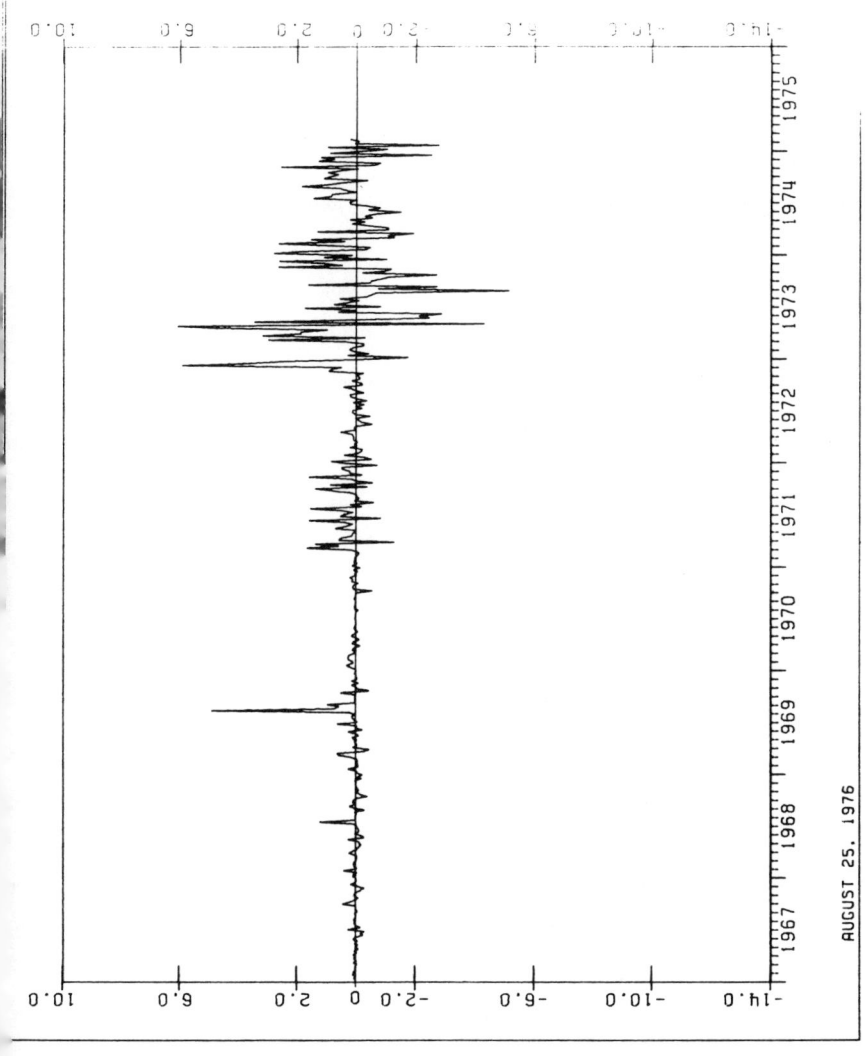

Figure 6.7.
Weekly Percentage Change in Spot Rate—Germany

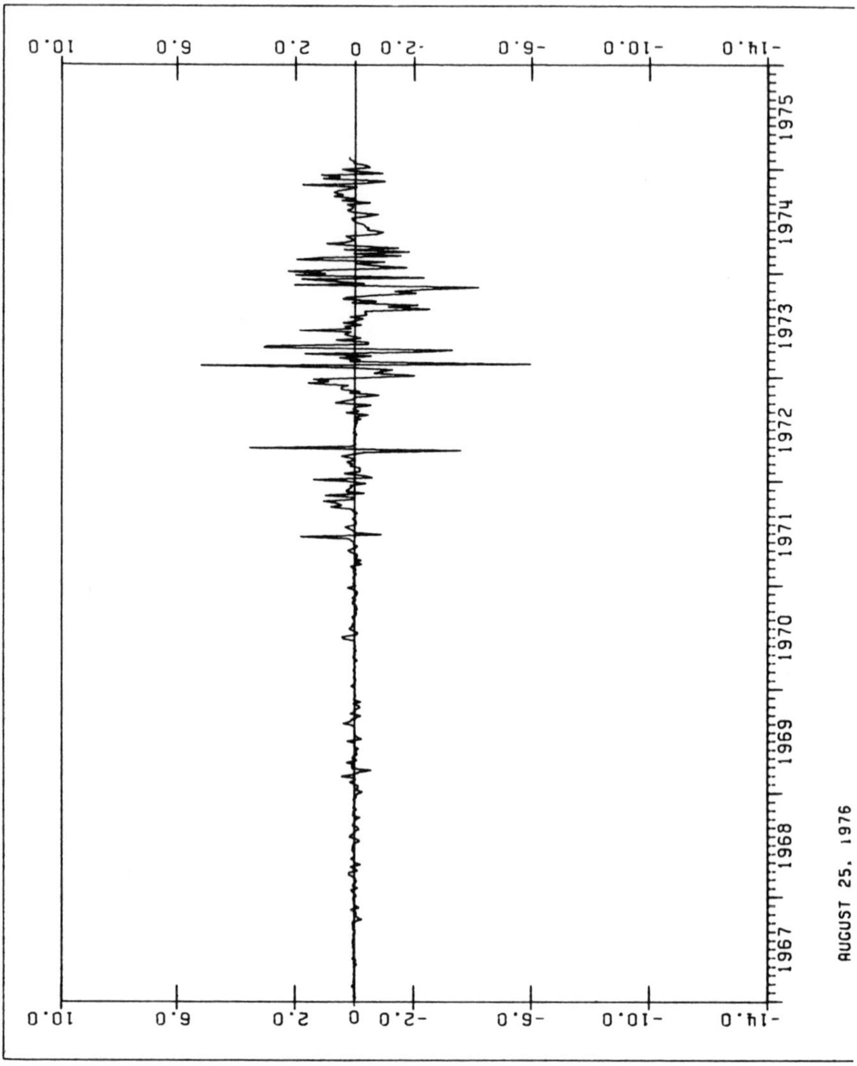

98 / *The International Money Market*

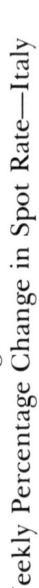

Figure 6.8.
Weekly Percentage Change in Spot Rate—Italy

Time Series Behavior of Spot and Forward Exchange Rates / **99**

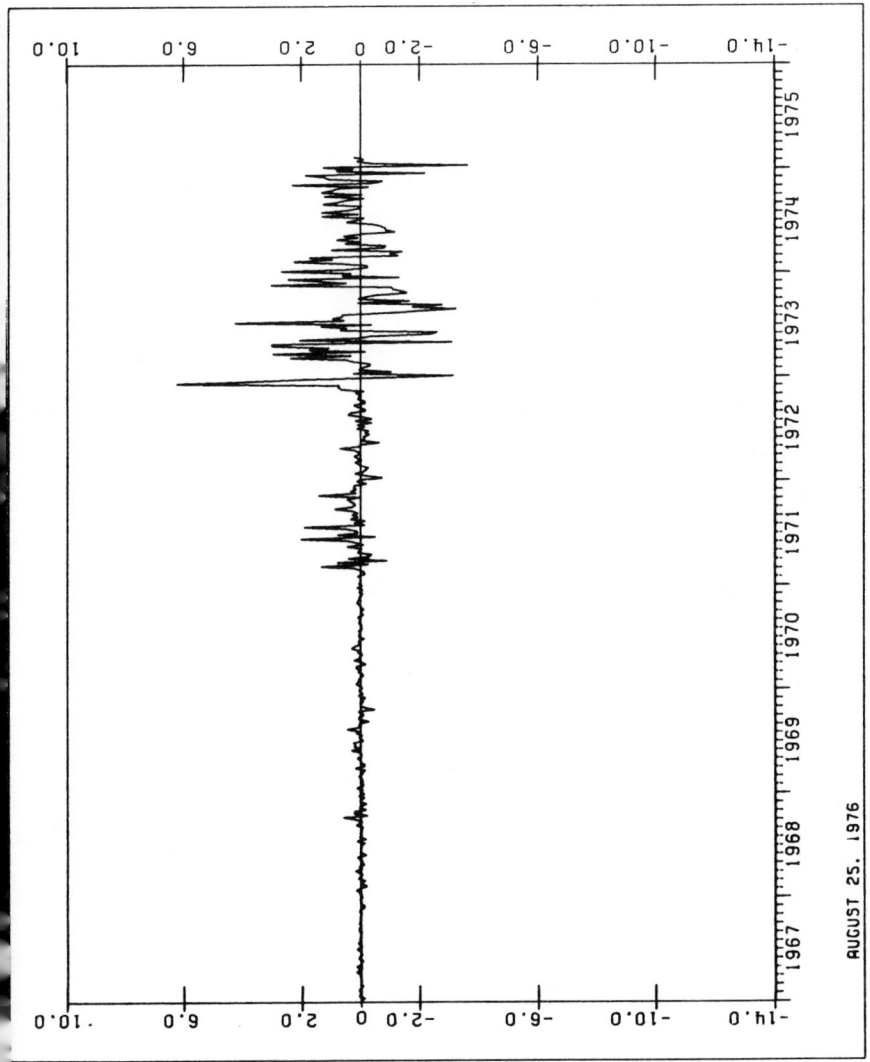

Figure 6.9.
Weekly Percentage Change in Spot Rate—Netherlands

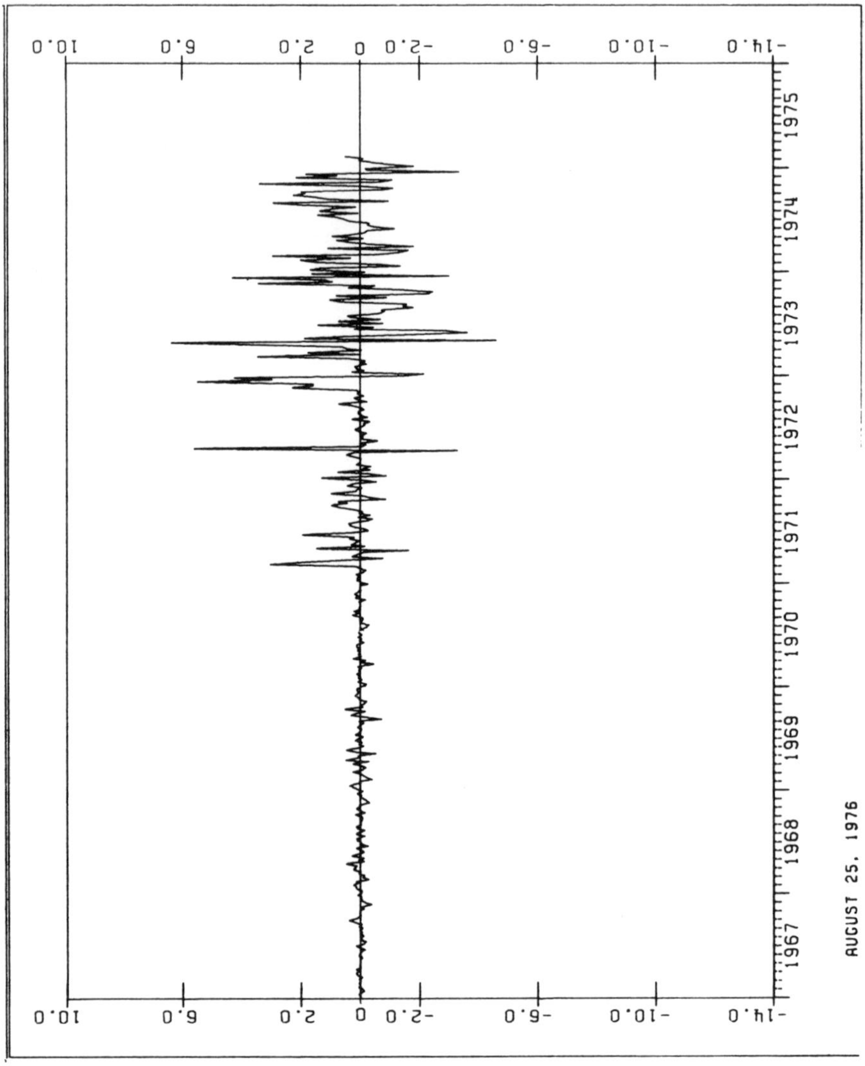

100 / *The International Money Market*

Figure 6.10.
Weekly Percentage Change in Spot Rate—Switzerland

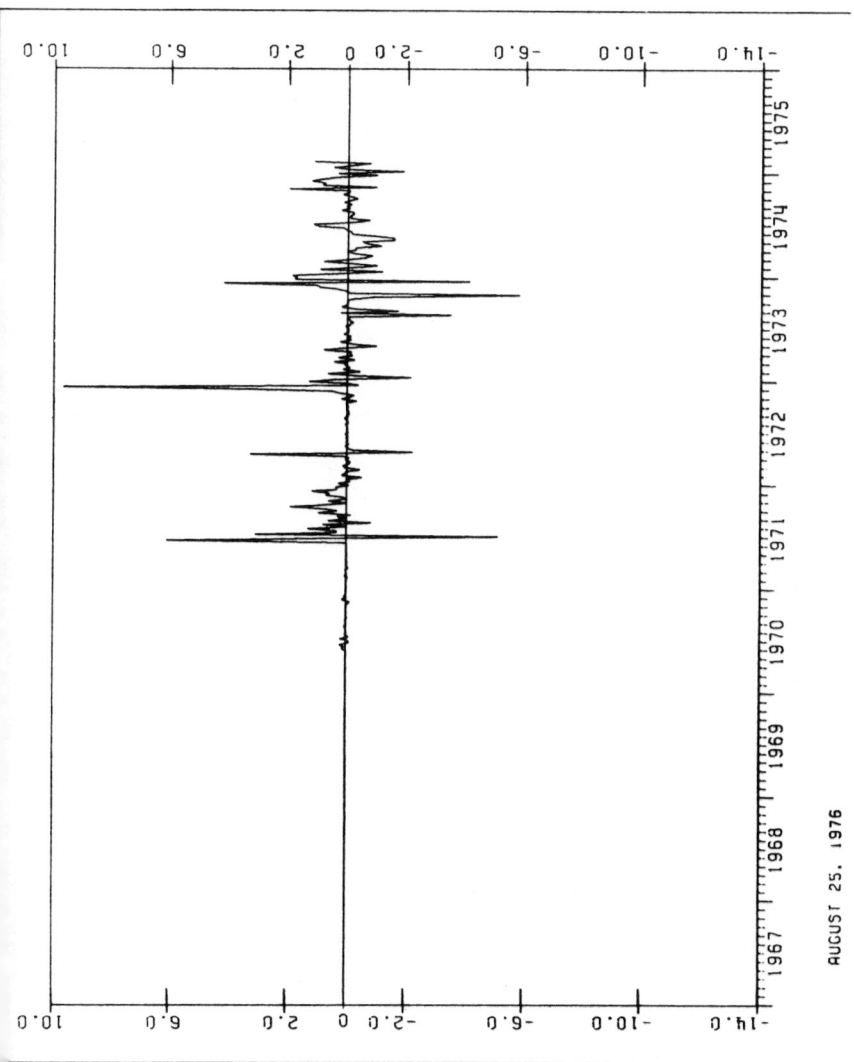

Figure 6.11.
Weekly Percentage Change in Spot Rate—Japan

Table 6.4. Summary Statistics for Weekly Percentage Changes ($X_{i,t}$)

Country	Statistic	Peg I	Float I	Peg II	Float II
Canada	Mean	0.003	0.002	N.A.	N.A.
	S.E.	0.104	0.295	N.A.	N.A.
	Nobs	172	256	0	0
United Kingdom	Mean	−0.057	0.175	−0.050	−0.036
	S.E.	0.856	0.306	0.772	0.841
	Nobs	235	17	26	148
Belgium	Mean	0.004	0.454	0.213	0.124
	S.E.	0.142	0.537	1.042	1.359
	Nobs	235	17	64	110
France	Mean	−0.004	0.049	0.230	0.099
	S.E.	0.674	0.179	1.044	1.500
	Nobs	235	17	64	110
Germany	Mean	0.050	0.292	0.225	0.175
	S.E.	0.406	0.666	1.029	1.615
	Nobs	221	31	64	110
Italy	Mean	0.003	0.090	0.043	−0.073
	S.E.	0.109	0.364	0.751	1.367
	Nobs	235	17	59	115
Netherlands	Mean	0.008	0.264	0.182	0.184
	S.E.	0.148	0.603	1.103	1.400
	Nobs	221	31	64	110
Switzerland	Mean	0.028	0.170	0.073	0.335
	S.E.	0.323	0.403	0.959	1.769
	Nobs	235	17	56	118
Japan	Mean	0.006	0.350	0.138	−0.080
	S.E.	0.067	1.642	0.714	1.096
	Nobs	60	17	59	115

stationary process dominates each series during the Float II period, a time series analysis seems possible.

THE BOX-JENKINS TECHNIQUE FOR ANALYZING TIME SERIES DATA

The time series processes of interest are those that are generated by a stationary stochastic process. It is possible to forecast in this case since the probability distribution generating future observations is the same as for past observations. The conditional probability distribution for future observations can be estimated from past data.

Box and Jenkins (1970) show that a stationary series can be written as an infinite sum of random variables:

(6.3) $$Z_t = a_t + \psi_1 a_{t-1} + \psi_2 a_{t-2} + \psi_3 a_{t-3} + \ldots$$
where $E(a_t) = 0$
$V(a_t) = \sigma_a^2$
$Cov(a_t, a_{t\pm i}) = 0; i \neq 0.$

In the jargon of time series analysis, a linear filter (the ψ weights) transforms a series of random shocks or white noise (the unobserved a's) into a series of observations (the observed Z's).

The following backshift operator notation will simplify the exposition.

$$B Z_t \equiv Z_{t-1}$$
$$B^k Z_t \equiv Z_{t-k}.$$

Therefore, (6.3) becomes

$$Z_t = (1 + \psi_1 B + \psi_2 B^2 + \ldots) a_t$$
$$= \psi(B) a_t.$$

Box and Jenkins analyze (6.3) extensively. They show that (6.3) can be rewritten as

(6.4) $$Z_t = \phi_1 Z_{t-1} + \phi_2 Z_{t-2} + \cdots \phi_p Z_{t-p} + \theta_0$$
$$+ a_t - \theta_1 a_{t-1} - \theta_2 a_{t-2} - \ldots \theta_q a_{t-q}.$$

Using the backshift operator notation, (6.4) becomes

(6.5) $$\phi(B) Z_t = \theta(B) a_t + \theta_0$$

or $$Z_t = \frac{\theta(B)}{\phi(B)} a_t + \theta_0$$

where $$\theta(B) = (1 - \theta_1 B - \ldots - \theta_q B^q)$$
$$\phi(B) = (1 - \phi_1 B - \ldots - \phi_p B^p).$$

The rational function of two polynomials, $\theta(B)$ and $\phi(B)$, in (6.5) approximates the infinite distributed lag function $\psi(B)$ in (6.3). The q values of θ are called "Moving Average" (MA) terms and the p values of ϕ are called "AutoRegressive" (AR) terms; θ_0 is a constant parameter. The series (6.5) is called an ARMA process of order (p,q).

If the raw data series is not stationary, Box and Jenkins suggest differencing the data until a transformed variable, W_t, such that

$$W_t = Z_t - Z_{t-d}$$

is stationary. In this case, the differenced (or integrated) series

(6.6) $$W_t = \frac{\theta(B)}{\phi(B)} a_t + \theta_0$$

is said to follow an ARIMA process of order (p,d,q).

In the special case where all MA and AR equal zero and d = 1, the model

(6.7) $$Z_t = Z_{t-1} + a_t + \theta_0$$

is of order (0,1,0)—the random walk model with drift parameter θ_0. The (0,1,0) model is a convenient model to test against higher order (p,d,q) models, since it tests the null hypothesis that higher order MA and AR terms equal zero.[6]

Techniques for model identification and estimation are analyzed in great detail by Box and Jenkins (1970). In brief, the approach is to difference the series Z_t until it appears stationary. Then estimates of the autocorrelation and partial autocorrelation function are computed. By comparing these sample functions with their theoretical counterpart it may be possible to identify the order (p,d,q) of the process and initial estimates of the parameters $\phi(B)$ and $\theta(B)$. Final parameter estimates are obtained during a nonlinear estimation procedure which minimizes the residual sum of squares in the fitted model.

DIAGNOSTIC TESTS FOR SELECTING A TIME SERIES MODEL

The decision to accept or reject a particular model is subjective. There is no single test statistic or diagnostic check to indicate the adequacy of a particular model. In selecting a model we are concerned with several factors: (a) We do not want to "over-fit" the series. There is a presumption that a low order (p,d,q) model can be found to adequately represent the data. (b) The coefficients in the $\phi(B)$ and $\theta(B)$ polynomials should be significantly different from zero. (c) The residuals from the fitted model should be serially uncorrelated white noise.

To deal more objectively with the first issue, Zellner and Palm (1974) propose the following likelihood ratio test. Under the null hypothesis, the time series follows the ARMA(p,q) process.

(2) $$\phi(B) Z_i = \theta(B)\epsilon_i, \quad i = 1,\ldots,N$$

where the error process ϵ_i is NID$(0,\sigma^2)$. The alternative hypothesis is the ARMA (p_a,q_a) representation

(1) $$\phi_a(B) Z_i = \theta_a(B)\epsilon_{ai}, \quad i = 1,\ldots,N$$

where the error process ϵ_{ai} is NID$(0,\sigma_a^2)$.

Final parameter estimates for both models are obtained using maximum likelihood procedures. Letting L represent the likelihood function, the likelihood ratio λ is

$$\lambda = (\max_{\phi,\theta,\sigma} L(\phi,\theta,\sigma|Z))/(\max_{\phi_a,\theta_a,\sigma_a} L(\phi_a,\theta_a,\sigma_a|Z)).$$

Zellner and Palm show that this ratio reduces to

$$\lambda = (\hat{\sigma}_a^2/\hat{\sigma}^2)^{N/2},$$

where $\hat{\sigma}_a^2$ and $\hat{\sigma}^2$ are maximum likelihood estimates.

Furthermore,

> If Model (1) is nested in model (2), i.e., $P_a \le p$ and/or $q_a \le q$, with at least one strict inequality, and under the assumption that (1) is the true model, 2 ln λ is approximately distributed as chi-square on r degrees of freedom with r being the number of restrictions imposed on (2) to obtain (1); that is r = p + q − $(p_a + q_a)$ (Zellner and Palm 1974, p. 34).

When the test statistic 2 ln λ is significant, the residual sum of squares $\hat{\sigma}_a^2$ will be significantly larger than $\hat{\sigma}^2$. In this case we reject the alternative model (1) in favor of model (2).[7]

To test the significance of the coefficients in the $\theta(B)$ and $\phi(B)$ polynomials, we rely on large sample standard error estimates and the usual t-tests.

Serial correlations of residuals may be tested for any given lag by using large sample standard errors and t-tests. Alternatively, we can compute the Q-statistic:

$$Q = N \sum_{i=1}^{k} \hat{r}_i^2$$

where $\hat{r}_i^2$ is the sample estimate of the serial correlation of residuals at lag i. Under the null hypothesis that there is no serial correlation ($\hat{r}_i = 0$ for all i), Q is distributed as chi-square with (k-p-q-d-1) degrees of freedom (Box and Pierce 1970).[8]

EMPIRICAL RESULTS

Spot Exchange Rate Series

Because percentage changes in the nine spot rate series appear stationary during the Float II period, models for the first difference (d = 1) of the natural logarithm of the spot rate are estimated. Analysis of the autocorrelation and partial autocorrelation functions for each series suggests that the transformed data $W_t = \ln Z_t - \ln Z_{t-1}$ can be described by an ARMA process of order $p \leq 1$ and $q \leq 2$. In other words, for most cases the autocorrelation functions decay exponentially while the partial autocorrelation function drops near zero after a 3 period lag. The United Kingdom and Japan are exceptions where (0,1,3) and (0,1,6) models, respectively, are indicated. Tables 6.5 and 6.6 summarize the final parameter estimates and diagnostic statistics for the models tentatively entertained.

For two countries (Italy and Switzerland) evidence for the random walk model (0,1,0) is strong. When we fit higher order models, for example (0,1,1), the first order moving average term is not significant with t-statistics of 1.0 for Italy and 1.3 for Switzerland. Note that the residual sum of squares for the (0,1,1) model is actually *higher* than for the (0,1,0) model—a seemingly anomalous result which arises because of our estimation technique.[9] Given that the residual sum of squares in-

Table 6.5. Parameter Estimates for Alternative ARIMA (P,D,Q) Models of the Spot Rate

Country	(P,D,Q)	Identified Model	SS	$\hat{\sigma}_a^2$	Q	d.f.	N
Canada	(0,1,0)		.223 E-2	.865 E-5	—	—	257
	(0,1,0)	$W_t = a_t + .161 a_{t-1}$ (2.7)	.216 E-2	.857 E-5	15.0	23	256
United Kingdom	(0,1,0)		.581 E-1	.390 E-3	—	—	149
	(0,1,1)	$W_t = a_t + .093 a_{t-1}$ (1.1)	.573 E-1	.390 E-3	34.0	23	148
	(0,1,3)	$W_t = a_t + .15 a_{t-3}$ (1.84)	.540 E-1	.372 E-3	19.2	21	148
Belgium	(0,1,0)		.145 E-4	.131 E-6	—	—	111
	(0,1,1)	$W_t = a_t + .134 a_{t-1}$ (1.42)	.142 E-4	.130 E-6	14.4	23	110
	(1,1,1)	$W_t = .71 Z_{t-1} + a_t - .55 a_{t-1}$ (2.6) (1.7)	.139 E-4	.128 E-6	11.1	22	110
France	(0,1,0)		.122 E-2	.110 E-4	—	—	111
	(1,1,2)	$W_t = .48 Z_{t-1} + a_t - .52 a_{t-1} + .25 a_{t-2}$ (1.64) (1.81) (2.64)	.114 E-2	.106 E-4	15.7	21	110
Germany	(0,1,0)		.463 E-2	.417 E-4	—	—	111
	(0,1,1)	$W_t = a_t + .06 a_{t-1}$ (0.6)	.460 E-2	.422 E-4	28.6	23	110
	(0,1,2)	$W_t = a_t + .012 a_{t-1} + .207 a_{t-2}$ (.13) (2.20)	.441 E-2	.408 E-4	17.0	22	110

continued

108 / *The International Money Market*

Table 6.5. continued

Country	(P,D,Q)	Identified Model	SS	$\hat{\sigma}_a^2$	Q	d.f.	N
Italy	(0,1,0)		.593 E-7	.511 E-9	—	—	116
	(0,1,1)	$W_t = a_t - .09a_{t-1}$ (1.0)	.598 E-7	.513 E-9	19.4	23	115
Netherlands	(0,1,0)		.311 E-2	.280 E-4	—	—	111
	(0,1,2)	$W_t = a_t + .13a_{t-1} + .20a_{t-2}$ (1.4) (2.1)	.293 E-2	.271 E-4	18.2	22	110
Switzerland	(0,1,0)		.422 E-2	.352 E-4	—	—	120
	(0,1,1)	$W_t = a_t + .12a_{t-1}$ (1.3)	.426 E-2	.361 E-4	16.3	23	119
Japan	(0,1,0)		.173 E-6	.149 E-8	—	—	116
	(0,1,6)	$W_t = a_t + .20a_{t-6}$ (2.6)	.143 E-6	.128 E-8	22.4	18	115

Notes: $W_t = Z_t - Z_{t-1}$
SS: sum of squared residuals after estimating parameters
σ_a^2: residual variance
Q: $Q = N \sum_{i=1}^{k} \hat{r}_i \sim$ chi-square (k-p-q-l)
Box-Pierce test for randomness of residuals
d.f.: degrees of freedom for Q statistic
N: sample size

Selected values of chi-square distribution:
Significance level by degrees of freedom

X^2	d.f.				
	23	22	21	20	18
10%	32.0	30.8	29.6	28.4	26.0
5%	35.2	33.9	32.7	31.4	28.9

Table 6.6. Likelihood Ratio Analysis of Alternative ARIMA (P,D,Q) Models Versus the Random Walk Model

Country (N)	Alternative (P,D,Q) Model	$\lambda = \left(\dfrac{\hat{\sigma}_a^2}{\hat{\sigma}^2}\right)^{N/2}$	$2 \ln \lambda$	r	Critical Points for X^2 $\alpha = .05$	$\alpha = .10$
Canada (257)	(0,1,1)	71.60	8.54	1	3.84	2.71
England (149)	(0,1,3)	236.24	10.93	1[a]	3.83	2.71
Belgium (111)	(0,1,1)	3.72	2.63	1	3.84	2.71
	(1,1,1)	12.16	5.00	2	5.99	4.61
France (111)	(1,1,2)	45.13	7.62	3	7.81	6.25
Germany (111)	(0,1,2)	14.73	5.38	2	5.99	4.61
Italy (116)	(0,1,1)	2.16	1.54	1	3.84	2.71
Netherlands (111)	(0,1,2)	26.40	6.55	2	5.99	4.61
Switzerland (120)	(0,1,1)	0.60	−1.02	1	3.84	2.71
Japan (116)	(0,1,6)	58620.	21.96	1[b]	3.84	2.71

[a] 2 MA parameters suppressed.
[b] 5 MA parameters suppressed.

creases, the likelihood ratio test statistics (in Table 6.6) are *negative*. The Q-statistics (in Table 6.5) indicate that the residuals are not significantly autocorrelated. All of the diagnostic tests therefore indicate that we cannot reject the (0,1,0) model for Italy and Switzerland.

For four countries (Canada, United Kingdom, Netherlands, and Japan) there is strong evidence to reject the (0,1,0) model. Each of these countries contains an MA term that has a significant t-value. For example, a θ_3 parameter in the British series has a t-value of 1.84.[10] In each of these countries, the MA parameter is positive although the length of the lag varies from one week for Canada to six weeks for Japan. This is consistent with a view that exchange rates *underadjust* to new information. For example, the British result indicates that if a 1% shock hits the spot exchange rate, on average, three weeks later the spot rate will rise an additional 0.15%.

In these four countries, the likelihood ratio test statistics (in Table 6.6) are significant which indicates that the reduction in residual variance is not the result of chance. Serial correlation of residuals which was significant in the lower order models is reduced to insignificant levels in the higher order models. All of the diagnostic tests therefore indicate that we can reject the (0,1,0) model for Canada, United Kingdom, Netherlands, and Japan in favor of higher order models.

For the final three countries (Belgium, France, and Germany) the evidence is not conclusive. Coefficients of the higher order terms are sometimes significant. However, the likelihood ratio tests indicate that the improvement over the (0,1,0) model is significant only at the 10% level. The higher order models, of course, reduce the serial correlation of the residuals. But this serial correlation was not statistically significant in the (0,1,0) model in the first place. The diagnostic tests therefore leave some doubt as to which models are most appropriate for these three countries.

In developing the likelihood ratio test, Zellner and Palm suggest that the loss from rejecting the unrestricted, higher order model (when it is true) probably exceeds the loss from accepting the unrestricted, higher order model (when it is false). Therefore, Zellner and Palm argue that a 5% or a 10% rejection region is more appropriate than a 0.1% or 1.0% value. Following this reasoning, we would reject the random walk model for Belgium, France, and Germany in favor of alternative, higher order models.

Forward Exchange Rate Series

If forward rates are an accurate reflection of future spot rates, then forward rates and spot rates should follow a similar time series representation.[11] To test this hypothesis, Box-Jenkins time series analysis is applied to a weekly series of 90-day forward exchange rates. The sample period and sample countries are the same as for the spot rates analyzed in the previous section.

The first difference of the natural logarithm of the forward rate appears stationary. Analysis of the autocorrelation and partial autocorrelation functions for each series suggests that in most cases the transformed data $W_t = \ln Z_t - \ln Z_{t-1}$ can be described by an ARMA process of order $p \leq 1$ and $q \leq 2$.

The results in Table 6.7 indicate that the coefficients for the spot and forward series of a given country are very similar. For example, $\theta_1 = -.16$ in the Canadian spot series; $\theta_1 = -.13$ in the forward series. For the Netherlands, $\theta_1 = -.13$ and $\theta_2 = -.20$ in the spot series, while $\theta_1 = -.11$ and $\theta_2 = -.20$ in the forward series. In Germany, the coefficients in the (0,1,2) model are nearly the same in both spot and forward rate series although the t-values are different.

For the spot series, currencies were classified on the basis of empirical

Table 6.7. Parameter Estimates for Alternative ARIMA (P,D,Q) Models of the 90-Day Forward Rate

Country	(P,D,Q)	Identified Model	SS	$\hat{\sigma}_a^2$	Q	d.f.	N
Canada	(0,1,0)			.805 E-5	—	—	257
	(0,1,1)	$W_t = a_t + .13a_{t-1}$ (2.2)	.203 E-2	.794 E-5	16.3	23	256
United Kingdom	(0,1,0)			.445 E-3	—	—	149
	(0,1,3)	$W_t = a_t + .07a_{t-1} + .03a_{t-2} + .24a_{t-3}$ (0.9) (0.3) (2.9)	.645 E-1		23.4	21	148
Belgium	(0,1,0)			.105 E-6	—	—	111
	(0,1,2)	$W_t = a_t + .24a_{t-1} + .23a_{t-2}$ (2.6) (2.4)	.103 E-4	.958 E-7	15.0	22	110
France	(0,1,0)			.126 E-4	—	—	111
	(0,1,2)	$W_t = a_t - .09a_{t-1} + .27a_{t-2}$ (0.9) (2.9)	.128 E-2	.119 E-4	11.9	22	110
Germany	(0,1,0)			.434 E-4	—	—	110
	(0,1,2)	$W_t = a_t + .01a_{t-1} + .21a_{t-2}$ (2.3)	.458 E-2	.424 E-4	18.1	23	110
	(1,1,2)	$= .61\nabla Z_{t-1} + a_t - .58a_{t-1} + .22a_{t-2}$ (2.5) (2.4) (2.1)	.445 E-2	.416 E-4	13.8	21	110
Italy	(0,1,0)			.660 E-9	—	—	115
	(0,1,1)	$W_t = a_t - .13a_{t-1}$ (1.4)	.751 E-7	.658 E-9	18.2	23	115
Netherlands	(0,1,0)			.283 E-4	—	—	110
	(0,1,2)	$W_t = a_t + .11a_{t-1} + .20a_{t-2}$ (1.2) (2.1)	.296 E-2	.273 E-4	19.7	22	110
Switzerland	(0,1,0)			.374 E-4	—	—	119
	(0,1,1)	$W_t = a_t + .13a_{t-1}$ (1.4)	.451 E-2	.382 E-4	15.3	23	119
Japan	(0,1,0)			.126 E-8	—	—	115
	(0,1,1)	$W_t = a_t + .18a_{t-1}$ (2.2)	.144 E-6	.121 E-8	21.0	23	115

evidence favoring the (0,1,0) model. A similar analysis is performed on the forward rate series. The evidence for the random walk model is strong for only two countries—Italy and Switzerland. All of the diagnostic checks—t tests of coefficients, likelihood ratio tests, Q test for serial correlation of residuals—reject alternative higher order models.

For two countries, Belgium and France, there is strong evidence against a random walk in forward rates. For these countries, higher order terms have significant coefficients, likelihood ratio tests reject the (0,1,0) model at the 5% level (or better) and residual correlation drops to insignificant levels in the higher order models. These two countries are in the set for which the evidence is mixed on the random walk model in spot prices.

For the final four countries—Canada, United Kingdom, the Netherlands, and Japan—the evidence on the random walk of forward rates is mixed. The likelihood ratio tests indicate that we can reject the (0,1,0) model in favor of a higher order model at approximately the 10% level.

In general, it seems that, given a particular currency, the time pattern of forward rates is similar to the time pattern of spot rates. This is suggested by the order (p,d,q) of the fitted models and the magnitude of the coefficients. This evidence is consistent with a view that forward speculators have knowledge of the time pattern of spot rates. By their activity, forward speculators make the time pattern of forward rates correspond to the time pattern of spot rates.

Table 6.8. Likelihood Ratio Analysis of Alternative ARIMA (P,D,Q) Models Versus the Random Walk Model of the 90-Day Forward Rate

Country (N)	Alternative (P,D,Q) Model	$\lambda = \left(\frac{\hat{\sigma}_a^2}{\hat{\sigma}^2} \right)^{N/2}$	$2 \ln \lambda$	r	Critical Points for $X^2 (r)$ $\alpha = .05$	$\alpha = .10$
Canada (257)	(0,1,1)	5.86	5.86	1	3.84	2.76
England (149)	(0,1,3)	26.45	6.55	3	7.81	6.25
Belgium (111)	(0,1,2)	162.26	10.18	2	5.99	4.61
France (111)	(0,1,2)	23.86	6.34	2	5.99	4.61
Germany (111)	(0,1,2)	3.65	2.59	2	5.99	4.61
	(1,1,2)	10.50	4.70	3	7.81	6.25
Italy (116)	(0,1,1)	1.19	0.35	1	3.84	2.76
Netherlands (111)	(0,1,2)	7.36	3.99	2	5.99	4.61
Switzerland (120)	(0,1,1)	0.28	−2.54	1	3.84	2.76
Japan (116)	(0,1,1)	10.47	4.70	1	3.84	2.76

CONCLUSIONS

This chapter analyzed the time series behavior of exchange rates during the sample period. The data indicate that the first two moments of the level of the spot rate ($S_{i,t}$) and its rate of change ($X_{i,t}$) are not stationary. The general trend is toward increasing volatility of S_i and X_i.

This result precludes a time series analysis of exchange rates extending over the sample period. However, low order time series models are estimated successfully for the Float II period. Models for the forward and spot rates are often similar, which indicates that the forward rate reflects the serial dependence in the spot rate series.

TIME SERIES ANALYSIS OF EXCHANGE RATES IN THREE PERIODS

The analysis in Chapter III suggests the three time periods (1962/67, 1968/69, and 1973/75) reflect markedly different patterns of behavior. The time series plot of the variable 100 · F/S reveals that in the period 1962/67 forward premia are relatively small in comparison to the 1968/69 period. The dichotomy is of interest because both periods are characterized by pegged rates. In the 1973/75 managed float period, the variable 100 · F/S becomes even more volatile than in the earlier periods.

In Chapter IV, the analysis of covered arbitrage flows indicates that the two periods 1962/67 and 1973/75 appear similar in that a similar fraction of observations fall within a neutral band generated by transaction costs. Transaction costs explain a much smaller fraction of observations in the 1968/69 period.

In this section, exchange rate series in each of the three periods are analyzed using time series methods. Underlying this approach is the presumption that a time series representation is consistent with a particular set of structural and behavioral relationships in the economy. Changes in structural or behavioral relationships may lead to changes in the order of the fitted time series model or changes in the magnitude of parameters (Nelson 1973).

A problem with this approach is that it may be difficult to make precise predictions on how changes in structure or behavior will affect the fitted time series model. In this section, however, inferences are drawn in the reverse direction. If a time series model changes across periods, we infer that the underlying structure has changed (albeit in some unspecified way).

To examine the three periods, Box-Jenkins time series models are fit for both spot and forward exchange rate series in the sterling, Deutsch mark, the Canadian dollar markets. Estimation and identification techniques described in Chapter VI are used. The results are summarized in Tables 6.9 and 6.10.

In the first and last periods the random walk formulation is rejected by the log-likelihood test at the 5% level in nine of the twelve series. In the middle, 1968/69 period, the random walk model is not rejected in any of the six series.

Table 6.9. Time Series Models for Spot Exchange in Three Periods[a]

Time Period	Country	Moving Average Coefficients			$\hat{\sigma}_a^2$	Q (k)	2 ln λ (r)
		θ_1	θ_2	θ_3			
1962/67	United Kingdom	−.06	−.06	−.11	.209 E-6	22.8	1.46
(N = 306)		(1.0)	(1.1)	(1.9)		(21)	(3)
	Germany	−.10	−.14	—	.498 E-6	17.2	6.08*
		(1.6)	(2.3)			(22)	(2)
	Canada	−.10	−.17	—	.334 E-5	12.4	9.92*
		(1.6)	(3.1)			(22)	(2)
1968/69	United Kingdom	−.10	−.07	+.15	.167 E-5	16.2	1.18
(N = 99)		(0.9)	(0.7)	(1.5)		(21)	(3)
	Germany	−.10	—	—	.342 E-4	6.9	−2.05
		(0.9)				(23)	(1)
	Canada	+.14	−.16	—	.123 E-5	12.3	1.60
		(1.4)	(1.7)			(22)	(2)
1973/75	United Kingdom	−.16	+.10	−.40	.748 E-4	16.3	10.22**
(N = 96)		(1.6)	(1.0)	(4.1)		(21)	(3)
	Germany	+.10	−.47	+.18	.205 E-3	18.4	16.32*
		(1.0)	(5.5)	(2.0)		(21)	(3)
	Canada	−.10	−.24	—	.852 E-5	18.1	4.19**
		(1.0)	(2.3)			(22)	(2)

[a] Moving average coefficients in the model

$$W_t = \ln S_t - \ln S_{t-1} = a_t + \theta_1 a_{t-1} + \theta_2 a_{t-2} + \theta_3 a_{t-3}$$

with t-statistics in parentheses.
$\hat{\sigma}_a^2$ = residual variance in series.
Q = Box-Pierce test statistic for autocorrelation of residuals. Distributed as χ^2 with k degrees of freedom.
2 ln λ = Zellner-Palm test statistic for significance of fitted model against null hypothesis that the series is a random walk. Distributed as X^2 with r degrees of freedom.
 * = significant at 5% level.
 ** = significant at 20% level.

Table 6.10. Time Series Models for Forward Exchange in Three Periods [a]

Time Period	Country	Moving Average Coefficients			$\hat{\sigma}_a^2$	Q (k)	2 ln λ (r)
		θ_1	θ_2	θ_3			
1962/67 (N = 306)	United Kingdom	−.08 (1.4)	+.02 (0.4)	−.25 (4.5)	.333 E-6	31.3* (21)	12.60* (3)
	Germany	−.13 (2.2)	—	—	.412 E-6	20.3 (23)	4.42* (1)
	Canada	−.05 (0.9)	−.16 (2.9)	—	.354 E-5	11.0 (22)	6.84* (2)
1968/69 (N = 99)	United Kingdom	−.05 (0.5)	−.04 (0.4)	−.05 (0.5)	.190 E-4	18.9 (21)	−2.64 (3)
	Germany	−.07 (.07)	—	—	.318 E-4	14.6 (23)	−2.20 (1)
	Canada	+.07 (0.7)	—	—	.169 E-4	16.2 (23)	−0.59 (1)
1973/75 (N = 96)	United Kingdom	−.06 (0.6)	+.02 (0.2)	−.37 (3.8)	.980 E-4	19.4 (21)	8.43* (3)
	Germany	+.05 (0.5)	−.40 (4.5)	—	.223 E-4	14.3 (22)	16.38* (2)
	Canada	−.10 (1.0)	−.22 (2.1)	—	.788 E-5	18.2 (22)	3.12 (2)

[a] For an explanation see footnotes on Table 6.9.
* = significant at 5% level.
** = significant at 20% level.

A closer examination of the series reveals further similarities between the first and third periods. The series describing forward sterling are good examples. In 1962/67, the point estimates of the moving average coefficients are (−.08,+.02,−.25) while in the 1973/75 period the estimates are (−.06,+.02,−.37). The similarity in the sign and magnitude of these numbers suggests that the two periods may reflect similar economic and structural relationships.[12] The series stand in contrast to the random behavior of forward sterling during the 1968/69 period. Spot sterling displays a similar pattern—the θ_3 term is significant in the first and last periods but not in 1968/69.

Movement in the Canadian dollar exchange rates provide another good example. In the first and last periods, the second order moving average coefficient is significant in both spot and forward rate series. In the 1968/69 period, however, these coefficients are not significant and the random walk formulation appears to be an adequate representation of each series.

The close analogy between first and last subperiods breaks down somewhat in the case of Deutsch mark. For example, in the spot series, a (0,1,2) model appears adequate in the 1962/67 period while a (0,1,3) model is required in 1973/75. For forward DM, the order of the model changes from (0,1,1) to (0,1,2) over the same periods. These longer lags in adjustment are consistent with higher transaction costs observed in these markets. However, even in the Deutsch mark case, the periods 1962/67 and 1973/75 appear similar in that the data reject the random walk description of percentage changes in the spot and forward rates. In the 1968/69 period, both spot and forward Deutsch mark appear to move randomly.

Overall, the data are consistent with the interpretation that underlying structural and behavioral relationships were similar in the two periods 1962/67 and 1973/75. This interpretation is based on the observation that fitted time series models for the two periods are similar to each other and markedly different from a third period, 1968/69. This finding is important because the two periods, 1962/67 and 1973/75, are characterized by different formal exchange rate regimes. One interpretation of this finding is that the formal exchange rate system does not change the manner in which underlying structural and behavioral relationships are reflected in the time series of exchange rates.

TIME SERIES ANALYSIS OF CANADIAN EXCHANGE RATES 1950/62

The behavior of the Canadian spot exchange rate during the floating time period 1950/62 has been studied extensively by Poole (1966) and others. In part, Poole was interested in detecting departures from randomness to determine if speculators had a stabilizing effect on the market. His conclusion was that speculation did have a stabilizing impact. Furthermore, while statistically significant departures from randomness were detected, Poole doubted their economic significance.

> With a (first order serial) correlation of .172, only 3 percent of the variance of the (daily percentage) changes can be explained by the ... model. Given that the variance of the daily percentage changes of the exchange rate is only .017 to begin with, it appears that the serial correlation can be of little practical importance (p. 31).

Table 6.11. Parameter Estimates for Alternative ARIMA (P,D,Q) Models of Canadian Spot Rate, 1950/62

Series	(P,D,Q)	Identified Model	SS	$\hat{\sigma}_a^2$	Q	d.f.	N
1	(0,1,0)		11.061	—	—	—	400
	(0,1,1)	$W_t = .015 + a_t + .29a_{t-1}$ $(1.4) \quad (6.1)$	10.318	.259 E-1	34.4	22	399
	(0,1,2)	$W_t = .015 + a_t + .25a_{t-1} - .08a_{t-2}$ $(1.6) \quad (5.0) \quad (1.6)$	10.269	.259 E-1	32.5	21	398
	(0,1,3)	$W_t = .015 + a_t + .26a_{t-1} - .09a_{t-2} - .12a_{t-3}$ $(1.8) \quad (5.3) \quad (1.8) \quad (2.5)$	10.107	.255 E-1	26.4	20	397
2	(0,1,0)		7.673	—	—	—	400
	(0,1,1)	$W_t = .004 + a_t + .17a_{t-1}$ $(.5) \quad (3.5)$	7.435	.187 E-1	22.9	22	399
	(0,1,2)	$W_t = .004 + a_t + .18a_{t-1} + .03a_{t-2}$ $(.4) \quad (3.5) \quad (.7)$	7.427	.188 E-1	22.2	21	398
(a)	(0,1,3)	$W_t = .004 + a_t + .18a_{t-1} + .04a_{t-2} - .01a_{t-3}$ $(.4) \quad (3.5) \quad (.7) \quad (.2)$	7.426	.188 E-1	22.2	20	397
3	(0,1,0)		3.408	—	—	—	400
	(0,1,1)	$W_t = -.004 + a_t + .16a_{t-1}$ $(.7) \quad (3.2)$	3.325	.837 E-2	28.1	22	399
	(0,1,2)	$W_t = -.004 + a_t + .16a_{t-1} + .01a_{t-2}$ $(.7) \quad (3.1) \quad (.2)$	3.324	.839 E-2	28.1	21	398
(b)	(0,1,3)	$W_t = -.004 + a_t + .15a_{t-1} + .01a_{t-2} + .08a_{t-3}$ $(.6) \quad (3.0) \quad (.3) \quad (1.6)$	3.306	.837 E-2	26.3	20	397

continued

Table 6.11. continued

Series	(P,D,Q)	Identified Model	SS	$\hat{\sigma}_a^2$	Q	d.f.	N
4	(0,1,0)		2.473	—	—	—	400
	(0,1,1)	$W_t = .007 + a_t + .30a_{t-1}$ $(1.4)(6.3)$	2.270	.572 E-2	33.9	22	399
	(0,1,2)	$W_t = .007 + a_t + .30a_{t-1} + .008a_{t-2}$ $(1.4)(5.9)(.2)$	2.270	.573 E-2	34.1	21	398
(c)	(0,1,3)	$W_t = .007 + a_t + .28a_{t-1} - .03a_{t-2} - .07a_{t-3}$ $(1.6)(5.6)(.5)(1.4)$	2.26	.572 E-2	33.3	20	397
5	(0,1,0)		6.063	—	—	—	400
	(0,1,1)	$W_t = -.005 + a_t + .18a_{t-1}$ $(.6)(3.6)$	5.889	.148 E-1	31.4	22	399
	(0,1,2)	$W_t = -.005 + a_t + .18a_{t-1} + .01a_{t-2}$ $(.6)(3.6)(.1)$	5.889	.149 E-1	31.4	21	398
(d)	(0,1,3)	$W_t = -.005 + a_t + .18a_{t-1} + .01a_{t-2} + .01a_{t-3}$ $(.6)(3.6)(.2)(.2)$	5.887	.149 E-1	31.1	20	397
6	(0,1,0)		5.087	—	—	—	400
	(0,1,1)	$W_t = .003 + a_t + .1a_{t-1}$ $(.5)(2.0)$	5.043	.127 E-1	17.5	22	399
	(0,1,2)	$W_t = .003 + a_t + .09a_{t-1} - .03a_{t-2}$ $(.5)(1.8)(.7)$	5.037	.127 E-1	16.5	21	398
	(0,1,3)	$W_t = .003 + a_t + .10a_{t-1} - .03a_{t-2} - .07a_{t-3}$ $(.5)(2.1)(.6)(1.4)$	5.014	.127 E-1	14.3	20	397

Series	(P,D,Q)	Identified Model	SS	$\hat{\sigma}_a^2$	Q	d.f.	N
7	(0,1,0)		12.960	—	—	—	400
	(0,1,1)	$W_t = -.020 + a_t + .10a_{t-1}$ (2.0)	12.825	.323 E-1	25.2	22	399
	(0,1,2)	$W_t = -.020 + a_t + .10a_{t-1} + .03a_{t-2}$ (1.9) (.7)	12.809	.324 E-1	23.4	21	398
	(0,1,3)	$W_t = -.020 + a_t + .09a_{t-1} + .03a_{t-2} + .12a_{t-3}$ (1.7) (.5) (2.5)	12.593	.319 E-1	15.1	20	397

Notes: $W_t = Z_t = Z_{t-1}$
SS: sum of squared residuals after estimating parameters
σ_a^2: residual variance
Q: $Q = N \sum_{i=1}^{k} f_i \sim$ chi-square (k-p-q-1)
Box-Pierce test for randomness of residuals
d.f.: degrees of freedom for Q statistic
N: sample size
(a) Significant spike in autocorrelation of residuals at lags 20, 21.
(b) Significant spike in autocorrelation of residuals at lags 9, 10, 12.
(c) Significant spike in autocorrelation of residuals at lags 4, 17, 19.
(d) Significant spike in autocorrelation of residuals at lags 4, 10.

Selected values of chi-square distribution:
Significance level by degrees of freedom

	d.f.		
χ^2	22	21	20
10%	30.8	29.6	28.4
5%	33.9	32.7	31.4

Maximum profits from a filter rule trading strategy were about 2.5% per year before transaction costs which similarly suggests a lack of economic significance.

A deficiency in this work is that we lack a general model for the process generating spot prices. Combining Box-Jenkins time series analysis with log-likelihood ratio testing provides a more rigorous method for specifying and estimating the nature of the Canadian spot series.

Using daily data published by Poole (1966), we follow the identification and estimation procedure described in Chapter VI. Since the program which estimates the sample autocorrelation and partial autocorrelation function has a limit of 400 observations, the sample period, 1950/62 is divided into 7 periods of 400 observations. In general, the sample autocorrelation and partial autocorrelation functions indicated that low order moving average processes would fit the data. Models (0,1,1); (0,1,2); and (0,1,3) were estimated, with a constant term, for each subperiod. The results appear in Table 6.11.

For all periods, we can reject the random walk (0,1,0) model since θ_1 is significantly nonzero. In the initial and final periods, the departure from the random walk model is more acute since θ_3 terms become significant, which is consistent with the interpretation that price changes become more random after an initial adjustment period and they were pre-

Table 6.12. Likelihood Ratio Analysis of Alternative ARIMA (P,D,Q) Models Versus the Random Walk Model for Canada 1950/62

Series[a]	Alternative (P,D,Q) Model	$\lambda = \left(\frac{\hat{\sigma}_a^2}{\hat{\sigma}^2}\right)^{N/2}$	$2 \ln \lambda$	r	Critical Points for χ^2 (r) $\alpha = .05$	$\alpha = .10$
1	(0,1,1)	109×10^4	27.8	1	3.84	2.71
	(0,1,3)	62.3	8.3	2	5.99	4.61
2	(0,1,1)	545.6	12.6	1	3.84	2.71
3	(0,1,1)	138.5	9.9	1	3.84	2.71
4	(0,1,1)	275×10^5	34.3	1	3.84	2.71
5	(0,1,1)	338.2	11.6	1	3.84	2.71
6	(0,1,1)	5.7	3.5	1	3.84	2.71
7	(0,1,1)	8.1	4.2	1	3.84	2.71
	(0,1,3)	312.7	11.5	3	7.81	6.25
	(0,1,3)[b]	38.5	7.3	2	5.99	4.61

[a] Each series has 400 daily observations.
[b] Versus the (0,1,1) model.

vented from being random because of government intervention in the final period.

Likelihood ratio tests are computed for the various models. The results in Table 6.12 indicate that the (0,1,3) model is a significant improvement over the (0,1,0) model in periods 1 and 7. The (0,1,1) model is a significant improvement in the other five subperiods. Higher order models are not significant in these five subperiods.

The data supplement Poole's conclusion that the Canadian spot rate displays serial dependence. However, the moving average terms are small and Poole's conclusion that the serial dependence is not economically significant is not challenged.

NOTES

1. Transformation (6.1) allows us to analyze currency trends relative to a nondollar standard. For example, let the French franc be the numeraire currency instead of the U.S. dollar. Table 6.1 indicates that the currencies of Belgium, Germany, Netherlands, Switzerland, and Japan appreciated relative to the French franc, while the currencies of the United States, Canada, United Kingdom, and Italy depreciated relative to the French franc.

2. The joint float began in April 1972, when the six original EEC members (Belgium, France, Germany, Italy, Luxembourg, and the Netherlands) agreed to stabilize the dollar value of their currencies within a 2.25% range. In March 1973, stabilization vis-à-vis the dollar was abandoned. The snake was allowed to float and member countries agreed to stabilize their currencies vis-à-vis each other. A difference greater than 2.25% between the high and low currency in the snake is a signal for intervention.

Two non-EEC countries, Norway and Sweden, have been associate members of the snake since May 1972 and March 1973, respectively. England and Italy left the snake in May 1973. France withdrew from the snake in January 1974 and returned in July 1975 (after the sample period). Switzerland requested to join the snake in 1975 but France vetoed the application. The other sample countries, Canada and Japan, have had no formal ties with the joint float.

3. In principle, all the hypotheses in this monograph could be examined using the German mark or any other currency as the numeraire. However, the dollar is a natural choice for numeraire because of its major role in international trade and finance. More important, choosing the dollar as numeraire allows a wider study of floating exchange rates, since through the joint float, some of our currencies are pegged to the German mark.

4. Mathematically, a stationary series is one in which each observation, Z_t, is generated by some function, F, which does not vary over time. That is, $F_t(Z_t,...,Z_{t+k}) = F_{t+i}(Z_{t+1},...,Z_{t+k+i}) = F_t(Z_t,...,Z_{t+k})$. Since the function, F, is constant over time, the moments of the functions are also constant. For example, $E(\tilde{Z}_t) = E(\tilde{Z}_{t+1}) = \mu$, and $V(\tilde{Z}_t) = V(\tilde{Z}_{t+1}) = \sigma^2$.

Unfortunately, there is no generally accepted mathematical technique to test for stationarity. Most researchers resort to the "eye-ball" technique. For alternative tests see Priestley and Rao (1969) and Melnick (1974).

5. The distributional properties of the $X_{i,t}$ are also analyzed for the Float II period. In general, the skewness statistic is small, indicating a symmetric distribution, while the kur-

tosis statistic is large, indicating a peaked distribution with fat tails. A Kalmogorov-Smirnov test for normality results in chi-square statistics that are significant at the 5% level for six countries (Canada, United Kingdom, France, Germany, Italy, Japan) and at the 10% level for two others (Netherlands and Switzerland). Similar results are reported in Westerfield (1975).

6. If $Z_t = \ln P_t$ where P_t is the price of a financial asset, then $W_t = Z_t - Z_{t-1}$ is the continuous rate of return on the asset. However, the time series models are investigated only for descriptive and forecasting purposes. Without further assumptions on the return generating process, there is no correspondence between the order (p,d,q) of a model and market efficiency.

7. The random walk (0,1,0) model is selected for the null hypothesis since this is consistent with the second diagnostic criterion—significant coefficients in the $\theta(B)$ and $\phi(B)$ polynomials. The test is purely description and not a test of market efficiency.

8. In small samples, this estimate of Q is biased downward. The exct statistic is $Q = N(N + 2)/[N-k/2] \Sigma_{i=i}^{k} \hat{r}_2$. If $N = 120$ and $k = 24$, sample estimates of Q should be multiplied by 1.15.

9. Theoretically, this result is not possible since adding another explanatory variable (in this case another MA term) should not reduce our ability to explain the Z_t. In practice, this result may occur because parameter estimation relies on an algorithm which seeks to minimize the unconditional sum of squares. If the initial guess values are quite far from the final estimates or if the sum of squares function is rather flat, the estimation routine may stop before it finds the global minimum sum of squares. In these cases, empirical evidence may suggest that adding additional variables reduces explanatory power.

10. Evidence for a three-week cycle is also reported in Grubel (1966) and Upson (1972).

11. Another approach for analyzing the relationship between the time pattern of spot and forward rates is developed in Bilson and Levich (1976).

12. In the 1962/67 period, the Q-statistic (31.3) indicates autocorrelation in the residuals. This indicates that higher order moving average terms might be significant.

Chapter VII

Forecasting Models—Empirical Results

PURPOSE

This chapter presents a test of hypothesis two—that prices of financial claims imply accurate and consistent forecasts of future spot exchange rates. To make this test, alternative forecasting models are analyzed across currencies, time periods, and forecast horizons. If the forecast errors display particular statistical properties (i.e., the errors are in a narrow band around zero, serially uncorrelated through time and with MSE proportional to the forecast horizon), then we cannot reject hypothesis two.

The most important overall results are that (1) forecast errors appear to be serially uncorrelated; (2) while forecasting bias or currency preference does appear significant for the total sample period, it does not appear to be predictable within the sample period; and (3) MSE rises in proportion to forecasting horizon. These results are consistent with the view that the market efficiently reflects information concerning future exchange rates. Thus, we cannot reject hypothesis two.

Tests for bias in the forward rate forecast and composite models are analyzed in the final two sections. Consistent with our theory, forward rates significantly underestimate (overestimate) the future spot rate when the spot rate is rising (falling). Composite forecasting models significantly reduce forecast errors. The gain may be the result of information costs, search costs, or government intervention which tend to separate financial markets.

AN OVERVIEW OF THE STATISTICAL METHODOLOGY

The data for this chapter are taken exclusively from the Harris Bank *Weekly Review*. Data for nine countries (Canada, United Kingdom, Belgium, France, Germany, Italy, Netherlands, Switzerland, and Japan) and the United States are reported. End-of-week bid quotations from the interbank market are reported for the spot rate and the external or Euro-currency deposit rate. All quotations reported as a percent per annum are converted to their per period equivalents.[1]

Forecasts of the future spot exchange rate, $\hat{S}$ (i,j,k,l) in U.S. dollars per foreign unit are generated for i = 1, ... 9 countries, j = 1, ... 4 forecasting models, k = 1, ... 3 forecasting horizons, and l = 1, ... 430 weekly observations.

The four forecasting models are

(1a) $\hat{S}_{t+n} = S_t \left(\dfrac{1 + r_{us,n}}{1 + r_{f,n}} \right)^n$, domestic interest rates;

(1b) $\hat{S}_{t+n} = S_t \left(\dfrac{1 + r_{us,n}}{1 + r_{f,n}} \right)^n$, external interest rates;

(2) $\hat{S}_{t+n} = F_{t,n}$;

(3) $\hat{S}_{t+n} = S_t$.

Model (1a) is the Fisher Open model using domestic interest rates (Fisher domestic) and model (1b) is Fisher Open using Euro-currency deposit rates (Fisher external). Model (2) is the current forward rate and model (3) is the current spot rate.[2]

The 430 weeks cover the period January 3, 1967 to May 9, 1975. The forecasting horizons analyzed are one, three, and six months. These horizons are consistent with the maturity of interest rates and forward contracts in the data base. However, since the *Weekly Review* is published weekly, it is necessary to translate the forecasting horizons to 4, 13, and 26 weeks. For example, today's one-month forward rate is compared to the spot rate 4 weeks from today. The three- and six-month forward rates are compared to spot rates 13 and 26 weeks in the future. This compromise may increase the magnitude of forecast errors at the one-month horizon. For the three- and six-month horizon, the effect should be small.

Percentage forecast errors, e_t, are calculated using

$$e_t = (S_{t+n} - \hat{S}_{t+n})/S_{t+n}.$$

Therefore, positive (negative) forecast errors indicate underestimation (overestimation). Note also that the forecast errors are subscripted for time t, the time when the forecast was made. Therefore, when forecasts are aggregated over some time period, say 1974, the summary statistics describe errors of forecasts which were formulated in 1974.

In the case of missing observations, the forecast is omitted. Data points are not interpolated or estimated using other sources. Missing observations sometimes resulted because official markets were closed during an exchange "crisis." At other times, the Harris Bank observed that no single number could adequately represent the hectic trading observed during the day.[3] Omitting observations of this type does not bias the results in any apparent way.

For all countries, methods and horizons for which data are available, a forecast and a percentage forecast error are calculated. If all the data for all 430 weeks were available, we could construct 426 four week ahead forecasts, 417 thirteen week ahead forecasts, and 404 twenty-six week ahead forecasts for each of the nine countries and four forecasting methods, for a total of 44,892 forecasts. Because of missing observations (mainly one- and six-month domestic interest rates), the number of forecasts actually constructed is 37,393.

STATISTICAL PROPERTIES OF FORECAST ERRORS

Forecasting Performance and Forecasting Model

The forecasts that are generated can be analyzed across the four alternative models. Table 7.1 displays the Mean Squared Error (MSE) statistic for each model. From Table 7.1 it appears that, given the currency, time period, and horizon, MSE is similar across models. Considering the entire sample period, Table 7.1 indicates that there is little difference among the models. For all 27 country-horizon episodes, the average ratio of the highest MSE to the lowest MSE is 1.05. Therefore, in their overall performance, the models are very similar.

Nevertheless, for most countries, the model which produces the lowest

Table 7.1. MSE Across Forecasting Horizons: 1967/75

Country	Horizon (Months)	Fisher Domestic	Fisher External	Forward	Lag Spot
Canada	1	0.374	0.380	0.385	0.365*
	3	1.491	1.486	1.517	1.463*
	6	3.501	3.179*	3.291	3.243
United Kingdom	1	3.968*	4.144	4.052	3.982
	3	15.520	15.924	15.983	15.065*
	6	33.180	29.779*	33.783	32.039
Belgium	1	—	4.406	4.434	4.110*
	3	17.247	18.064	17.935	16.714*
	6	—	36.087	38.525	34.093*
France	1	—	6.277	5.881	5.460*
	3	32.053	22.803	22.280	21.493*
	6	—	53.252	54.189	50.555*
Germany	1	—	5.590*	5.636	5.687
	3	24.122	23.550*	23.737	24.501
	6	—	45.158*	45.415	49.972
Italy	1	—	2.094	2.241	2.067*
	3	13.421	8.557	8.395	7.408*
	6	—	12.909	13.907	12.110*
Netherlands	1	—	4.481*	4.554	4.545
	3	16.681	15.282*	15.385	16.135
	6	—	28.728*	32.717	31.768
Switzerland	1	—	5.448*	5.469	5.458
	3	1.255†	20.864*	21.057	20.952
	6	—	45.881*	46.347	47.819
Japan	1	—	5.623*	5.671	5.704
	3	24.248	23.605*	23.788	24.500
	6	—	46.687	45.892*	49.947
Column Total of [a]		1	13	1	12

Note:
*- entries marked (*) are lowest MSE given country and horizon.
†- based on only 34 observations.
MSE is in units of percent squared.

MSE at one horizon also produces the lowest MSE at other horizons. For example, the Fisher external model leads to the lowest MSE forecast for Germany, Netherlands, and Switzerland. For Belgium, France, and Italy, the lagged spot forecast leads to the lowest MSE at all horizons. One interpretation of this result is that the markets are integrated across maturities. Investors in external security markets set prices so that the term structure of relative interest rates reflects their term structure of exchange rate expectations. If their expectations about one horizon are correct, internal consistency of prices suggests that they may be correct about other horizons as well. In this sense, many models may be *horizon blind*—they work well regardless of forecast horizon.

It does not follow that a model is "time blind." The model which produces the lowest MSE in the overall sample does not necessarily produce the lowest MSE in every subperiod. For example, in forecasting the German mark the Fisher external forecast (1b) produces the lowest MSE for all horizons in the overall, 1967/75 sample period. However, in several yearly subperiods, Table 7.2 indicates that there is often a model with a lower MSE.

The data in Table 7.1 can be collapsed further. The lowest MSE model in each of the 27 country-horizon episodes is marked with an asterisk. The totals indicate that on 13 episodes, the Fisher external model has the lowest MSE, 12 for the lagged spot model, and one each for the remaining two models.

This is a surprising result given the empirical evidence on interest parity. If interest parity holds exactly, then the Fisher external and forward rate forecasts are identical. Therefore, it was anticipated that the two models would be very similar. While the Fisher external regularly outperforms the forward rate, the difference is generally small enough to be explained by transaction costs or sampling errors. One inference from the data is that if forecasting must rely on a single model, then either the Fisher external or lagged spot model should be selected. Across all countries, horizons, and time periods, these two models tend to produce the lowest MSE forecast.

Forecasting Performance and Currency

In this section, forecast errors are analyzed in the currency dimension. This classification raises the intuitive question: Which currency is "easiest" to forecast? A more careful analysis suggests that an unambiguous standard for comparison is lacking, and therefore the question cannot be answered.

In part, forecast errors are a function of transaction costs and risk premia. If these factors differ across currencies, then the conclusion that a currency is difficult to forecast is not necessarily justified. Investors may have formed accurate expectations; but they have decided that it is not profitable to act on these expectations. Therefore, prices remain unchanged and (apparent) forecast errors result.

Table 7.2. MSE by Year and Horizon—Germany

Period	Model	Horizon		
		1 Month	3 Months	6 Months
1967	(1a)	—	0.455	—
	(1b)	0.096	0.291	0.451
	(2)	0.089	0.297	0.431
	(3)	0.076*	0.181*	0.198*
1968	(1a)	—	1.222	—
	(1b)	0.300	1.250	2.506
	(2)	0.265	1.161	2.457
	(3)	0.192*	0.526*	0.282*
1969	(1a)	—	10.842	—
	(1b)	2.695*	9.641*	14.662
	(2)	2.798	9.799	14.364*
	(3)	3.057	13.224	29.667
1970	(1a)	—	0.228*	—
	(1b)	0.098*	0.447	2.170*
	(2)	0.105	0.470	2.258
	(3)	0.098	0.462	2.380
1971	(1a)	—	12.066	—
	(1b)	1.614*	10.363*	33.110*
	(2)	1.637	10.605	33.680
	(3)	1.860	11.710	37.144
1972	(1a)	—	17.360*	—
	(1b)	0.424	17.724	70.886
	(2)	0.430	17.512	69.823*
	(3)	0.312*	17.900	78.154
1973	(1a)	—	100.050*	—
	(1b)	30.121	100.691	186.070
	(2)	30.059*	100.691	185.989*
	(3)	31.255	105.544	193.670
1974	(1a)	—	46.822*	—
	(1b)	9.272	48.219	47.366*
	(2)	9.447	48.552	47.424
	(3)	8.844*	47.448	55.220
1975	(1a)	—	3.070*	—
	(1b)	3.842	3.188	—
	(2)	3.837	3.148	—
	(3)	3.702*	3.488	—

Note:
*- lowest MSE given year and horizon.

To argue the same point in another way, it is observed that some exchange rate series are (statistically) more volatile than others. In part, this is because changes in exchange rates reflect underlying variables including changes in monetary policy. Monetary policies differ widely

Table 7.3. Lowest MSE and Ranking for Country and Horizon

Country	1 Month	Horizon 3 Months	6 Months
Canada	0.365 (1)	1.463 (1)	3.179 (1)
United Kingdom	3.968 (3)	15.065 (3)	29.779 (4)
Belgium	4.110 (4)	16.714 (5)	34.093 (5)
France	5.460 (7)	21.493 (7)	50.555 (9)
Germany	5.590 (8)	23.550 (8)	45.158 (6)
Italy	2.067 (2)	7.408 (2)	12.110 (2)
Netherlands	4.481 (5)	15.282 (4)	28.728 (3)
Switzerland	5.448 (6)	20.864 (6)	45.889 (7)
Japan	5.623 (9)	23.605 (9)	45.892 (8)

Note: rank in parentheses.

across countries and over time. As a purely theoretical matter, the increased variability in underlying (monetary) factors will not (necessarily) lead to a decrease in forecasting precision. The reason is that some of this variability can be anticipated and therefore reflected by forecasters. It is therefore possible for a series to become more volatile (statistically) and yet the forecast errors for that series may decline. For these reasons, intercountry comparisons must be viewed with caution.

Table 7.3 presents data on the lowest MSE forecast for each country and horizon. Canada has the lowest MSE of all countries at each horizon. The MSE for the one-month horizon is 0.365% which implies an average forecast error (or root mean squared error) of 0.6%. At the six-month horizon the MSE increases to 3.179% and the average error increases to 1.78%. Four countries (France, Germany, Switzerland, and Japan) have MSEs greater than 5.0% at the one-month horizon and 45.0% at the six-month horizon, or approximately 15 times as great as for Canada. It follows that the average forecast error is three to four times as great for these countries than Canada.

An alternative approach is to record the percentage of forecast errors falling within a neutral band. In Table 7.4, the data for the 1967/75 period indicate that the forecast errors for Canada and Italy fall within narrower bounds than for the United Kingdom, France, Germany, or Japan. The methods therefore differ in their rankings of Switzerland and the United Kingdom. Table 7.4 indicates that nearly twice as many forecasts fall within the 1% or 2% bounds for Canada as for Japan. This is an alternative measure of the relative difficulty in forecasting currencies.

Table 7.4. Percentage of 3-Month Forward Rate Forecasts Within 0.5%, 1.0%, and 2.0% of Future Spot Rate

Country	1967				1971				1972				1973				1974				1975				1967/75			
	0.5	1.0	2.0		0.5	1.0	2.0		0.5	1.0	2.0		0.5	1.0	2.0		0.5	1.0	2.0		0.5	1.0	2.0		0.5	1.0	2.0	
Canada	57	83	100		45	61	100		31	43	92		33	60	87		16	36	92		0	17	83		44	66	90	
United Kingdom	66	68	70		4	37	50		12	24	34		2	6	14		6	14	38		17	34	67		25	44	61	
Belgium	91	100	100		34	38	42		47	68	86		6	14	20		4	8	16		17	34	83		48	60	69	
France	57	100	100		53	61	71		22	47	75		4	10	16		2	4	26		0	0	0		28	48	63	
Germany	54	98	100		8	12	24		29	56	72		6	8	12		4	10	16		17	50	67		28	45	60	
Italy	98	100	100		36	42	74		59	69	85		10	20	34		8	18	40		0	0	0		48	62	75	
Netherlands	94	100	100		14	28	42		22	42	77		6	10	20		6	10	20		17	34	100		36	56	70	
Switzerland	64	94	100		25	29	56		12	30	72		4	8	16		4	8	14		17	50	67		38	58	70	
Japan	—	—	—		47	57	57		15	28	43		10	14	31		10	18	30		17	17	34		29	36	46	
Average	73	93	96		30	41	57		28	45	71		9	17	28		7	14	32		11	26	56		36	53	67	

Forecasting Performance and Currency Preference

In Chapter V, it was demonstrated that if investors prefer to hold assets denominated in a particular currency, then exchange rate forecasts based on interest rates may result in forecast errors that are systematically positive or negative. In this section, the mean forecast errors are analyzed. When the mean error is significantly different from zero, forecast bias exists. According to the Fisherian theory, if the forecast exchange rate change is larger than the actual exchange rate change, then the foreign currency is preferred. If the forecast exchange rate change is smaller than the actual exchange rate change, then the domestic currency (U.S. dollar) is preferred. In this study, negative forecast errors correspond to a preference for the foreign currency; positive forecast errors correspond to a preference for the domestic currency.

Information on the t-statistic of the mean forecast error is summarized in Table 7.5.[4] Entries marked with an asterisk are *not* significantly different from zero at the 5% level. Therefore, it appears that in most cases, the forecasts display a positive bias, indicating that the U.S. dollar was the preferred currency during this period.[5] The most prominent clustering of unbiased forecasts are in the United Kingdom. Both Fisher forecasts and the forward rates appear to be unbiased forecasters in the United Kingdom. The lagged spot forecast also appears to be unbiased in France and Italy.

Estimates of transaction costs in the spot and 90-day foreign exchange market range between approximately .05% in the 1962/67 period to about 0.5% in the 1973/75 period. Transaction costs in Euro-currency deposits are smaller, between 0.03% and 0.1%. During the period 1967/75, it seems likely that a bias of 0.5% or 1.0% would be consistent with transaction costs. Most mean forecast errors at the three-month horizon fall within this range. It is therefore possible to conclude that while the bias may be statistically significant, it is not economically significant.

Note also that there is a general tendency for bias to increase approximately in proportion to horizon. This agrees with the result in Moses (1969) that currency preferences may be expressed as a constant rate per unit time.

In Table 7.5 the country-horizon episodes which did not contain an unbiased forecasting model are considered separately. In this group (of 16) the model with the smallest bias (in absolute value) is marked by the

Table 7.5. Mean Forecasting Error Across Forecasting Horizon: 1967/75

Country	Horizon (month)	Fisher Domestic	Fisher External	Forward	Lag Spot
Canada	1	0.062	0.004*	0.043	0.050*
	3	0.309	0.107a	0.178	0.212
	6	0.640	0.345a	0.458	0.487
United	1	0.017*	0.005*	0.054*	−0.184
Kingdom	3	0.073*	−0.001*	0.078*	−0.567
	6	0.088*	0.166*	−0.021*	−1.229
Belgium	1	—	0.262a	0.340	0.309
	3	1.027	0.941a	1.040	1.029
	6	—	1.784a	2.145	1.976
France	1	—	0.194*	0.339	0.137*
	3	1.027	0.862	0.937	0.402*
	6	—	1.313	1.644	0.568*
Germany	1	—	0.269*	0.292	0.453
	3	1.167	1.031a	1.060	1.520
	6	—	2.130a	2.156	3.036
Italy	1	—	0.118	0.238	−0.021*
	3	0.070	0.283	0.527	−0.075*
	6	—	0.359	0.802	−0.245*
Netherlands	1	—	0.212a	0.247	0.352
	3	0.695a	0.844	0.899	1.195
	6	—	1.691a	2.026	2.314
Switzerland	1	—	0.263a	0.291	0.468
	3	−1.017a	1.075	1.096	1.587
	6	—	2.219a	2.251	3.136
Japan	1	—	0.233a	0.254	0.444
	3	1.082	0.984a	1.015	1.510
	6	—	2.317	2.294a	3.060
Column total of (* and a)		5	19	4	7

Note:
* - entries marked (*) are *not* significantly different from zero at 5% level.
a - model with lowest absolute mean bias.

letter "a." In 13 of these 16 cases the Fisher external model produces the smallest bias. This result could be expected since the Fisher external models tended to have low MSE and bias is one of the two components in MSE.

The data in Table 7.5 can be collapsed further by adding the number of entries that are marked (* or a) in each column. There are 19 entries marked for the Fisher external model; the next highest is the lag spot model with 7. This result indicates that overall, the Fisher external model leads to a greater number of unbiased or smallest bias forecasts among the models that are tested. In this overall sense, the Fisher external model appears to be best.

From a purely forecasting viewpoint, bias is important as a correction factor for the naive model. For example, a watch which is consistently five minutes fast is a very good forecaster of the correct time. If Fisher external consistently overestimates the future spot rate by 1%, it will be a very helpful forecasting model. In both of these examples the important factor is the consistency or stationarity of the forecast errors over time.

This issue is analyzed using two approaches. First, weekly Fisher external forecasts for the three-month horizon were aggregated by calendar year. Significant positive mean forecast errors are recorded as (+); significant negative mean forecast errors are recorded as (−). When the mean forecast error is not significantly different from zero, a (0) is entered. Table 7.6 summarizes these results.

Table 7.6 indicates that the sign of forecast errors changes over time. Significant positive and negative errors exist for each country during some time period. The bias does not appear to follow any recognizable time pattern. A formal runs analysis of the series in Table 7.6 was not performed, however, since a dependent sample of weekly forecasts was aggregated to calculate yearly bias. Instead, the second approach calculates the serial correlation of forecast errors in an independent sample. For example, at the one-month horizon, the sample consists of every fourth weekly forecast error; at the three-month horizon, the sample

Table 7.6. Time Pattern of Forecasting Bias with the Fisher External Model—Three-Month Horizon

Country	1967	1968	1969	1970	1971	1972	1973	1974	1975	1967/75
Canada	0	+	−	+	0	0	0	−	−	0
United Kingdom	−	+	+	+	+	−	0	+	0	0
Belgium	+	−	+	−	+	+	0	+	+	+
France	0	0	−	+	+	+	0	+	+	+
Germany	−	−	+	+	+	0	0	+	0	+
Italy	−	−	−	+	+	+	−	+	+	+
Netherlands	0	−	−	0	+	0	0	+	+	+
Switzerland	−	−	−	−	+	+	0	+	−	+
Japan	NA	NA	NA	+	+	0	0	−	0	+

[a]Note: + = significant (at 5% level) positive forecast bias.
− = significant (at 5% level) negative forecast bias.
0 = forecast bias not significantly different from 0.
NA = not available.

Table 7.7. Q-Statistic to Test Serial Correlation of Forecast Errors

	Horizon		
Country	1 Month	3 Months	6 Months
Canada	47.4	17.4	7.5
United Kingdom	—	20.4	11.5
Belgium	—	18.1	12.2
France	49.9	11.3	8.6
Germany	47.4	11.3	8.6
Italy	—	14.8	15.6
Netherlands	25.5	12.9	9.5
Switzerland	48.1	19.5	9.4
Japan	—	—	—
	N = 105	N = 32	N = 15

Note: Entry in table is $Q = N \sum_{i=1}^{k} \hat{r}_i$
where k = 24 for 1-month and 3-month forecast and k = 12 for 6-month forecast. Entry is for method (2), and forward rate. Results for other methods were very similar. Sample points from the chi-square distribution are:

		d.f.	
	χ^2	23	10
significance level	10%	32.0	17.3
	5%	35.2	19.7

consists of every thirteenth weekly forecast error, etc. Table 7.7 summarizes these results.

At the three-month and six-month horizons, serial correlation of forecast errors is not significant. At the one-month horizon, serial correlation is significant. However, it seems likely that this correlation is the result of using one-month interest rates to forecast spot exchange rates four weeks in the future. If forecast errors are serially uncorrelated, as the data suggest, the implication is that bias (i.e., significant forecast errors) cannot be predicted; currency preferences are likely to be random. In this case, the standard approach of correcting the naive forecasting model for bias will not necessarily improve forecasting performance because the bias is not stationary.

Forecasting Performance and Horizon

The relationship between forecasting accuracy and forecast horizon is easily developed using time series methods. A standard result is that the variance of the forecast error is proportional to the forecast horizon. It follows that the MSE is also proportional to the forecast horizon.

Table 7.8. Ratio of MSE for Pairs of Forecast Horizons

Country	Ratio[a]	Fisher Domestic	Fisher External	Forward	Lag Spot
Canada	3:1	3.99	3.91	3.94	4.01
	6:3	2.35	2.14	2.17	2.22
United Kingdom	3:1	3.91	3.84	3.94	3.78
	6:3	2.14	1.87	2.11	2.13
Belgium	3:1	—	4.10	4.04	4.07
	6:3	—	2.00	2.15	2.04
France	3:1	—	3.63	3.79	3.94
	6:3	—	2.34	2.43	2.35
Germany	3:1	—	4.21	4.21	4.31
	6:3	—	1.92	1.91	2.04
Italy	3:1	—	4.09	3.75	3.58
	6:3	—	1.51	1.66	1.63
Netherlands	3:1	—	3.41	3.38	3.55
	6:3	—	1.88	2.13	1.97
Switzerland	3:1	—	3.83	3.85	3.84
	6:3	—	2.20	2.20	2.28
Japan	3:1	—	4.20	4.19	4.30
	6:3	—	1.98	1.93	2.04

[a] 3:1 = Ratio of 3-month to 1-month MSE.
6:3 = Ratio of 6-month to 3-month MSE.

The data in Table 7.1 are used to test the theoretical relationship between MSE and horizon. First, the ratio of three-month MSE to one-month MSE is calculated; the theoretical value of this ratio is 3.0. Second, the ratio is calculated for six-month and three-month forecasts; the theoretical value of this ratio is 2.0. Table 7.8 summarizes the results.

The three-month to one-month ratio is consistently greater than 3.0. In part, this may be because we are comparing 13 week and 4 week forecasts, and so, the theoretical value of the ratio may be 3.25. However, the sample ratios are even larger than this number.

The results of the six-month and three-month comparison are more nearly consistent with theory. The sample values are generally near two. At these maturities, the data support the hypothesis that MSE rises in proportion to the forecast horizon. The economic significance of this result is that the market-based forecasts display a property of a time series forecast which is a minimum MSE forecast. This is another piece of evidence to support the view that market prices efficiently forecast the future spot rate.

An alternative technique for measuring the horizon effect is illus-

Table 7.9. Percentage of Forward Rate Forecast Errors within Neutral Bands[a]

Width of Neutral Band	Horizon		
	1-Month	3-Month	6-Month
0.5%	47	28	13
1.0%	68	45	26
2.0%	80	60	47
3.0%	87	66	55
4.0%	92	72	59
5.0%	94	77	66

[a] Germany only, 1967 to 1975.

trated in Table 7.9, which reports the percentage of forward rate forecast errors inside given neutral band. As the forecast horizon lengthens, this percentage decreases. For example, the percentage of forecast errors within a 0.5% band drops from 47% to 13% as the forecast horizon increases from one to six months. For a 2.0% band, the decrease is not as sharp—from 80% to 47%.

Forecasting Performance and Time

In this section, forecast errors are analyzed in the time dimension. Figures 7.1 through 7.9 present a time series plot of weekly forecast errors using the three-month forward rate for the nine currencies. These graphs are representative of the other forecasting models and horizons. The vertical axes are scaled alike so intercountry comparisons are possible.

The graphs suggest several qualitative observations. First, for each country, large forecast errors are associated with discrete changes in exchange rates or exchange rate systems (e.g., United Kingdom, 1967; France, 1969; Germany, 1969). Second, forecast errors tend to be smaller during pegged rate periods—except when there is a discrete change in the rate. In the managed float period forecast errors have become larger and more volatile. The graphs for Belgium, France, Germany, Italy, and Netherlands show the large forecast errors associated with the oil crisis of 1973/74. However, both positive and negative errors are observed; the errors tend to fluctuate about some value near zero. The graphs for the United Kingdom, Germany, Netherlands, and Japan indicate that forecast errors have decreased during the managed float period.

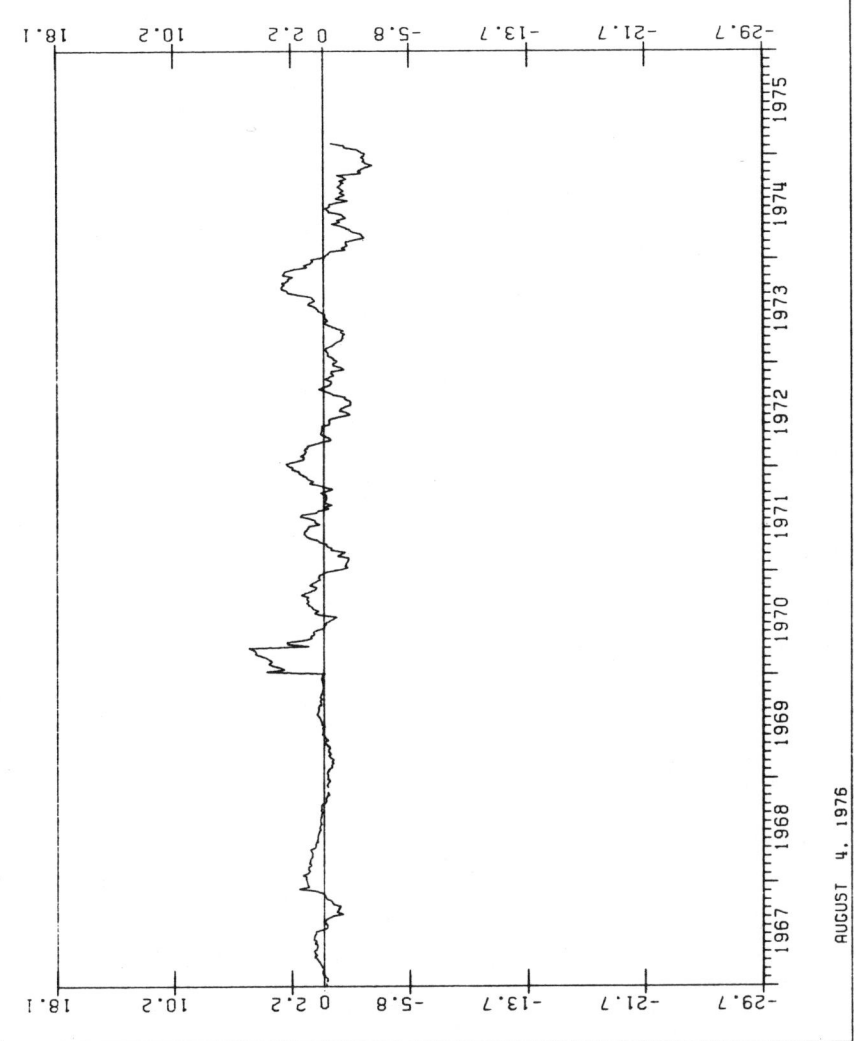

Figure 7.1.
Forecast Errors, Forward Rate 3-Month—Canada

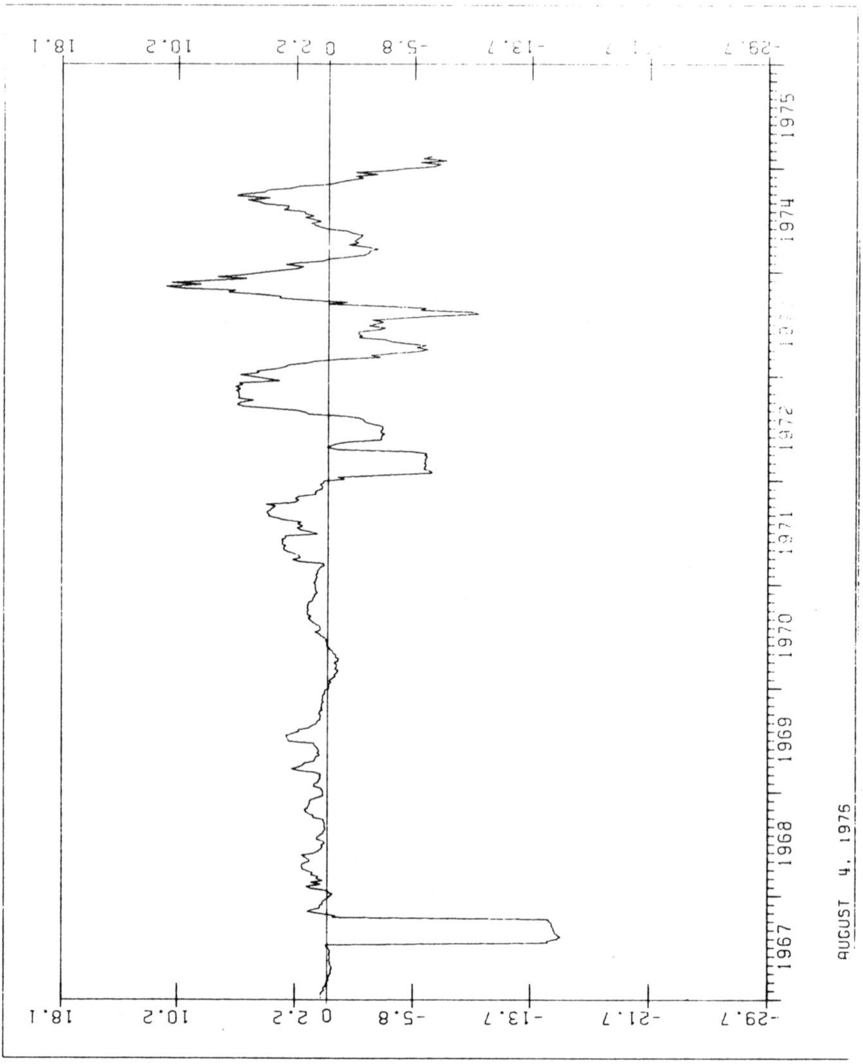

138 / *The International Money Market*

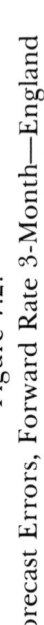

Figure 7.2.
Forecast Errors, Forward Rate 3-Month—England

Forecasting Models—Empirical Results / **139**

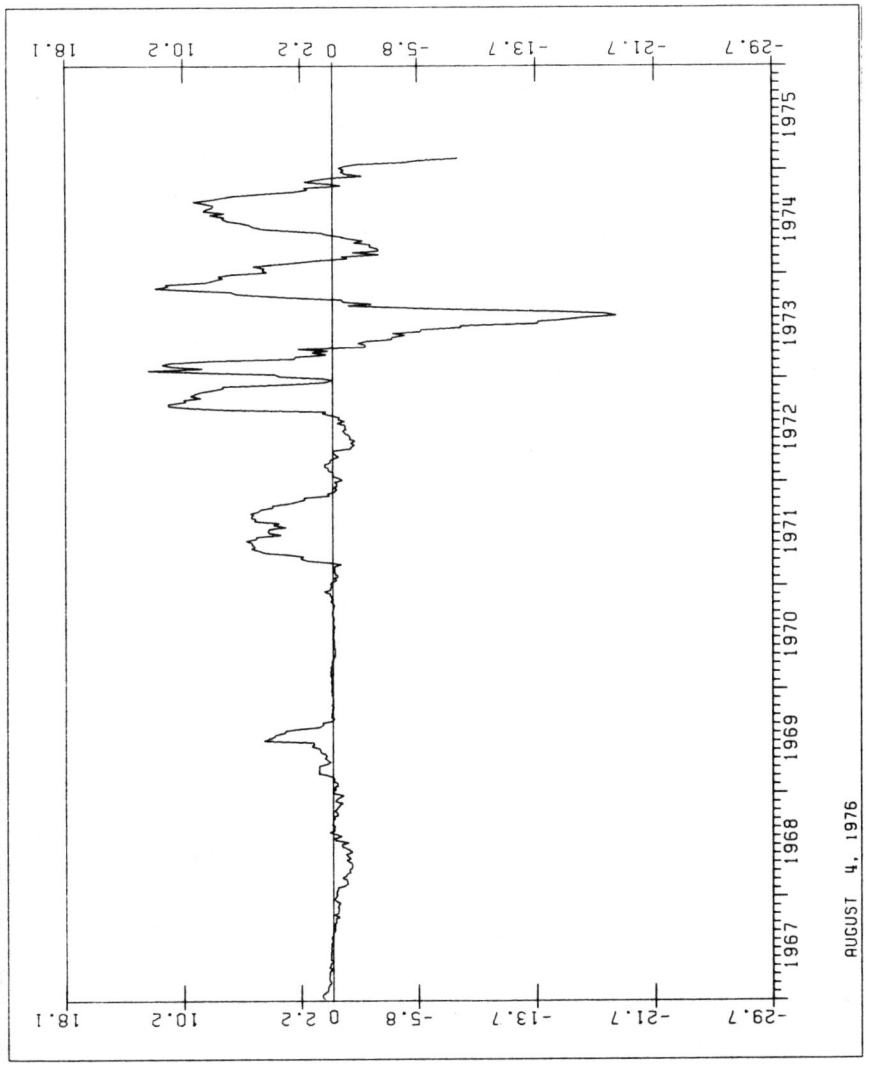

Figure 7.3.
Forecast Errors, Forward Rate 3-Month—Belgium

140 / *The International Money Market*

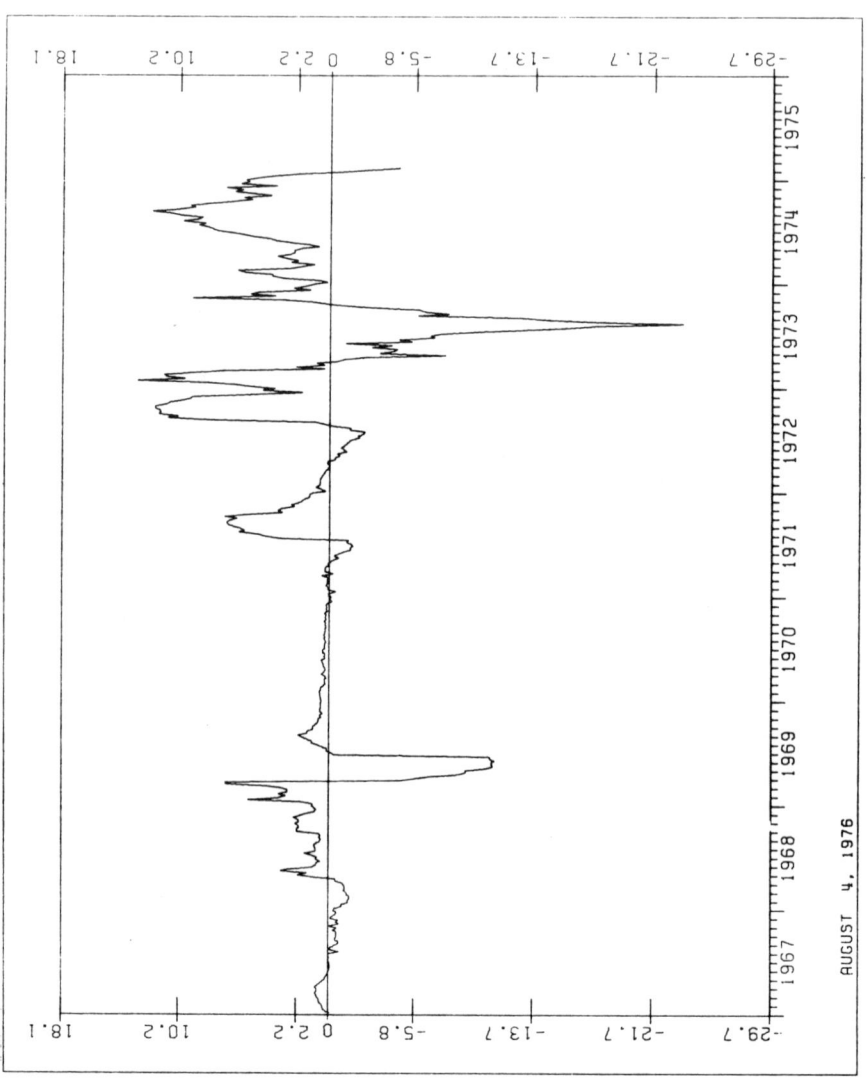

Figure 7.4.
Forecast Errors, Forward Rate 3-Month—France

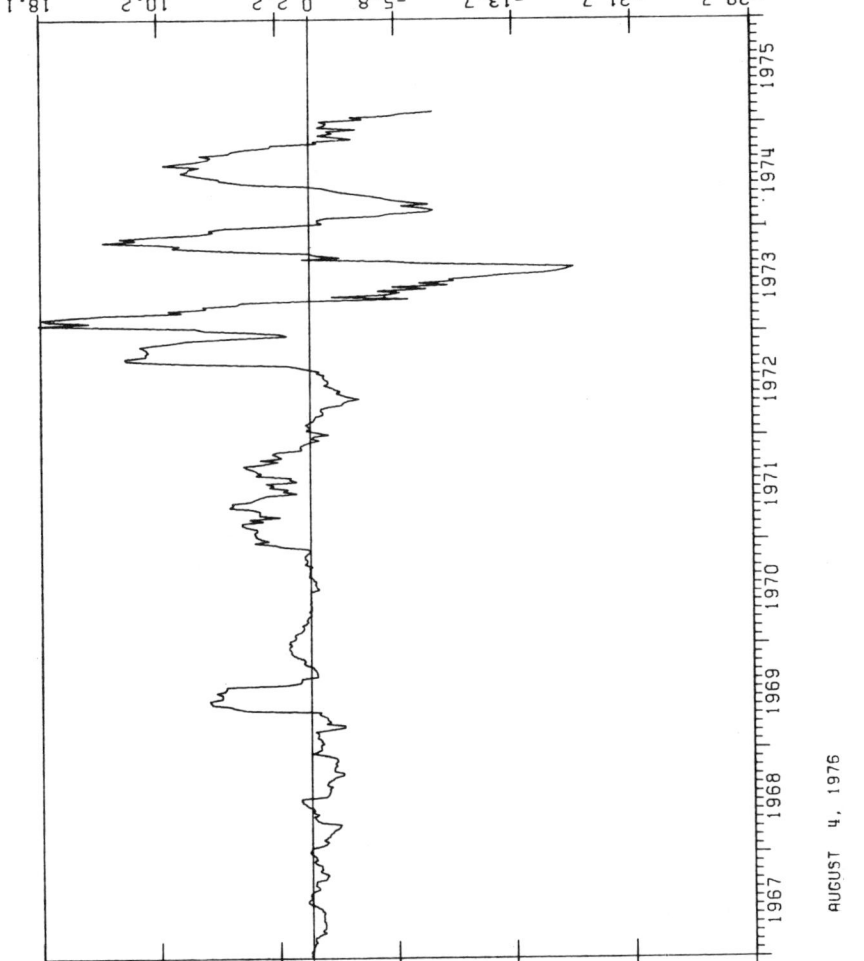

Figure 7.5.
Forecast Errors, Forward Rate 3-Month—Germany

142 / *The International Money Market*

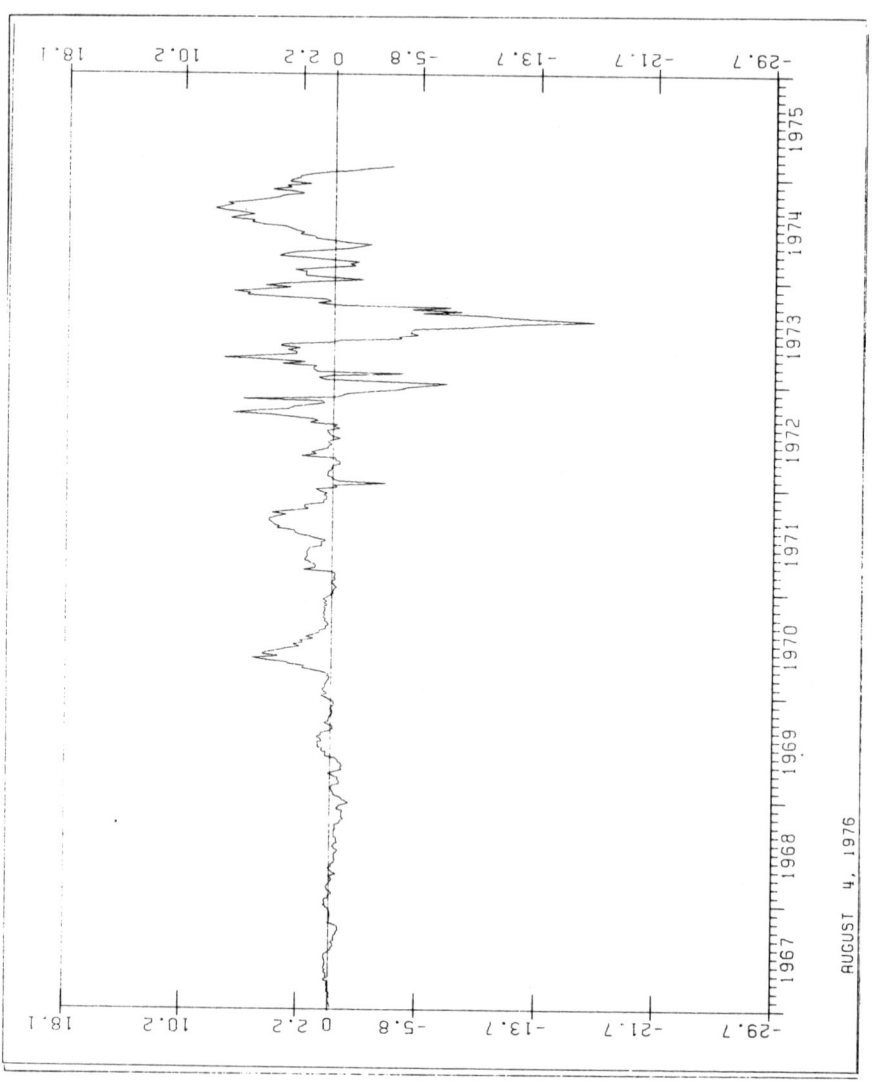

Figure 7.6.
Forecast Errors, Forward Rate 3-Month—Italy

Forecasting Models—Empirical Results / **143**

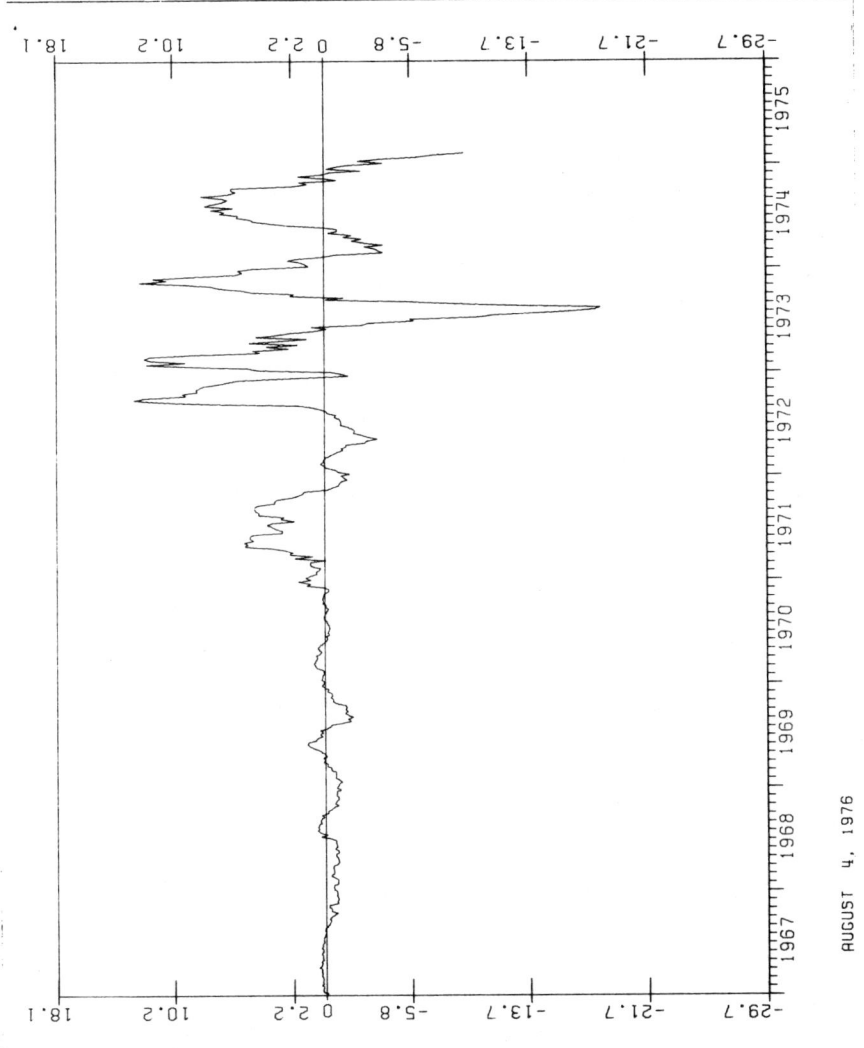

Figure 7.7.
Forecast Errors, Forward Rate 3-Month—Netherlands

144 / *The International Money Market*

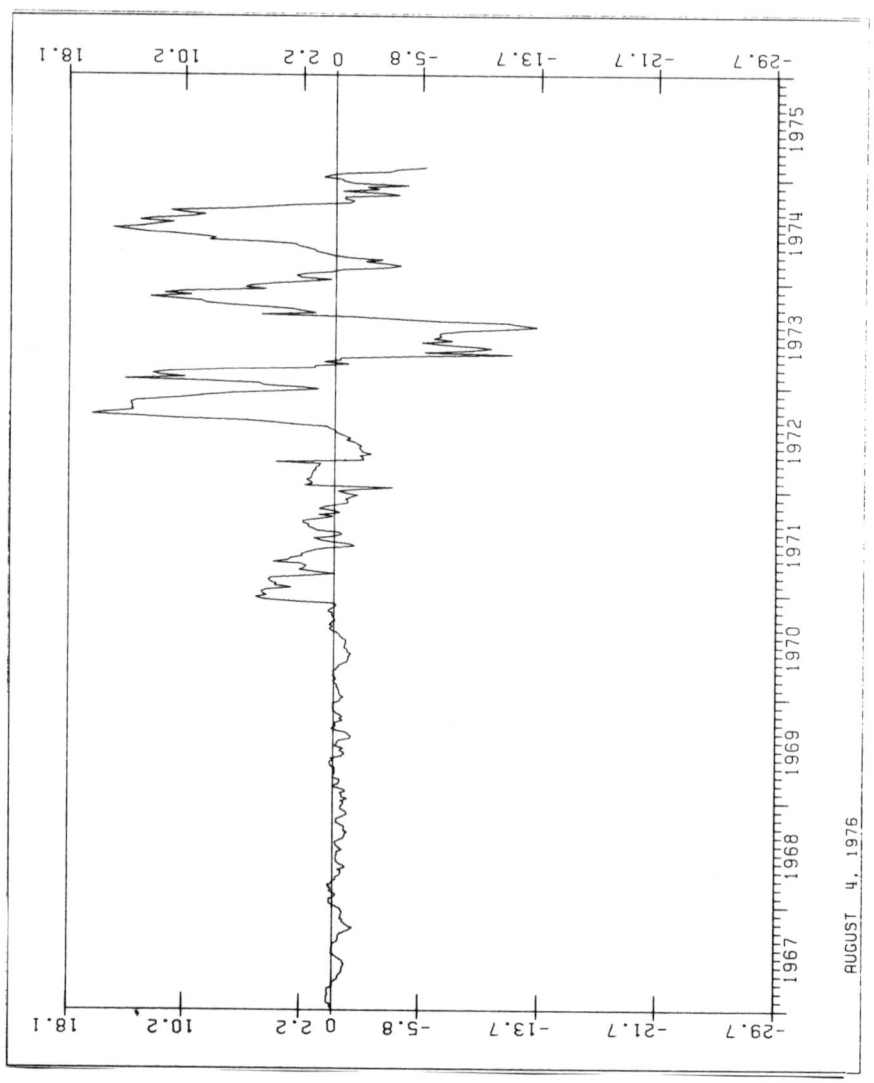

Figure 7.8.
Forecast Errors, Forward Rate 3-Month—Switzerland

Forecasting Models—Empirical Results / **145**

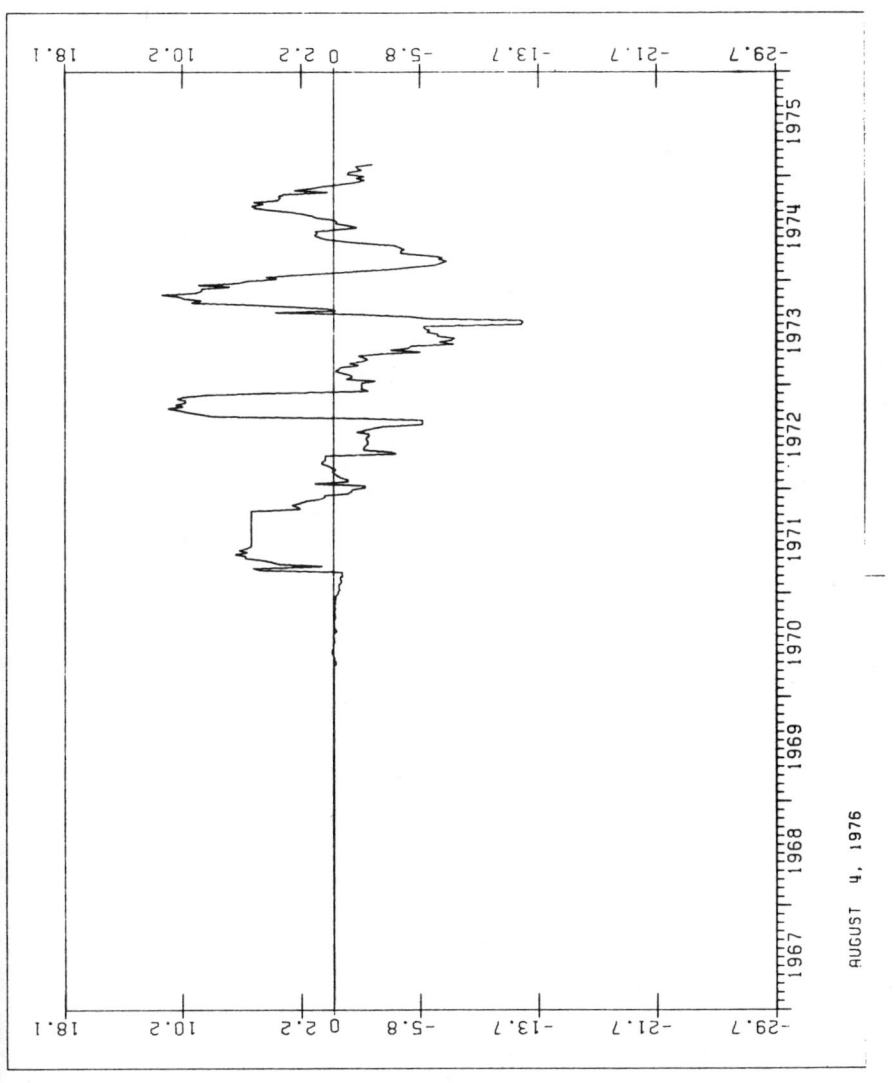

Figure 7.9.
Forecast Errors, Forward Rate 3-Month—Japan

A quantitative examination of the time dimension begins with Table 7.4, which reports the fraction of forecast errors within a neutral band. The estimates of transaction costs presented in Chapter III (Tables 3.1, 3.3, and 3.4) suggest a neutral band of no more than 0.5% during the quiet period. With transaction costs increasing during speculative periods and during the managed float, a 2.0% neutral band is a reasonable estimate.

Table 7.4 indicates that in 1967, the three-month forward rate was within 0.5% of the future spot rate in 73% of the sample weeks. As the width of the band increases to 1% and 2%, the number of forecasts meeting this tolerance rises to more than 90%.

In later periods, 1971 and 1973, the spot exchange rate is more volatile. Concurrently, the forward rate becomes a less precise forecast of the future spot rate. In 1973, the first year of managed floating, the number of forecast errors within the 2% band is 34% compared with 72% in the previous year. In 1974, forecasting performance is unchanged and in 1975, accuracy improves so that 50% of the weekly forecasts fall within a 2% band. Statistically, therefore, there is some evidence that forecast errors are becoming smaller as the managed float continues.

Since the percentage of forecast errors inside a 0.5% neutral band has decreased over the sample period, we could conclude that the predictive power of the forward rate has declined. However, transaction costs have increased over the period. The data suggest that transaction costs account for a similar, large percentage of forecast errors in most yearly subperiods. In many cases, therefore, the forward rate will be an accurate forecast of the future spot rate.

Table 7.2 conveys a similar picture. The MSE statistic is smallest during pegged rate periods except in years when the exchange rate changes. MSE tends to increase with the introduction of floating rates. However, MSE tends to decline in 1974 and 1975 from the levels reached during 1973.

Figures 7.1–7.9 indicate a positive serial correlation in the weekly series of three-month (13 week) forecast errors, which is expected since the observations are a dependent series.[6] Therefore, an independent sample of forecast errors is selected to check for serial correlation. The calculation for the Q-statistic appears in Table 7.7. At the three-month and six-month horizon, serial correlation is not significant. Significant autocorrelation is present in the one-month forecasts. It was suggested earlier that this may be because the forward rate and interest rate maturities are one-month while the differencing interval for spot rates is four weeks. It should be reiterated that serial correlation of forecast errors is not a sufficient condition to reject market efficiency. Serial correlation of unprofitable investment opportunities is consistent with market efficiency. Since the mean forecast error at the one-month horizon is very small (see Table 7.5), it is possible that this serial correlation is not economically significant.

FORWARD RATE FORECASTS—TESTS FOR BIAS

In Chapter V, a theory of the time pattern of forecast errors was developed. The theory predicts that positive forecast errors (underestimates) will be more frequent when the spot rate is rising and negative forecast errors (overestimates) will be more frequent when the spot rate is falling.

Figures 7.10, 7.11, and 7.12 plot the spot exchange rate and the lagged forward rate at the 1-, 3-, and 6-month maturities. The data are for Germany and are representative of the experience of other countries. The graphs support the theory. It is especially clear in the managed floating period that the forward rate is an underestimate (overestimate) of the future spot rate when the spot rate is rising (falling).

One way to test the theory statistically is to classify each time period along two dimensions: (1) the forecast error, positive or negative; and (2) the change in the spot rate, positive or negative. Accordingly a 2×2 contingency table can be constructued for each country-horizon episode. A sample table for the German one-month episode appears in Table 7.10. The null hypothesis is that the sign of the forecast error is independent of the sign of the rate of change in the spot rate. The test statistic

$$\sum_{I=1}^{2} \sum_{J=1}^{2} (A(I,J) - E(I,J)^2/E(I,J)$$

is approximately chi-square on one degree of freedom. The chi-square value for Table 7.10 is 67.0, which is highly significant.

Table 7.11 summarizes these chi-square statistics for all nine sample

148 / *The International Money Market*

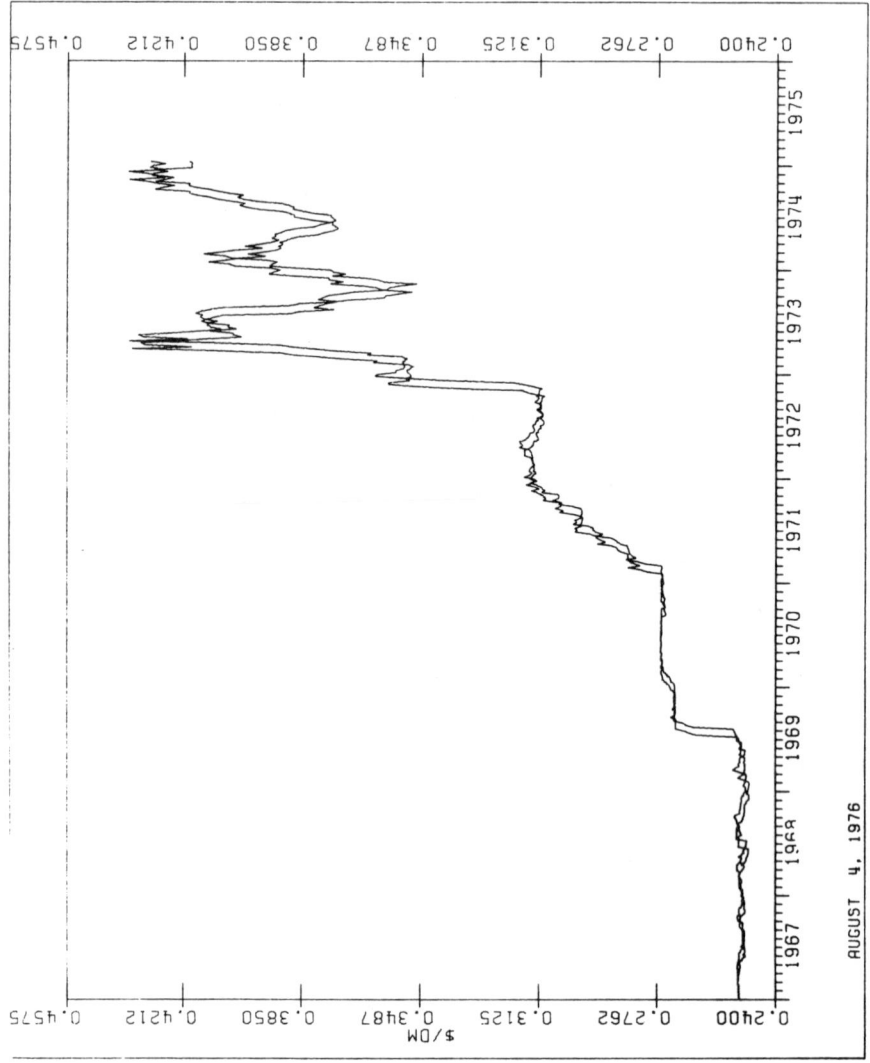

Figure 7.10.
Germany, Spot Rate and Forward Rate Forecast—1-Month Horizon

Forecasting Models—Empirical Results / **149**

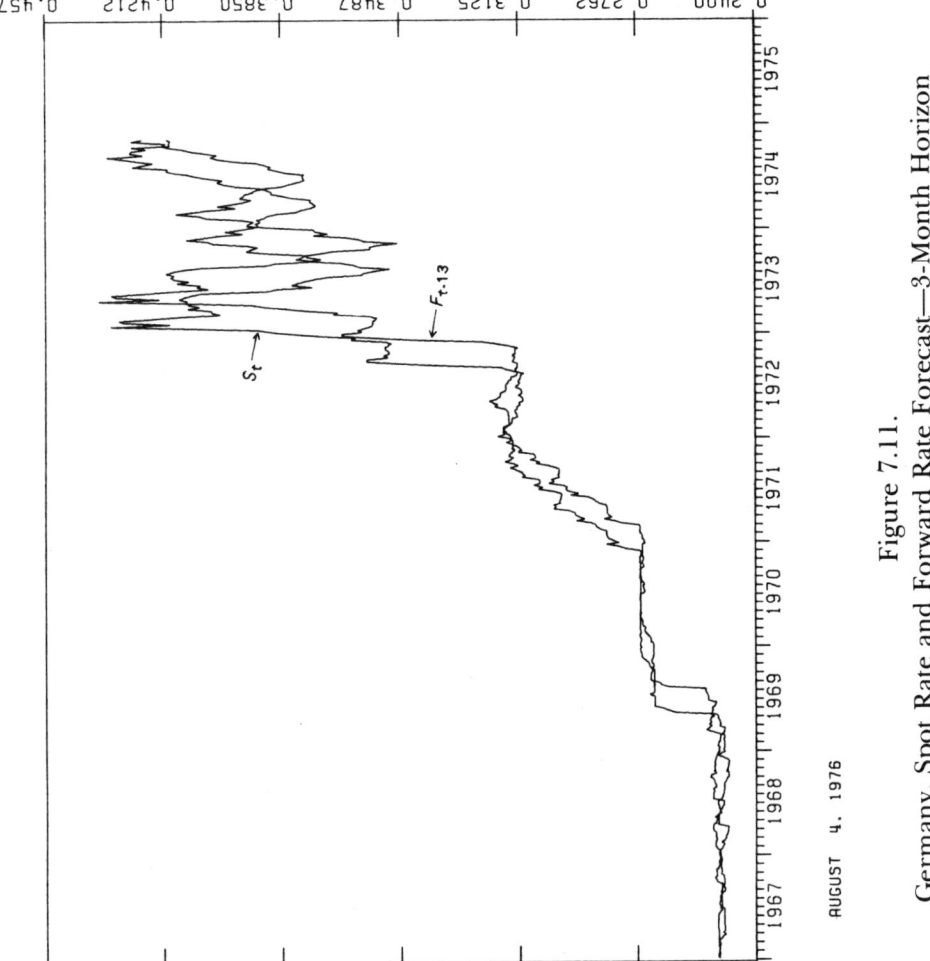

Figure 7.11.
Germany, Spot Rate and Forward Rate Forecast—3-Month Horizon

150 / *The International Money Market*

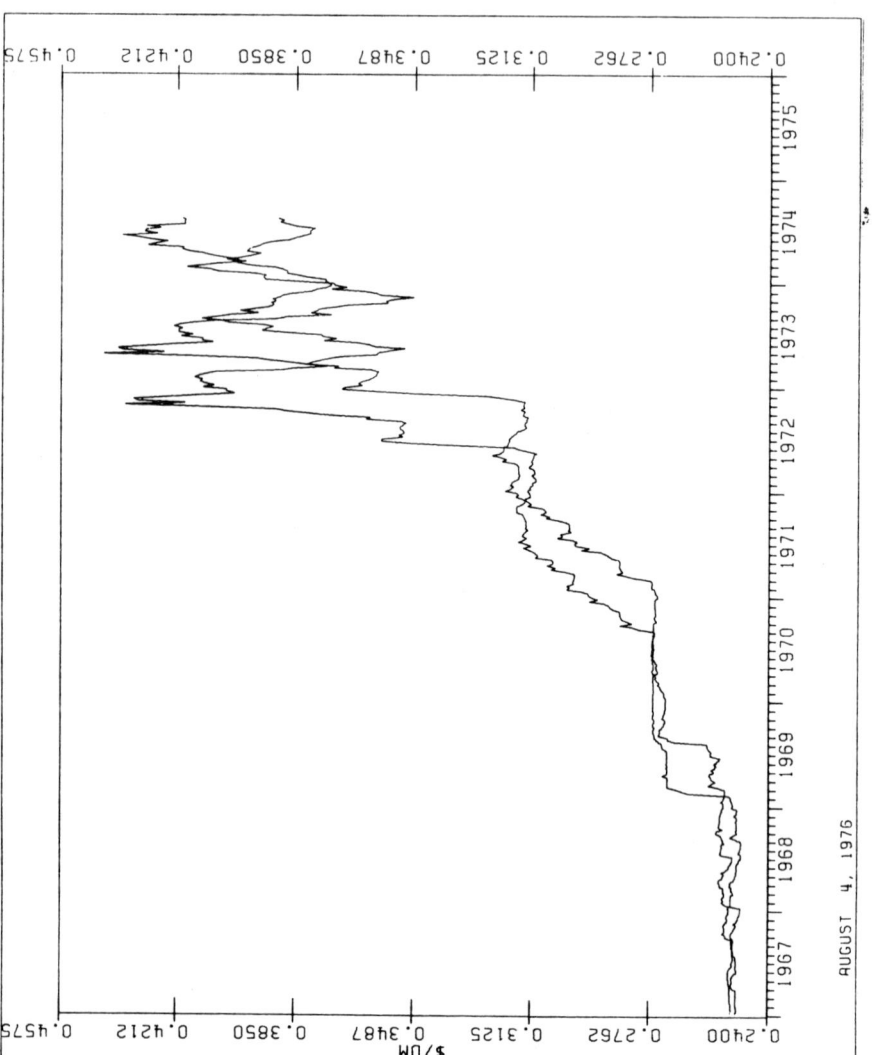

Figure 7.12.
Germany, Spot Rate and Forward Rate Forecast—6-Month Horizon

Table 7.10. Forward Rate Bias in Germany—One-Month Horizon

	$S_{t+1} > S_t$	$S_{t+1} \leq S_t$	Row Total
$S_{t+1} > F_t$	$A_{11} = 60$ $E_{11} = 40$	$A_{12} = 6$ $E_{12} = 26$	66
$S_{t+1} \leq F_t$	$A_{21} = 4$ $E_{21} = 24$	$A_{22} = 35$ $E_{22} = 15$	39
Column Total	64	41	105

A_{ij} = Actual number of observations in cell (i,j).
E_{ij} = Expected number of observations in cell (i,j).

countries. Independent samples were selected for each horizon so the observations are nonoverlapping. At the 5% level, all country-horizon episodes are consistent with the forward rate bias described by the theory. The results are particularly significant for the one-month maturity.[7]

Although the data support our theory, this pattern does not imply profit opportunities since the forecast errors are a function of transaction costs. The theory will be useful for currencies following a trend rate of growth. In these cases, the forecast can be improved by adjusting the forward rate for transaction costs.

COMPOSITE MODELS

The theory of composite forecasting is to combine several alternative forecasts of the future spot rate. Even if the overall results are similar across models, the composite forecast can increase accuracy if the corre-

Table 7.11. Summary of χ^2 Tests for Forward Bias[a]

Country	1-Month	3-Month	6-Month
Canada	71.2	20.7	10.9
England	—	15.2	8.0
Belgium	—	6.4	11.4
France	37.3	14.8	3.2
Germany	67.0	21.1	11.2
Italy	—	9.7	6.6
Netherlands	44.7	12.6	5.6
Switzerland	63.2	14.5	15.0
Japan	—	—	—
NOBS	105	32	15

[a] Critical values of $\chi^2(1) = 3.84$ at 5%, and 6.63 at 1% level.

lation of error terms across models is less than one. The composite model provies a framework for analyzing a prospective forecasting technique. If the new forecast reflects information that is not reflected in the existing models, the new forecast will lead to a significant reduction in MSE in the composite model.[8]

Regression analysis is used to construct the composite forecast ($\hat{S}_t$) using the four forecasting models ($\hat{S}_{i,t}$) analyzed in this study.

$$\hat{S}_t = b_0 + b_1\hat{S}_{1,t} + b_2\hat{S}_{2,t} + b_3\hat{S}_{3,t} + b_4\hat{S}_{4,t}.$$

This equation is estimated for every country-horizon episode in the sample. A dependent sample of observations is selected from two subperiods: the pre-Float II period and the Float II period.[9]

A null hypothesis consistent with the extreme efficient markets view is that composite forecasting will have no effect, since all information is reflected simultaneously in all markets. An alternative view is that when information is costly, prices will never fully reflect information (Grossman and Stiglitz 1976). In this case, composite forecasting may be helpful since an analysis of more markets may exploit more information.

To examine the impact of the composite forecast, the ratio of the composite forecast MSE to the MSE from a single forecasting model is

Table 7.12. Ratio of Mean Squared Forecasting Error—Composite Model/Forward Rate Model

| | \multicolumn{6}{c}{Horizon} | | | | | |
| | 1-Month | | 3-Month | | 6-Month | |
Country	Prefloat	Float	Prefloat	Float	Prefloat	Float
Canada	.93	.92	.81	.93	.75	1.00
United Kingdom	1.00	.78	.95	.71	.89	.77
Belgium	.95	.88	.84	.77	.80	.66
France	.96	.83	.92	.74	.78	.49
Germany	.96	.97	.78	.96	.77	.94
Italy	—	.88	—	.88	—	.77
Netherlands	.63	.71	.94	.86	.83	.87
Switzerland	.98	.92	.92	.69	.88	.48
Japan	—	.81	—	.60	—	.31
Average	.92	.86	.88	.79	.81	.70

Table 7.13. Ratio of Mean Squared Forecasting Error—Composite Model/Lagged Spot Model

	\multicolumn{6}{c}{Horizon}					
	1-Month		3-Month		6-Month	
Country	Prefloat	Float	Prefloat	Float	Prefloat	Float
Canada	.96	.98	.83	.96	.80	.95
United Kingdom	.98	.88	.95	.82	.92	.89
Belgium	.95	.93	.79	.83	.74	.76
France	.94	.92	.88	.84	.68	.60
Germany	.90	.97	.67	.94	.66	.90
Italy	—	.96	—	.91	—	.76
Netherlands	.64	.69	.86	.81	.72	.81
Switzerland	.94	.92	.86	.69	.78	.48
Japan	—	.97	—	.89	—	.57
Average	.90	.91	.83	.85	.76	.75

calculated. A ratio less than 1.0 implies that MSE has been reduced in the composite model. The results appear in Table 7.12.

Composite forecasting appears to have a greater impact during the Float II period and when the forecasting horizon is longer. For some countries (Canada and Germany) the improvement is negligible. For others, Netherlands (at the one-month horizon) and France, Switzerland, and Japan (at the six-month horizon), the improvement is large and significant. The largest reduction in MSE is 69% for the six-month forecast of the Japanese yen. Most of the reductions are in the 10–30% range. Composite forecasting does not appear to have a smaller impact on those spot series that move randomly over time. For example, although the Swiss franc and Italian lira appear to follow a random walk, a six-month composite forecast reduces the MSE by 52% and 24% respectively, during the Float II period.

Generally, it appears that composite forecasting can lead to substantial reductions in MSE especially as the forecast horizon lengthens. One interpretation is that exchange rate expectations are not reflected equally in all market sectors. This may be due to efforts by central banks to restrict price movements or to differential transaction costs or information costs across markets. When the markets are segmented and the forecast horizon is longer, the data indicate that a composite model can significantly reduce forecast errors.

CONCLUSIONS

In this chapter a set of simple models for forecasting the future spot rate was tested on a uniform data base. The most important results are that (1) forecast errors appear to be serially uncorrelated, (2) forecasting bias or currency preference does not appear to be predictable, and (3) mean squared forecasting error rises in proportion to forecasting horizon. Furthermore, in a large percentage of cases, forecast errors are bounded by a neutral band which depends on transaction costs. In general, the mean of forecast errors is significantly nonzero. However, since the mean is usually small relative to transaction costs, the forecast errors may not be economically significant.

These results are consistent with the view that the market efficiently reflects information concerning future exchange rates. The analysis of the mean forecast error indicates that the forecasts are accurate relative to a standard that depends on transaction costs. Furthermore, a large percentage of forecast errors fall within a neutral band consistent with transaction costs. The tests for serial correlation of forecast errors indicate that investors efficiently use the past information in this series. Tests of the dependence of MSE on the length of the forecasting horizon suggest that financial markets are integrated across maturity, resulting in forecast errors that are consistent with minimum mean squared error prediction. Overall, the results suggest that the prices of financial claims can be used to form accurate and consistent forecasts of future spot exchange rates. Therefore, we cannot reject hypothesis two.

Two additional tests were performed in this chapter. First, forward rates significantly underestimate (overestimate) the future spot rate when the spot rate is rising (falling). This result is not economically significant since the forecast errors depend on transaction costs. Second, a composite forecasting model can significantly reduce forecast errors. The gain from composite forecasting, which is larger for longer horizon forecasts, may be the result of information costs, search costs, or government intervention which tend to separate financial markets. More generally, the model provides a framework for analyzing prospective forecasting techniques.

NOTES

1. These data are described more fully in the Appendix.
2. This forecast is consistent with the spot series being generated by a random walk process with zero drift. The random walk description of the exchange rate is only one

model consistent with market efficiency. Equation (3) is selected because it is a naive model that may have been postulated by market participants during this period. A more general time series description of the entire sample period is not available.

3. For example, in the week ending 11/21/67 a number of forward quotations were omitted. The *Weekly Review* commented, "The foreign exchange markets this week were steadier and more real than they have been since the devaluation of the Pound Sterling on November 18. The forwards, however, were still quoted rather than traded." On 3/1/68 most forward quotations were omitted with the warning "the Forward Market was too erratic for a meaningful quotation." A number of quotations were omitted for the week of 3/18/68 when the two-tier gold system was introduced. Finally, during the week ending 11/22/68 the *Weekly Review* reported that most forward prices were "By Negotiation." They commented "The markets were nervous as the week opened and became chaotic by Tuesday.... By Wednesday the major European foreign exchange markets were closed and remained closed for the week."

4. Higher moments of the distribution of forecast errors were also estimated. In most cases the skewness statistic is small (near zero) indicating a symmetric distribution of forecast errors. The kurtosis statistic is large indicating a peaked distribution with fat tails. A Kalmogorov-Smirnov test confirms that for most currencies the distribution is nonnormal. The economic significance of this result is that exchange risk management models that rely on a normal distribution of speculative returns or forecast errors will not be appropriate. Similar results on the distribution of exchange rate changes are reported in Chapter VI, footnote 5.

5. The one exception is Swiss Treasury Bills. Holders of these securities yielded about 1% less per three-month period than if they had held U.S. Treasury Bills.

6. Using time series models, it is easily shown that the weekly (dependent) series of k-week ahead forecasts follows a moving average process of order k-1. Using a dependent sample, Bilson and Levich (1976) demonstrate that the forward rate efficiently reflects the time dependence in the spot exchange rate.

7. The blanks in Table 7.11 indicate that because of missing observations, an independent sample could not be formed. In similar tests using a dependent sample of weekly observations, all χ^2 statistics were significant at the 5% level.

It should be noted that the use of the word bias in this section is not in exact agreement with the usual statistical definition. For example, if the spot rate increases for 10 periods and then decreases for 10 periods, the underestimates in the first 10 periods may cancel the overestimates in the second 10 periods. Overall, the forward rate may appear unbiased while in each subperiod, an apparent bias develops.

8. For a discussion of the theory and an application, see Nelson (1972).

9. We do not use the Peg I, Float I, Peg II, Float II breakdown from Chapter VI since there are too few observations in the Float I, Peg II periods for a regression analysis.

Chapter VIII

Forecasts and Risky Investment Opportunities

PURPOSE

In the previous chapters, the possibility of using data-based models to generate consistent and accurate forecasts of the future spot exchange rate was investigated. Having shown that there are models which can forecast the future spot rate within an error term that depends on transaction costs and a risk premium, our concern shifts to the applicability of these models. Can these models be used to make an unusual profit?

A general profit opportunity that is available to all investors is forward speculation. By taking an open forward position, investors gain a profit that is proportional to the difference between the future spot rate, S_{t+n}, and today's n-period forward rate, $F_{t,n}$.[1] The purpose of this chapter is to test hypothesis three, to test if forecasting models based on publicly available information can lead to unusual profits in forward speculation.

TRADITIONAL METHODOLOGY FOR ANALYZING UNUSUAL PROFITS

A framework for testing for unusual profits in a domestic equity market is developed by Fama, Fisher, Jensen, and Roll (1969). This technique relies on an asset pricing model to estimate expected returns. Actual returns in excess of expected returns are unusual.

In the foreign exchange literature, no consensus exists on a model relating speculative returns with risk. One way to proceed is to assume that the Sharpe-Lintner model of asset pricing applies to the international money market.[2] Then forward speculation is just another investment activity and the rate of return from this activity is defined as

(8.1) $$R_{FS,t} = d_t (F_t - \tilde{S}_{t+1})/F_t$$

where the subscript *FS* indicates forward speculation and d_t is a dummy variable defined by:

$$d_t = +1 \text{ for forward sales,}$$
$$= -1 \text{ for forward purchases.}$$

Speculative returns should therefore be generated according to

(8.2) $$\hat{R}_{FS} = R_F + \beta_{FS} (R_M - R_F)$$

where R_M is the return on an international portfolio of risky assets and R_F is the international risk-free rate. Return in excess of $\hat{R}_{FS}$ is defined as unusual.

Two methodological problems arise. First, the model requires an estimate of the returns on an international portfolio of risky assets, defined as the average return on all possible investment opportunities using market value weights. This is primarily a measurement problem. The second problem is to identify a unique international asset (or portfolio) that is risk-free. Investors face political risk as long as countries reserve the power to erect barriers to the international flow of goods and capital. Since governments may discriminate between investors using a resident/nonresident or citizen/noncitizen criterion, investors may associate different political risks with a given investment.

Similarly, an international risk-free asset should be free of exchange risk. Assume that the objective of investors is to maximize utility from consumption. If all investors face consumer prices denominated in dollars, this objective is equivalent to maximizing the net present *dollar* value of wealth. In this case, a dollar bond issued by the U.S. government is free of exchange risk and default risk and therefore could serve as the risk-free asset. However, the assumption that *all* investors face a dollar denominated set of prices is unrealistic. This suggests that it will be difficult to identify a single asset which investors from all currency areas consider "risk-free."

While a single risk-free asset may not exist, it may be possible to construct a risk-free international portfolio (i.e., the zero beta portfolio) following Black's (1972) methodology. Using a combination of long and short positions in risky assets that are imperfectly correlated, a risk-free portfolio can be constructed. What is the economic interpretation of this constructed portfolio?

Consider Ruthenia, a small, open economy whose local currency is the Pengo. Ruthenian consumers face Pengo prices since they live and consume in Ruthenia. But since Ruthenia is a small country, it is a *price-taker*, the prices of its trading partners (United States, Germany, England, and others) are translated at the exchange rate to calculate Pengo prices. If Ruthenian investors hold a portfolio of the risk-free assets of their trading partners where the portfolio weights are proportional to the trade mix, exchange risk is eliminated. The strategy is similar to that of a multinational corporation with cash flows (positive and negative) in several currencies. A sufficient condition for eliminating this cash flow exposure to exchange risk is to balance the positive and negative cash flows on a currency-by-currency basis (Dufey 1972). Given zero transaction costs, all consumers in each country face the same set of prices. Given similar tastes, the country and currency composition of consumption bundles will also be similar. In this case, the construction of a unique risk-free portfolio applicable to all investors seems justified. As these assumptions are dropped it becomes difficult (if not impossible) to construct a (zero beta) portfolio that residents of each currency area consider to be risk-free.

Theoretical problems, measurement problems and data limitations restrict the application of a traditional approach to analyzing unusual profits in forward speculation. Therefore, an alternative methodology is developed.

AN ALTERNATIVE METHODOLOGY FOR TESTING THE PROFITABILITY OF FORECAST RULES

Assume the speculator has made a forecast, $\hat{S}_{t+n}$, of the future spot rate. Observing $\hat{S}_{t+n} > F_{t,n}$ is a signal to buy the foreign currency forward;

$\hat{S}_{t+n} < F_{t,n}$ is a signal to sell the foreign currency. Assume that the speculator buys one unit of currency forward independent of the amount of the deviation between his forecast and the forward rate observed in the market. The speculator is therefore *risk-neutral*—he gambles a fixed amount after comparing the expected value of his forecast with the forward rate. Assuming 100% margin, the mean profit rate from following this strategy for M periods can be calculated as

$$(8.3) \qquad \sum_{i=1}^{M} d_i (S_{t+n,i} - F_{t,i})/(M \cdot F_{t,i})$$

where
$$d_i = +1 \text{ if } \hat{S}_{t+n} > F_{t,n}$$
$$ -1 \text{ if } \hat{S}_{t+n} < F_{t,n}.$$

If the investor has "perfect information," he can gain a profit in every period with the proper selection of d_i. Profits assuming perfect information are calculated as

$$(8.4) \qquad \sum_{i=1}^{M} |S_{t+n,i} - F_{t,i}|/(M \cdot F_{t,i}).$$

In Levich (1976c) it is shown that the ratio

$$(8.5) \qquad H = \sum_{i=1}^{M} d_i (S_{t+n,i} - F_{t,i}) / \sum_{i=1}^{M} |S_{t+n,i} - F_{t,i}|$$

has expected value $(2p-1)$ and variance $4p(1-p)/M$, where p is the probability of choosing d_i correctly in any period and M is the number of independent sample observations. For example, a rule which is correct half of the time has $p = 0.5$ and $E(H) = 0.0$. "Unusual" profits correspond to the case where H is greater than zero or p is greater than one-half.

In this chapter, five rules for selecting the d_i are considered:
(1) Select d_i using a forecast based on traditional interest rates.
(2) Select d_i using a forecast based on external interest rates.
(3) Select d_i using a forecast based on the lagged spot rate.

(4) Select $d_i = +1$ for all i.
(5) Select $d_i = -1$ for all i.

Each rule is compared to rule (6):

(6) Select d_i assuming perfect information.

EMPIRICAL RESULTS

Table 8.1 displays the mean percentage profit from three-month forward speculation for each rule. Note that the results describe a dependent sample of observations for the entire sample period. In other words, we assume the investor makes a three-month investment decision in every week of the sample. The reported profits are per three-month period; they are not annualized.[3]

The several rules lead to a substantial difference in mean profit for each currency. For example, there are six currencies where one rule results in negative profits while another rule results in statistically significant positive profits.[4] For the other three countries, the difference between profits from following the worst rule and the best rule is at least a factor of two.

Of the three forecast based rules (1, 2, and 3), rule (3) is consistently dominated by rule (2) or rule (4)—the "always buy foreign currency"

Table 8.1. Mean Percentage Profit from Speculation Following Alternative Rules

Country	Alternative Rules					
	1	2	3	4	5	6
Canada	−.103	.203[a]	.175	.178	−.178	.878
United Kingdom	.676[a]	.327	.044	.078	−.078	2.438
Belgium	.186	.486	.498	1.040[a]	−1.040	2.430
France	−.869	1.126[a]	.679	.937	−.937	2.912
Germany	−.322	.555	−.312	1.060[a]	−1.060	3.042
Italy	.371	.721[a]	.431	.527	−.527	1.669
Netherlands	−.537	.760	−.531	.899[a]	−.899	2.277
Switzerland	−.327	1.331[a]	.500	1.096	−1.096	2.603
Japan	.382	−.457	.601	1.015[a]	−1.015	3.295

Note: The entries are percentage profit per three-month period. The sample period is 1967/75.
For explanation of numbering, see text.
[a] Most profitable rule for this country.

rule. This is true even for countries (e.g., United Kingdom and Italy) whose currency generally depreciated over the sample period. Similarly, rule (1) generally leads to negative or near zero speculative profits.

Overall, there are four cases where rule (2) is the most profitable, four cases for rule (4), and one for rule (1). In each of these cases, the mean profit is significantly greater than zero.[5] With the possible exception of Canada, these profits appear to be in excess of transaction costs. If the profits are annualized, the rates of return are in the range 0.8% to 5.3%. These profits are small relative to the risk-free yield on U.S. Treasury Bills over this period.[6]

In Table 8.1 observe that perfect information profits (column 6) vary across currencies. These profits are largest for Japan (which also has the highest mean squared forecast error) and lowest for Canada (which had the lowest mean squared forecast error). This observation only confirms a definition. Potential profits from forward speculation are greatest when the forward rate is a poor forecaster of the future spot rate.

Statistics for analyzing the unusualness of these speculative profits are presented in Table 8.2. For the most profitable rules, the H ratio ranges between 0.23 for Canada and 0.51 for Switzerland; the corresponding probabilities (p) range between 0.62 and 0.76. While these estimates of p are larger than 0.5, they are based on a sample of 32 independent observations. Therefore, no estimate of p is significantly larger than 0.5 at the 5% confidence level. These rules do not result in unusual profits and therefore we cannot reject hypothesis three.

Table 8.2. A Test for Unusual Speculative Returns

| | Alternative Rules | | | | | | | |
| | 1 | | 2 | | 3 | | 4 | |
Country	H	p	H	p	H	p	H	p
Canada	−.12	.44	.23[a]	.62	.20	.60	.20	.60
United Kingdom	.28[a]	.64	.13	.57	.02	.51	.03	.51
Belgium	.08	.54	.20	.60	.02	.51	.43[a]	.71
France	−.30	.35	.39[a]	.69	.23	.62	.32	.66
Germany	−.11	.45	.18	.59	−.10	.45	.35[a]	.67
Italy	.22	.61	.43[a]	.72	.26	.63	.32	.66
Netherlands	−.24	.38	.33	.67	−.23	.38	.39[a]	.70
Switzerland	−.12	.44	.51[a]	.76	.19	.60	.42	.71
Japan	.12	.56	−.14	.43	.18	.59	.31[a]	.65

[a] Most profitable rule for this country.

CONCLUSIONS

This chapter has developed a methodology for testing the profitability of forecast rules. The methodology was applied using the forecasts developed in earlier chapters. The results indicate that speculative profits are small relative to a risk-free rate and small relative to the level of perfect information profits. The forecasting models do not lead to unusual profits from risky foreign exchange positions. Another interpretation of these results is that the alternative models are not significantly better forecasters than the forward rate. If they were better forecasters, the probability (p) would be significantly greater than 0.5. Therefore, the forward rate prediction of the future spot rate is as good as the prediction based on the other naive models.

Since the forecasting models are based on publicly available information, the results are consistent with the efficient market theory; the data do not reject hypothesis three. The results should be considered only as indicative since we have abstracted from a portfolio measure of risk.

NOTES

1. Testing our forecasts or any other forecasts in this way does not imply that the firm does or should speculate in foreign exchange. The issues of the accuracy of the forecast and the firm's use of the forecast are separable. Assume that the firm uses the forward rate as its estimate of the future spot rate. A new forecast, which is more accurate than the forward rate (and therefore leads to speculative profits) should increase the profits of the firm.

2. An alternative model of speculative returns is developed in Solnik (1973) and Roll and Solnik (1975). In this model, the return from forward speculation (in currency j) is directly related to the average speculative return available to the investor (from country i) scaled by a risk factor for currency j. For a review of this model, see Levich (1976b).

3. A similar set of calculations were made for one-month and six-month forward speculation. The results for the three-month horizon appear representative of the other two periods. Since the data base consists of bid prices for both spot and forward rates, profits from speculative purchases of foreign currency are overestimated while profits from speculative sales of foreign currency are underestimated. Mean speculative profits may be unbiased and variability over-stated if long and short foreign currency positions balance out over time. However, if the investor has a consistent long position in one currency, the estimate of mean speculative profits will be biased by as much as the cost of two transactions.

4. A rule which leads to a negative profit can be adapted to result in a positive profit just by reversing the speculative activity indicated by the rule (i.e., reverse the d_i). In other words, if the forecast indicates that S_{t+n} will be greater (less) than F_t, we sell (buy) the foreign currency forward. None of these adapted rules results in higher profits than an alternative rule in Table 8.1.

5. The t-statistics for mean profit range between 3.3 for Canada and 5.6 for Switzerland.

6. The returns appear similar to those calculated by Grubel (1966). Over the period July 1955 to May 1961 Grubel calculated average annual rates of return between 16% and 27% for sterling speculation assuming a 10% margin. Adjusting our figures for a 10% margin implies rates of return in the range 8% to 53%. The rate of return from sterling speculation is 27% (.676·4·10). Grubel did not calculate an empirical measure of the riskiness of his speculative profits.

Chapter IX

Conclusions and Suggestions for Future Research

CONCLUSIONS

This study has investigated various aspects of the international money market. The principle motivation for this research was to see whether the efficient market hypothesis held when tested on a uniform set of international financial data. Three specific hypotheses were formulated: (1) Unusual profit opportunities in covered interest arbitrage are quickly eliminated. (2) Prices—spot rates, forward rates, and interest rates—of particular financial claims imply accurate and consistent forecasts of future spot exchange rates. (3) Speculative returns greater than the risk-adjusted rate of return should not be earned by investors who use exchange rate forecasts based on publicly available information. These hypotheses were tested in Chapters IV, VII, and VIII. Overall, the data cannot reject any of these hypotheses.

To supplement these tests, additional descriptive statistics and theoretical models were developed. Estimates of transaction costs in foreign exchange and securities markets were presented in Chapter III. Alternative models for exchange rate forecasting were presented in Chapter V. In Chapter VI, the time series behavior of exchange rates was analyzed.

The remainder of this chapter reviews and integrates the empirical results of this study. Descriptive statistics on transaction costs and the time series of exchange rates are reviewed in the next section. Conclusions concerning international money market efficiency are presented in the third section. The fourth section examines the implications of these findings for international financial managers. The chapter concludes with suggestions for future research.

DESCRIPTIVE STATISTICS FOR THE INTERNATIONAL MONEY MARKETS

To supplement the hypothesis testing, additional descriptive statistics were calculated. Chapter III presented alternative estimates of the cost of transacting. A new method of calculating foreign exchange transaction costs was developed that relies on triangular arbitrage. Estimates of transaction costs were based on the deviations from triangular parity in the foreign exchange market. Variation in these estimates over time was consistent with variation in other estimates based on the bid-ask spread. Estimates of transaction costs were shown to vary across markets and over time. As a theory of profit maximization given risk aversion would predict, transaction costs were larger the greater the uncertainty, the longer the maturity of instruments, and the smaller the volume of trading. While transaction costs remained small in absolute terms, they increased dramatically in the move to the managed float period. The rise in transaction costs was associated with an increase in the deviations from interest rate parity and an increase in forecasting errors.

Chapter VI analyzed the time series behavior of exchange rates. The data suggested that the first two moments of the level of the spot rate and its rate of change were not stationary. The general trend was toward an increasing volatility of exchange rates. The implication of this result was to rule out a time series analysis of the entire sample period. However, an analysis of the floating rate period indicated that low order time series models were sufficient to describe exchange rate movements. The economic interpretation of this result is that the foreign exchange market reacts quickly to new information. An innovation in the exchange rate series has its major effect contemporaneously with the remainder of the effect spread out over the following one or two or three periods. Furthermore, time series models for spot and forward rates were often similar, implying that the forward rate efficiently reflects the time series pattern in the spot rate.

Another descriptive theme in this research has been the identification of homogenous sample periods. Chapter III presented evidence that the level of speculative activity was not constant over the period 1962/75. For the purposes of estimating transaction costs, we concentrated on three periods (the quiet peg, 1962/67; the turbulent peg, 1968/69; and the managed float, 1973/75) that appeared homogeneous within each period and heterogeneous between periods.

The analysis in Chapter IV suggested that transaction costs played a similar role in accounting for deviations from interest parity during the quiet peg and the managed float periods. The middle, turbulent peg period was an exception. The analysis in Chapter VI suggested that, for each currency, the time series description of each series was similar during the quiet peg and managed float periods. For the turbulent peg period, the time series description of the exchange rate series was often a random walk, which differs from the other two periods.

One interpretation of these findings is that the formal exchange rate system does not change the manner in which underlying structural and behavioral relationships are reflected in international arbitrage and the time series of exchange rates. This suggests that sample periods can be defined by the level of uncertainty rather than the formal exchange rate system.

INTERNATIONAL MONEY MARKET EFFICIENCY

The tests of market efficiency were designed to proceed from simple to more complicated tests. Hypothesis one tests covered interest arbitrage between foreign exchange and securities markets. This arbitrage is essentially free of exchange risk since profit opportunities are calculated using *current* prices that are observed with certainty. Hypotheses two and three are more demanding since they rely on the expected *future* spot rate which the market estimates with uncertainty.

A test of hypothesis one was presented to Chapter IV and a model that explicitly accounts for transaction costs was developed. It was demonstrated that transaction costs led to a neutral equilibrium band, within which there are no profits from covered interest arbitrage. The model suggested a test statistic—the percentage of observations bounded within the neutral equilibrium band—that is a proper test of market efficiency. To conform to this model, data reported on a per annum basis were adjusted to their per period equivalents. Calculations using the adjusted data indicated that there were few unexploited profit opportunities. The profit opportunities which did appear were quickly bid away. Therefore, the data did not reject hypothesis one.

The section entitled "Covered Interest Arbitrage in the Period 1967/75" in Chapter IV examined the sensitivity of deviations from interest rate parity to the choice of currency, financial instrument, and maturity. Economic theory predicts that deviations from interest rate parity are smaller for currencies that trade in larger markets, for financial instruments that trade in wider unregulated markets, and for shorter term maturities. The data in this section confirmed these predictions.

Hypothesis two was tested in Chapter VII. A set of simple forecasting models was tested on a uniform data base. Since there is no single test statistic for testing hypothesis two, a variety of statistical calculations was performed. Specifically, the serial correlation of forecast errors, the mean forecast error, mean squared forecast error, and the percentage of forecast errors bounded within a neutral band were calculated. The results confirm that relative to the magnitude of transaction costs, the forecasts were accurate and consistent in different time periods as well as different forecasting horizons. Therefore, the data did not reject hypothesis two.

A test of hypothesis three was presented in Chapter VIII. A technique for measuring unusual speculative profits was developed and tested on a set of forecasts based on spot rates, forward rates, and interest rates—information that is publicly available. The results indicated that speculative profits were small relative to the U.S. risk-free rate and small relative to the level of "perfect information profits." Therefore, hypothesis three was not rejected.

IMPLICATIONS FOR FINANCIAL MANAGERS

When financial markets are efficient in reflecting available information, investors and financial managers should behave differently and follow different strategies than when markets are inefficient.[1] We will concentrate on two issues in the discussion of efficient markets: forecasting exchange rates and hedging exchange risk.

Financial managers often require a forecast of the future spot rate. When markets are inefficient, managers may invest in data collection and analysis, or outside forecasting services. The analysis in Chapter VII suggests that where developed financial markets exist, market prices can be used to formulate relatively accurate and consistent forecasts as far as the six-month horizon. These forecasts are likely to have desirable properties—for example, serially uncorrelated forecast errors with a mean that is near zero. Another desirable feature is that these forecasts are inexpensive; the necessary data to construct the forecast are published in daily newspapers.

For longer horizon forecasts, Chapter VII suggests that composite forecasting will reduce errors modestly. The composite technique will also be useful for measuring the marginal contribution of an additional forecast. If the new forecast is based on information not previously reflected in market prices, adding the new forecast to a composite model will significantly reduce MSE. If the market for new information is competitive, it is unlikely that a new forecast will be based on information or analysis not already reflected in market prices. The models analyzed in Chapter VII represent a naive standard that can be used for comparison with competing forecasting models.

A second problem faced by financial managers is the decision to hedge foreign exchange risk. There are basically two techniques: to borrow and lend in spot transactions in the international money market or to buy and sell forward currency contracts. As a theoretical matter, when the interest parity theorem holds, these two techniques are equivalent. Therefore, we consider hedging with forward contracts only.

Suppose a firm holds an asset denominated in foreign currency. The firm can avoid exchange risk by selling a forward contract (at F_t) or the firm can carry the exchange risk and sell the asset at the future spot rate (S_{t+1}). If the forward rate equals the future spot rate, the value of the firm does not depend on which action the firm takes. The analysis in Chapter VII suggests that the forward rate and future spot rate are very closely related. The mean deviation between the two numbers is near zero and, in many cases, less than transaction costs. Furthermore, the deviations are serially uncorrelated.

The implication of the close relationship between forward rates and future spot rates is that the firm's hedging strategy will not affect the long-run expected profits of the firm. However, continued hedging of the exchange risk exposure will reduce the volatility of earnings. If investors prefer firms with a lower volatility of earnings (*ceterus paribus*) hedging will increase the market value of the firm without altering its long-run expected profits. The more closely the forward rate equals the future spot rate, the less the cost of hedging and the more the firm should hedge.[2]

SUGGESTIONS FOR FUTURE RESEARCH

This research has examined the efficiency of the international money market. The hypotheses which were tested rely primarily on publicly available information. One extension of this research would be to consider hypotheses based on inside information. Commercial forecasters in banks or consulting groups may have access to inside information or superior analytical skills. If they do, their forecasts should be superior to the naive models analyzed in Chapter VII. Foreign exchange traders in commercial banks may also have access to inside information. If they do, their speculative profits should be greater than the profits from following a naive rule, such as those tested in Chapter VIII.

Another more demanding test of market efficiency is to test a specific pricing model. For example, we could formulate a specific short-run monetary model of the foreign exchange rate—perhaps Bilson's (1976) model. If the market is efficient and it uses this model for pricing, then observed foreign exchange rates should fluctuate randomly about their predicted value. Another example would formulate a specific model of foreign exchange risk pricing—perhaps Solnik's (1973) model. Once again, if the market is efficient and it uses this model for pricing exchange risk, then observed speculative returns should fluctuate randomly about the predicted return.

A final research issue is to explain the forecast errors generated in Chapter VII. This analysis would require a structural model of the fundamental determinants of exchange rates. We expect that forecast errors are associated with unanticipated disturbances in exogenous variables. One method to improve on the naive forecasts presented here is to build a structural model of the exchange rate and hope to anticipate the disturbances in exogenous variables.

NOTES
1. Black (1971) analyzes the impact of the efficient market hypothesis on domestic portfolio management. Levich (1975) extends this analysis to international financial management.
2. For a theoretical proof see Farber (1976).

Appendix

DATA SOURCES

Chapter III

Data on bid and ask prices for forward exchange are from the *International Monetary Market Year Book* and the *Daily Information Bulletin* published by the staff of the International Monetary Market (IMM) of the Chicago Mercantile Exchange. The IMM reports the closing rates from the New York interbank market.

Figure 3.3 which illustrates the time series behavior of the forward rates relative to spot rates is based on two sources. For the period 1962/69, the spot and forward rates ($/DM and $/$C) are taken from *International Financial Statistics (IFS)* (International Monetary Fund, Washington, D.C.), which published a daily series of prices during this period. (More detailed information on this source is given below.) Exchange rates for the period 1970/75 are from the *Weekly Review of International Money Markets* (Harris Bank, Chicago, Illinois). The *Weekly Review* publishes a closing bid price from the New York interbank market for the last trading day of each week.

Data necessary to calculate transaction costs using triangular arbitrage are collected from several sources. For the period 1962/69, exchange rates involving the U.S. dollar are taken from the *IFS*. The daily, midpoint exchange rates reported in the *IFS* are collected by the IMF from several other sources. For example, the $/£ rates are based on closing prices in London as reported in the *Financial Times*. The $/$C rates are based on noontime, interbank prices in Toronto as reported by the Bank of Canada. The $/DM rates are based on the 11:00 A.M. Official Session quotation of the Bundesbank in Frankfurt.

Also for the period 1962/69, the exchange rates involving the United Kingdom pound sterling (DM/£,)C/£) are based on information reported in the *Montagu Monthly Review* (Samuel Montagu and Co., Ltd., London, England). Montagu reports the daily range of spot prices during the London trading day. The midpoint of this range estimates spot exchange prices in London for the day. Montagu also reports the forward premium (bid-ask) over the spot rate at the close of London trading. The midpoint of the closing forward spread added to midpoint of daily range of spot prices forms an estimate of forward exchange prices in London for the day.

For the 1973/75 period, exchange rates involving the U.S. dollar are taken from the IMM. Closing bid and ask forward prices from the New York interbank market are reported; only the closing bid price is available for spot exchange. Sterling exchange rates, again, are taken from the *Montagu Monthly Review*. The characteristics of this data are the same as we described for the 1962/69 period.

The approach for estimating transaction costs described in Chapter III relies on midpoint prices for foreign exchange quoted at the same moment in time. The data sources described above do not meet these requirements precisely. For example, in the "$-$C-£ triangle," $/$C and $/£ prices are midpoint prices quoted at similar moments in time (noon in Toronto and closing in London), however, $C/£ prices are based on the midpoint of the daily range of spot prices in London. It is important to distinguish data bases and estimation techniques that lead to biased results from those that lead to imprecise (yet unbiased) results. A simple example will illustrate that the sample data base could lead to underestimates (as well as overestimates) of transaction costs. Therefore, a priori, it is not possible to predict the sign or magnitude of the estimation bias introduced as a result of the data.

To study the effect of using a midpoint of the daily range in the $C/£ market, fix the spot prices in the other two markets: $/$C = 1.00, $/£ = 2.00. Table A.1 illustrates two examples (cases 2 and 3) where use of a daily range in one market leads to an underestimate of the true deviation. The examples do not indicate that the sample data (i.e., daily range prices) and the estimation technique produce a clear pattern of bias.

Table A.1. Deviations from Triangular Parity Using Daily Range of Prices and True Prices

Case No.	Daily Range	% Deviation with Midpoint of Daily Range	$C/£ True Price	% Deviation with True Price
1	1.90–2.10	0	2.00	0
2	1.90–2.10	0	1.90	−5%
3	1.90–2.10	0	2.10	+5%
4	1.90–2.00	−2.5%	1.90	−5%
5	1.90–2.00	−2.5%	2.00	0
6	2.00–2.10	+2.5%	2.10	+5%
7	2.00–2.10	+2.5%	2.00	0

However, since overestimation is sometimes possible (cases 5 and 7) and to allow for the possibility of data errors, a conservative number (i.e., that number which bounds 95% of triangular deviations) is selected to represent transaction costs. It should be noted that if the sample numbers correspond to cases 2 and 3, the estimated deviations from triangular parity are already conservative.

Estimates of transaction costs in security markets are based on bid-ask prices from several sources. Data on the bid yield and ask yield on U.S. Treasury Bills for the period 1962/69 are from *Salomon Brothers Monthly Bond Report*. For the period 1973, this information on U.S. Treasury Bills is taken from the *Money Manager*. U.S. Treasury Bill yields are quoted using the bankers discount method. The bid price and the ask price (expressed as a percentage of par) are computed according to (1) bid price = 100 − (bid yield × days to maturity)/360, (2) ask price = 100 − (ask yield × days to maturity)/360. The percentage spread is (ask price-bid price)/ask price.

The cost of transacting in external security markets is estimated using bid and ask yields on nonnegotiable external deposit accounts. In this case, the spread is (ask yield-bid yield). For the period 1968/69, these quotations on Euro-dollar in London and Euro-sterling in Paris are reported in the *Bond Buyer*.[1] For the period 1973/75, quotations on Euro-dollar in Frankfurt and Euro-sterling in Frankfurt are selected from the *Money Manager*.

Chapter IV

This chapter deals primarily with covered interest arbitrage. The following table gives an overview of the data sources.

Table A.2. Overview of Data Sources in Chapter IV

Period	Exchange Rates	Treasury Bills	Euro-deposit Rates
1962/69	International Financial Statistics	Federal Reserve Bulletin	Bank of England Quarterly
1972/75	Harris Bank	Harris Bank	Harris Bank

The exchange rates reported by the *IFS* were described earlier. The *Federal Reserve Bulletin* reported weekly discount yields for the latest three-month bill. Therefore, some of the rates used are for bills that have maturities two or three days less than three months. The discount yields are converted to prices and then to holding period yields according to: yield = (100-price)/price. The *Bank of England Quarterly* reports middle closing rates for three-month Euro-dollar deposits in London and Euro-sterling deposits in Paris.[2]

All of the data reported by the Harris Bank are closing bid prices for the last trading day of the week. The Euro-currency rates are all for London deposits, except Euro-sterling deposits which are quoted in Paris.

The covered interest arbitrage calculations are based on data reported by the Harris Bank. The exchange rates and Euro-currency rates were described earlier. Quotes on three-month Treasury Bills are reported for the United States, Canada, United Kingdom, Belgium, and the Netherlands. For France and Italy the maturity is often one year; for Japan the maturity is 60 days. Capital controls restricted the purchase by foreigners of these Treasury Bills in Belgium, France, Germany, Italy, and Switzerland.

Chapters VI, VII, and VIII

The data for these chapters are taken almost exclusively from the Harris Bank *Weekly Review*. The data from this source on foreign exchange rates, Treasury Bill rates, and Euro-currency deposit rates have been described in previous sections. In Chapter VI, the section titled "Time Series Analysis of Exchange Rates in Three Periods," shows that the spot and forward exchange rates are from the *IFS*. This data also was described earlier.

NOTES

1. The *Bond Buyer* changed its name to the *Money Manager* in 1972. Otherwise, the publication remained essentially the same.

2. Ideally, one would prefer to use dollar and sterling deposits issued in the same external center. Aliber (1973) has argued that this compromise does not alter the results significantly.

References

Books and Articles

Aliber, Robert Z., ed. *The International Market for Foreign Exchange.* New York: Praeger, 1969.

———. "The Interest Rate Parity Theorem: A Reinterpretation." *Journal of Political Economy* 81, no. 6 (November/December 1973):1451–1459.

———. "A Short Guide to International Corporation Finance." University of Chicago, 1975. (Mimeographed.)

Bagehot, Walter. "The Only Game in Town." *Financial Analysts Journal* 27, no. 2 (March/April 1971):12ff.

Barnea, Amir and Dennis E. Logue. "The Effect of Risk on the Market Maker's Spread." *Financial Analysts Journal* 32, no. 6 (November/December 1975):45–49.

Bilson, John F. O. "Rational Expectations and the Exchange Rate: Theory and Estimation." Northwestern University, Working Paper, December 1975.

———. "A Monetary Approach to the Exchange Rate." Ph.D. disseration, University of Chicago, 1976.

Bilson, John F. O., and Richard M. Levich. "A Test of the Efficiency of the Forward Exchange Market." Federal Reserve System Board of Governors, August 1976. (Mimeographed.)

Black, Fischer. "Capital Market Equilibrium with Restricted Borrowing." *Journal of Business* 45:3 (July 1972):444–445.

———. "Implications of the Random Walk Hypothesis for Portfolio Management." *Financial Analysts Journal* 27, no. 2 (March/April 1971):16–22.

Black, Fischer, and Myron Scholes. "From Theory to a New Financial Product." *Journal of Finance* 29:2 (May 1974):399–412.

Box, G.E.P., and W. Jenkins. *Time Series Analysis.* San Francisco: Holden-Day, Inc., 1970.

Box, G.E.P., and David A. Pierce. "Distribution of Residual Autocorrelation in Autoregressive-Integrated Moving Average Time Series Models." *Journal of the American Statistical Association* 65, no. 332 (December 1970):1509–1526.

Branson, William H. "The Minimum Covered Interest Differential Needed for International Arbitrage Activity." *Journal of Political Economy* 77, no. 6 (November/December 1969):1028–1035.

Cournot, Augustin. *Mathematical Principles of the Theory of Wealth* (1838). Reprinted. New York: Kelly, 1971.
Cuneo, Larry J., and Wayne H. Wagner. "Reducing the Cost of Stock Trading." *Financial Analysts Journal* 32, no. 6 (November/December 1975):35–44.
Demsetz, Harold. "The Cost of Transacting." *Quarterly Journal of Economics* 82, no. 1 (February 1968):33–53.
Dooley, Michael P., and Jeffrey R. Shafer. "Analysis of Short-Run Exchange-Rate Behavior: March, 1973 to September, 1975." International Finance Discussion Papers, no. 76. Washington, D.C.: Federal Reserve System, February 1976.
Dufey, Gunter. "Corporate Finance and Exchange Rate Variations." *Financial Management* 1, no. 2 (Summer 1972):51–57.
Einzig, Paul A. *A Dynamic Theory of Forward Exchange*. London: Macmillan, 1961.
Fama, Eugene F. "Efficient Capital Markets: A Review of Theory and Empirical Work." *Journal of Finance* 25, no. 2 (May 1970):383–417.
———. *Foundations of Finance*. New York: Basic Books, 1976.
Fama, Eugene F., Lawrence Fisher, Michael C. Jensen, and Richard Roll. "The Adjustment of Stock Prices to New Information." *International Economic Review* 10, no. 1 (February 1969):1–21.
Farber, André L. "A Note on the Optimal Level of Forward Exchange Transactions." University of Belgium, September 1975. (Mimeographed.)
Fieleke, Norman S. "The Hedging of Commerical Transactions Between U.S. and Canadian Residents: A View from the United States." Federal Reserve Bank of Boston, *Conference Series* no. 6, September 1971.
———. "Exchange Rate Flexibility and the Efficiency of the Foreign Exchange Markets." *Journal of Financial and Quantitative Analysis* 10, nos. 3–5 (September 1975):409–426.
Fisher, Irving. "Appreciation and Interest." *Publication of the American Economic Association* 11, no. 4 (August 1896):331–442.
Frenkel, Jacob A. "Elasticities and the Interest Parity Theory." *Journal of Political Economy* 81, no. 3 (May/June 1973):741–747.
———. "The Forward Exchange Rate, Expectations and the Demand for Money: The German Hyperinflation." Center for Mathematical Studies in Business and Economics, no. 7623. University of Chicago, 1976.
Frenkel, Jacob A., and Richard M. Levich. "Covered Interest Arbitrage: Unexploited Profits?" *Journal of Political Economy* 83, no. 2 (April 1975):325–338.
———. "Transaction Costs and Interest Arbitrage: Tranquil versus Turbulent Periods." International Finance Discussion Paper, no. 87. Washington, D.C., Federal Reserve System, August 1976.
Giddy, Ian H., and Gunter Dufey. "The Random Behavior of Flexible Exchange Rates." *Journal of International Business Studies* 6, no. 1 (Spring 1975):1–32.
Goschen, Viscount. *The Theory of the Foreign Exchanges*. 3d ed. London, 1864. Reprinted 4th ed., London: Pitman House, 1932.
Grossman, Sanford J., and Joseph E. Stiglitz. "Information and Competitive Price Systems." *American Economic Review* 66, no. 2 (May 1976):246–253.
Grubel, Herbert G. *Forward Exchange Speculation and the International Flow of Capital*. Stanford: Stanford University Press, 1966.
Heagy, Thomas C. "The Term Structure of the Eurodollar Market." University of Chicago, 1970. (Mimeographed.)
Hodgson, John S. "An Analysis of Floating Exchange Rates: The Dollar-Sterling Rate, 1919–1925." *Southern Economic Journal* 38, no. 2 (October 1972):249–257.

Holmes, A.R., and F. H. Schott. *The New York Foreign Exchange Market.* New York: Federal Reserve Bank of New York, 1965.

Kaserman, David L. "The Forward Rate: Its Determination and Behavior as a Predictor of the Future Spot Rate." Proceedings of the American Statistical Association, 1973. Pp. 417-422.

Keynes, John M. *A Tract on Monetary Reform.* London: Macmillan, 1923.

Klein, Lawrence R. *An Essay on the Theory of Economic Prediction.* Chicago: Markham Publishing, 1971.

Kohlhagen, Steven W. "The Forward Rate as an Unbiased Estimator of the Future Spot Rate." University of California, Berkeley, 1975. (Mimeographed.)

Kouri, P. "International Investment and Interest Rate Linkages Under Flexible Exchange Rates." In R. Z. Aliber (ed.), *The Political Economy of Monetary Reform.* London: Macmillan, 1976.

Kraus, Alan and Hans Stoll. "Price Impacts of Block Trading on the New York Stock Exchange." *Journal of Finance* 27, no. 3 (June 1972):569-588.

Leamer, Edward E., and Robert M. Stern. "Problems in the Theory and Empirical Estimation of International Capital Movements." In *International Mobility and Movement of Capital.* Edited by Fritz Machlup et al. New York: National Bureau of Economic Research, 1972. Pp. 171-206.

Levi, Maurice D. "Taxation and 'Abnormal' International Capital Flows." *Journal of Political Economy* 85, no. 3 (June 1977): 635-646.

Levich, Richard M. "Efficient Markets and International Financial Management." New York University Working Paper no. 75-89, December 1975.

———. "Pure Gambles and Portfolio Theory." New York University, 1976a. (Mimeographed.)

———. "The Rewards for Bearing Foreign Exchange Risk." Federal Reserve System Board of Governors, 1976b. (Mimeographed.)

———. "A Note on Testing for Unusual Returns in Speculative Markets." New York University, 1976c. (Mimeographed.)

Magee, Stephen P. "The Empirical Evidence on the Monetary Approach to the Balance of Payments and Exchange Rates." *American Economic Review* 66, no. 2 (May 1976): 163-170.

McCormick, Frank. "Transaction Costs in the Foreign Exchange Markets Under Fixed and Floating Exchange Rates." University of California, Riverside, Working Paper, June 26, 1975.

McCulloch, J. Huston. "Operational Aspects of the Siegel Paradox: Comment." *Quarterly Journal of Economics* 89, no. 1 (February 1975):170-172.

Melnick, Edward L. "A Test for Weak Band with Stationarity." New York University, Working Paper no. 72-07, 1972.

Morgenstern, Oskar. *International Financial Transaction and Business Cycles.* Princeton: Princeton University Press, 1959.

Moses, Ronald. "Anticipations of Exchange Rate Changes." Ph.D. dissertation, University of Chicago, 1969.

Muth, John F. "Rational Expectations and the Theory of Price Movement." *Econometrica* 29, no. 3 (July 1961):315-335.

Nelson, Charles R. "The Prediction Performance of the FRB-MIT-PENN Model of the U.S. Economy." *American Economic Review* 62, no. 5 (December 1972):902-917.

———. *Applied Time Series Analysis.* San Francisco: Holden-Day, Inc., 1973.

———. "Rational Expectations and the Predictive Efficiency of Economic Models." *Journal of Business* 48, no. 3 (July 1975):331-343.

Officer, Lawrence H., and Thomas D. Willet. "The Covered-Arbitrage Schedule: A Critical Survey of Recent Developments." *Journal of Money, Credit and Banking* 2, no. 2 (May 1970):247–257.
Poole, William. "The Canadian Experiment with Flexible Exchange Rates." Ph.D. dissertation, University of Chicago, 1966.
———. "Speculative Prices on Random Walks: An Analysis of Ten Time Series of Flexible Exchange Rates." *Southern Economic Journal* 33, no. 4 (April 1967):468–478.
Porter, Michael G. "A Theoretical and Empirical Framework for Analyzing the Term Structure of Exchange Rate Expectations." *IMF Staff Papers* 18, no. 3 (November 1971):613–645.
Predex Corporation. *Predex Forecast.* New York, 1975.
Priestley, M. B., and T. S. Rao. "A Test for Non-Stationarity of Time Series." *Journal of the Royal Statistical Society,* Series B, 31, no. 1 (1969):140–149.
Ricardo, David. *Reply to Mr. Bosanquet's Practical Observations on the Report of the Bullion Committee.* London: N.p., 1811.
Roll, Richard and Bruno Solnik. "A Pure Foreign Exchange Asset Pricing Model." Centre d'Enseignement Superieur des Affaires, Working Paper, no. 75-31, August 1975.
Roper, Donald E. "The Role of Expected Value Analysis for Speculative Decisions in the Forward Currency Market: Comment." *Quarterly Journal of Economics* 89, no. 1 (February 1975):157–169.
Samuelson, Paul A. "Proof that Properly Anticipated Prices Fluctuate Randomly." *Industrial Management Review* 6 (Spring 1965):41–49.
Scholes, Myron S. "The Market for Securities: Substitution versus Price Pressure and the Effects of Information on Share Prices." *Journal of Business* 45, no. 2 (April 1972):179–211.
Siegel, Jeremy J. "Risk, Interest and Foreign Exchange." *Quarterly Journal of Economics* 86 (May 1972):303–309.
Solnik, Bruno H. *European Capital Markets.* Boston: D. C. Heath-Lexington, 1973.
Smidt, Seymour. "The Road to an Efficient Market." *Financial Analysts Journal* 27, no. 5 (September/October 1971):18ff.
Stein, Jerome L. *The Nature and Efficiency of the Foreign Exchange Market.* Essays in International Finance, no. 40. Princeton: Princeton University Press, 1962.
Stokes, Houston H. "The Crisis Index: An Empirical Test of the Degree of Tension in the Foreign Exchange Market." *Economic Notes* 1, no. 1 (January/April 1972):72–91.
Stoll, Hans R. "An Empirical Study of the Foreign Exchange Market Under Fixed and Flexible Exchange Rates." *Canadian Economic Journal* 1, no. 1 (February 1968):55–66.
Swoboda, Alexander K. "Vehicle Currencies: The Case of the Dollar." In *The International Market for Foreign Exchange.* Edited by Robert Z. Aliber. New York: Praeger, 1969.
Tanner, J. Ernest and Levis A. Kochin. "The Determinants of the Difference between Bid and Ask Prices on Government Bonds." *Journal of Business* 44, no. 4 (October 1971):375–379.
Theil, Henri. *Principles of Econometrics.* New York: John Wiley, 1971.
Tinic, Seha. "The Economics of Liquidity Services." *Quarterly Journal of Economics* 86, no. 1 (February 1972):79–93.
Tsiang, S. C. "The Theory of Forward Exchange and the Effects of Government Intervention on the Forward Market." IMF Staff Papers 7, no. 1 (April 1959):75–106.
Upson, Roger B. "Random Walk and Forward Exchange Rates: A Spectral Analysis." *Journal of Financial and Quantitative Analysis* 7, nos. 3–5 (September 1972):1897–1905.

Van Horne, James C. *Function and Analysis of Capital Market Rates.* Englewood Cliffs, N.J.: Prentice-Hall, 1970.
Walras, Leon. *Elements of Pure Economics.* Translated by W. Jaffe. 1st ed. 1870. New York: Kelly, 1969.
Wells, Chris. "The Computer Assault on New York's Foreign Exchange Market." *Institutional Investor* 10, no. 3 (March 1976):70-74.
West, Richard and Seha Tinic. *The Economics of the Stock Market.* New York: Praeger Publishers, 1971.
Westerfield, Janice M. "Empirical Properties of Foreign Exchange Rates Under Fixed and Floating Rate Regimes." Department of Research. Federal Reserve Bank of Philadelphia. December 1975.
Working, Holbrook. "New Concepts Concerning Futures Markets and Prices." *American Economic Review* 51 (May 1961):160-163.
Zellner, Arnold and Franz Palm. "Time Series Analysis and Simultaneous Equation Econometric Models." *Journal of Econometrics* 3 (1974):17-54.

Statistical Material

Bank of England. *Bank of England Quarterly Bulletin.* Various issues.
Federal Reserve System. *Federal Reserve Bulletin.* Various issues.
Harris Bank. *Weekly Review of International Money Markets.* Chicago, Ill. Various issues.
International Monetary Fund (IMF). *International Financial Statistics (IFS).* Washington, IMF, Monthly issues, 1962-67.
International Monetary Market (IMM). *International Monetary Market Year Book.* Chicago, Ill. Various issues.
Money Manager. New York. Various issues.
Montagu, Samuel and Co. *Montagu, Monthly Review.* London, England. Various issues.
Salomon Brothers. *Salomon Brothers Monthly Bond Report.* New York. Various issues.

Index

Adversary Theory, 7, 8, 24
Aliber, Robert Z., 9, 11, 37n, 69, 84n, 175
Appreciation:
 and forward rate forecasts, 19, 73
 and interest rate differentials, 18, 19, 73
 and nominal return on assets, 15
Arbitrage, covered interest, *See* Covered Interest Arbitrage.
 models, *See* Models, arbitrage-based.
 triangular, *See* Triangular Arbitrage.
Arbitragers, 11, 49, 72-73
 versus speculators, 84n
ARIMA, compared with FRB-MIT-PENN model, 85n
Asset Pricing Model, 157-159
Auto Regressive Moving Average Process (ARMA), 78, 104-106 passim, 110
Autocorrelation:
 of exchange rates, 13, 20, 106, 110, 120
 of forecast errors, 17, 147
 of residuals, 109, 122n
 and time series analysis, 81, 104

Bagehot, Walter, 8
Bank of England Quarterly, 174
Bankers Discount Method, 43, 63n, 173
Barnea, Amir, 7
Belgian, Franc, 61, 89, 92, 110, 121n, 126
 forecast errors, 136
 and random walk, 112
Bias, 4, 18, 19, 65, 122n, 123, 133, 155n, 163n, 172
 and currency preference, 4, 65, 69, 70, 131
 and exchange risk, 70, 73, 125
 and Fisher Open Model, 69-70, 132-133
 and forecasting errors, 81, 84n, 131, 133
 and forecasting horizon, 131
 of forward rate based forecasts, 19, 72-73, 82, 85n
 and interest rate based forecasts, 69-70
 and interest parity calculations, 45, 63n
 and political risk, 69-70
 predictability of, 134, 154
 sources of, 69-70, 72-73

181

Bias continued
  systematic risk premia and 4, 65
  time pattern of, 19
  transaction costs and, 38n, 45, 69
Bid-Ask Prices, 4, 13, 38n, 43, 74, 75, 124, 163n, 170, 172, 173
Bid-Ask Spread, 8, 9, 20n, 21n, 37n, 38n
  as cost of meeting immediate demand, 35
  in spot versus forward markets, 9, 27
  in transaction cost estimation, 24-28, 32, 33, 37n, 44, 166
Bilson, John F. O. 15, 19, 20, 22n, 84n, 122n, 155n, 170
Black, Fischer, 21n, 159, 170
Bond Buyer, 173, 175n
Box, G. E. P., 4, 5, 78, 106
Box-Jenkins Time Series Technique, 12, 20, 102-122
British Pound, 19, 20, 89, 90, 106, 114, 121n, 124, 131, 155n, 162, 172
  bid-ask spread in, 27
  forecasting errors, 129, 136
  forward-spot ratio, 30
  transaction costs in, 35
Branson, William H., 10
Broker, foreign exchange, 37n
Brokerage fees, 9, 29, 33, 37n, 75. *See also* Transaction Costs.
Bundesbank, 38n, 172
Business Risk, See Risk, business.
Buy-and-Hold Strategy, 11, 14, 21n

Canada, 12, 20, 84, 124
  Bond Market in, 21n
  Government Debt, 17
  T-Bill Maturity, 174
  Term Structure of Interest Rates, 18-19
Canadian Dollar, 18, 19, 61, 92, 110, 112, 114, 120, 121n, 153, 162, 163n
  Bid-Ask Spread in, 27
  Forecast Errors, 127, 129
  Forecast Spread in, 27
  Random Walk and, 109, 115
  Transaction Costs in, 32
Canadian Float, deviations from random behavior, 87, 116
Capital Controls, 174
Capital Flows, 14, 63n
  barriers to, 159
  cost of, 40
Central Bank Intervention, 12, 153
  (See government intervention)
Chi-Square Test, 105, 106, 147
Commercial Paper, deviations from interest parity, 62
Composite Forecasting Model, 4-6 passim, 78-79, 123, 151-154, 169
"Consensus" data, 47
Corporate Cash Management Model, and use of exchange rate forecasts, 86n
Correlation;
  of forecast errors, 4-6 passim, 79 (See forecast errors)
  of residuals, 20 (See residuals)
  serial correlation (See serial correlation)
Cost of Liquidity Services, 7, 24, 63n
Cournot, Augustin, 37n
Covariance, of exchange rates, 70
  Exchange Risk, 12, 70, 73, 75
  and forward as predictor of spot, 73
Covered Interest Arbitrage, 4, 10-11, 21n, 168, 173, 174 *See also* Neutral Band
  in comparable securities, 48
  flows, and market efficiency, 3, 4, 10, 39-62, 62n, 113, 167
  profit opportunities and, 1, 39, 47, 140, 165
  risk-free profit in, 33, 49
  timing and risk, 47

transaction costs and. *See* Transaction Costs.
Covered Interest Differential, 9, 16. *See also* Interest Rates.
Crisis Index, 37n
Cuneo, Larry J., 21n
Currency Preference, 4, 18, 65, 69, 70, 123
  and bias in transaction costs, 69, 70, 131
  exchange risk and, 69
  and Fisher Open, 70
  and forecasting performance, 131–134

Daily Information Bulletin, 171
Demsetz, Harold, 7, 8, 20n, 25, 33, 35, 37n
Depreciation, and forward rate forecasts, 19
  and nominal return on assets, 15
  and profits from different forecast rules, 162
Determinants of exchange rates, 15
  see also Structural Economic Relationships; and Forecasting Models, Structural
Deutsch Mark, 89, 90, 110–116 passim, 121n, 153
  bid-ask spread in, 27
  forecasting errors, 19, 126, 127, 129, 136
  and joint float, 90, 121n
  ratio of forward to spot, 30
  transaction costs in, 32
Dollar, as numeraire, 121n
  time series behavior of currencies vis-a-vis, 89
Dooley, Michael P., 13, 38n
Dufey, Gunter, 12, 15, 20, 82, 159
"Drift" Parameter, 79, 154n

Dutch Guilder, 89, 92, 109–126 passim, 153
  forecasting errors, 136
Dynamic price/inventory adjustment theory, 7, 8, 24

Efficient Market Hypothesis, 1–6 passim, 39, 78, 163, 165, 170n. *See also* Market Efficiency
Einzig, Paul A., 21n
Elasticity for Arbitrage Funds, 11
Equilibrium Band (See Neutral Band)
Equilibrium Line (See Parity Line)
Equity Market Risk, 70
Eurocurrency deposits, transaction costs in, 131
Eurocurrency market, 11
  arbitrage within, 46
  cost of transacting in, 35, 45
  risk comparability spread in, 27, 35, 39
Eurodollar and Eurosterling deposits, 11, 173, 174
Exchange Controls, 86n. *See also* Political Risk.
Exchange Rate, 171, 174
  See also Forecasting, Forward Rates, Spot Rates, and Structural Models
  adjustment to new information, 109
  cross, 28
  determination, 13–15 passim, 66, 79, 170
  equilibrium, 12
  Fisherian relationship between interest rates and. *See* Fisher Open
  ratio of spot to forward, 30
  speculation. *See* Speculation
  systems, 5, 87
  time series behavior of. *See* Time Series Analysis.
  volatility, 5, 128, 166

Exchange Rate Changes, 11-20, 21n, 155n
  and bid-ask spread, 9
  expected versus actual, 18
  and interest rate differentials, 17, 70. See also Forecasts.
  and random walk, See Random Walk.
  and rates of return, 70
Exchange Rate Expectations, 69, 126
Exchange Rate Quotations, 155n. See also Bid-Ask Prices.
Exchange Rate Systems
  Flexible, 46
  Managed Float, 30, 45, 46, 49
  Pegged, 46
  Quiet Peg, 30, 45, 46, 49
  Turbulent Peg, 30, 45, 46, 49
  See also Structural Economic Relationships.
Exchange Risk, 4, 14, 24, 75, 167-169 passim. See also Risk.
  and currency preference, 69
  and equity market risk, 70
  and international assets, 158
  management models, 155
  and portfolio management, 70, 159
  and uncovered interest arbitrage, 70
Exogenous Variables, 77
  and forecast errors, 170
  forecasts of, 84n
  in models of future spot, 83n
Expectations (exchange rate), 153
  forward rate as reflection of, 72, 84n
  and price determination, 127
Exposure to Exchange Risk
  Cash-flow Exposure, 159
  Hedging, See Hedging.

Fama, Eugene F., 1, 85n, 157
Farber, Andre L., 170n
Federal Reserve Bank of N.Y., 25

Federal Reserve Bulletin, 174
Fieleke, Norman S., 9, 21n, 25, 37n, 84n
Filter Rule, 11, 13, 14, 21n, 120. See also Trading Strategies.
Financial Times 171
Fisher, Irving, 15, 16, 17, 157. See also Fisher Closed and Fisher Open.
Fisher Closed, 84n
Fisher Open, 65, 66
  currency preference and, 70, 131
  exchange risk covariance and, 70
Fisher Domestic, 124
Fisher External, 124, 127
  forecast bias, 69, 70, 131-133
  forward rate forecasts compared to, 70-71
  interest parity and, 84n
  political risk and, 70
Floating Rates, 38n
  bid-ask spreads during, 9, 27
  forward-spot ratio during, 30
  time series behavior of exchange rates during, 3, 12, 13, 166
Forecasting (future spot rate). 4, 16, 19, 20, 21n, 66, 124, 154, 157
  See also Forecasts and Forecasting Models.
  of currencies, relative difficulty, 129
  efficient markets and, 168
  profitability of, 161-162. See also Forecasting Models.
  stationarity and, See Stationarity
Forecasting Accuracy, 68, 163n. See also Forecasting Bias.
  forecast horizon and, 134, 168, 169
  using structural information, 78
  variability of underlying monetary factors and, 129
Forecasting Bias, See Bias, Currency Preference, Political Risk and Transaction Costs.
Forecasting Errors, 6, 19, 79, 83, 85, 155n, 170

across forecasting models, 81, 125–127, 136
composite forecasting and, 4, 123, 153, 154
correlation of, 4, 123, 134, 146, 154, 168, 169
currency dimension of, 127–130
currency preference and, 131–134
deviations from covered arbitrage and, *See* Covered Arbitrage.
exchange rate system and, 136, 147
Fisher Open and, 17
and horizon, 6, 85n, 134–136, 153, 154
market efficiency and, 82, 147
neutral band analysis of, *See* Neutral Band.
profit opportunities and, 151
risk premia and, 65, 127
stationarity of, 133
time pattern of, 73–77, 136–147
transaction costs and, 65, 73–77, 85n, 127, 154, 166
volatility of exchange rates and, 19, 136, 129
Forecasting Horizon, 123, 124
composite forecasting and, 153, 154
Forecasting accuracy and, *See* Forecasting Accuracy
Forecasting errors and, *See* Forecasting Errors
Forecasting models and, *See* Forecasting Models
Forecasting performance and, *See* Forecasting Performance
Forecasting Models, 5, 65, 78, 123–125, 163–169 passim. *See also* Time Series Analysis
arbitrage models, 65
composite, *See* Composite Forecasting.
and forecasting errors, *See* Forecasting Errors

and forecasting horizon, 123, 127, 131, 134–136
forward rate based, 18–20, 70–77, 147–151
interest rate based, 15–20, 65–70
lagged spot, 126
and neutral band, 68
performance of, 81–83, 125–127
profits from, 162
pure, 4, 65, 77–79
structural, 14–15, 65, 78, 83n, 85n
and time, 123, 136, 146–147
utility functions and, 81
Forecasting Performance, 65, 146
correcting for bias, 134
and currency, 127–131
and currency preference, *See* Currency Preference
and horizon, 134–135
and forecasting model, 125–127
and time, 136–147
Forecasting Services, 168, 170
Foreign Exchange, 3, 71, 174. *See also* Exchange Rates.
Foreign Exchange Advisory Services, 21n. *See also* Forecasting Services.
Foreign Exchange Market, 8–9, 23, 37n, 46, 155n
bid-ask spread in, *See* Bid-Ask Spread.
efficiency of, *See* Market Efficiency.
elasticity of demand and supply in, 63n
transaction costs in, *See* Transaction Costs
Foreign Exchange Regulations, 83
Foreign Exchange Traders, 2, 36n, 84n
Forward Contract, 64n, 71, 72, 80
to hedge exchange risk, 169. *See also* Hedging Exchange Risk.
Forward Exchange Rate, 12, 27, 40, 43, 171, 172, 174

Forward Exchange Rate continued
  in the cost of hedging, 170. *See also* Hedging Exchange Risk.
  deviations from future spot, 169
  expectations reflected in, 84n–85n
  forecasting ability of, 18–20, 127, 168
  and forecasting bias, *See* Bias
  and forecasting error, *See* Forecasting Error
  and interest parity rate, 84n
  modern theory of. *See* Modern Theory.
  as predictor of future spot, 70–74, 84n, 85n, 110, 124, 131, 146, 147, 154, 162, 163, 163n, 164
  transaction costs and, 32. *See also* Transaction Costs.
Forward Market, 155n
  bid-ask prices in, 75. *See also* Bid-Ask Prices.
  discounts and premiums in, 3, 23, 36.
  See also Forward Premia.
  speculative pressures in, 46, *See also* Speculation
  spreads in, 27, 32
  transaction costs in, 32, *See also* Transaction Costs
Forward Premia, 3, 5, 40, 43, 44, 172
Forward Rate Bias, 72, 84n, 151, 154
  exchange risk covariance and, 73
  portfolio theory and, 73
Forward Speculation, *See* Speculation, Forward
FRB-MIT-PENN Model, compared with ARIMA, 85n
Franklin National Bank, 83, 86n
French Franc, 12, 20, 89, 90, 92, 110, 124, 131, 153
Frenkel, Jacob A., 11, 15, 19, 20, 64n
Futures Contracts, Currency, 21n, 85n
Futures Prices, reflecting available information, 84n

German Mark, *See* Deutsch Mark
Giddy, Ian H., 12, 15, 20, 82
Gold, 14–17 passim, 63n, 155n
Goschen, Viscount, 2, 21n, 63n
Government Intervention, 5, 6, 9, 123. *See also* Central Bank Intervention.
  and composite forecasting, 154
  and random walk, 121
  in the snake, 121n
Grossman, Sanford J. 5, 152
Grubel, Herbert G., 21n, 122n, 163n

H ratios, for different forecast rules, 162
Harris Bank, 121, 171, 174
Harris Bank Weekly Review, 60, 64n, 124, 155n, 174
Heagy, Thomas C., 38n
Hedging Exchange Risk Exposure, 168–170
Herstatt Bank, 38n, 83, 86n
Hodgson, John S. 14
Holmes, A. R., 21n, 37n
Horizon effect, 135–136

Indian rupee, 15, 16
Infinite distributed lag function, 85n 103
Information, 2, 4, 6, 8, 13, 47, 79, 85n
  arbitrage profits signaled by, 17
  and composite forecasting, 4–5, 169
  exchange rate adjustments to, 109
  inside information, 8, 21n, 24, 37n, 63n, 170
  and market efficiency, 1, 5, 67, 69, 123
  perfect information, 160, 161.
  See also Perfect Information Profits.
  price reflection of, 1, 5, 65, 84n, 154.
  See also market efficiency.
  publicly available, 6, 163, 165, 168,

170
  reaction time to, 49, 84n, 166
  structural, 4, 79
Information Costs, 4–6 passim, 123, 154
  and market efficiency, 152
  and MSE, 153
Interbank Market, 124
Interest Parity Equilibrium Condition, 43
Interest Parity Line, 10, 43, 44
Interest Rate Parity, 1, 21n, 40, 44–46, 49, 70, 127. *See also* Neutral Band
  asset selection and, 44
  data considerations, 43–44
  deviations from, 10–11, 43–44, 46, 49, 60, 62, 63n, 83, 167, 168
  empirical evidence, 44–46
  forward rate determination, 72
  and hedging exchange risk, 169
  maturity, effect of on, 61
  and market efficiency, *See* Market Efficiency.
  and transaction costs, 39–43, 49, 70, 166
  and uncovered interest arbitrage, 73
Interest Rates, 22n, 43, 44, 49, 60, 63n, 84n
  See also Treasury Bills.
  and bid-ask spread, 9
  and exchange rate expectations, 2, 18, 126
  Fisherian relationship, *See* forecasting exchange rates, Fisher Closed and Fisher Open
  forecasting based on, 15–20, 65, 66, 70, 124, 131, 134, 160, 168
Intermediate Currency, in triangular arbitrage, 32, 33
International Bank for Reconstruction and Development, 17
International Financial Statistics, 37n, 171, 174

International Monetary Fund, 171
International Monetary Market (IMM), 21n, 27, 37n, 171
International Monetary Market Newsletter, 25
International Monetary Market Year Book, 171
International Money Market, 1, 2, 23, 78, 158, 165, 166, 169
International Risk-Free Rate, 158
Italian Lira, 89, 92, 106, 112, 121n, 124, 126, 131, 162
  forecasting errors, 129, 136
  and joint float, 121n

Japanese Yen, 92, 106, 109, 121n, 124, 153, 162
  forecasting errors, 129, 136
Jenkins, W., 4, 5, 78
Jensen, Michael C., 157
Jensen's Inequality, 73, 84n
Joint Float, 89, 90, 121n

Kalmogorov-Smirnov Test, 122n, 155n
Kaserman, David L., 15, 19, 20
Keynes, John M., 10, 21n
Kochin, Levis A., 21n
Kohlhagen, Steven W., 15, 82
Kouri, Penti, 84n
Kraus, Alan, 21n
Kurtosis statistic, 122, 155n

Lagged Spot Model, 127, 131, 132, 160
Lags, 13, 20, 106
  and forecast errors. *See* Forecast Errors, time pattern of.
  and transaction costs, 166
Leamer, Edward E., 30
Levich, Richard M., 22n, 64n, 85n, 122n, 155n, 160, 170n
Likelihood Ratio Test, 105, 109, 110, 112, 121

188 / *Subject Index*

Linear Filters, 77, 103
Liquidity Theory, 7, 8, 21n
Lira. *See* Italian Lira.
Log Transformations, of exchange rates, 92
Log-likelihood test, 114
  with Box-Jenkins, 120
Logue, Dennis E., 7
Luxembourg, and joint float, 121n

Managed Float, 3, 38n
  transaction costs and, 33, 166
Margin Account, 71, 72
Market integration across maturities, 126
Market Efficiency, 2, 3, 5, 23, 30, 38n, 43–49 passim, 123, 166–168, 179
  and arbitrage, 30. *See also* Neutral Band
  and composite forecasting, 152
  and covered interest arbitrage, *See* Covered Interest Arbitrage
  and Fisher Open forecasts, 67
  and forecasting errors, *See* Forecasting Errors and market efficiency
  and interest rate parity, 44
  and the neutral band, *See* Neutral Band.
  and random behavior, 11, 12, 13, 155n, 170
  tests of, 1–6, 14, 81
  and time series analysis, 81
  and transaction costs, *See* Transaction Costs.
Market Makers, 36n, 47
  behavior, 8, 24, 27
  and forward bid-ask prices, 77
  and profit opportunities, 77
Martingale Process, 14
Maturity of Financial Instruments,
  and deviation from interest parity, 60
  effect on transaction costs, 61

McCormick, Frank, 9, 25, 27
McCulloch, J. Huston, 84n
Mean Squared Error (MSE), 125, 146. *See also* Forecasting Errors
  composite forecasts and, 152–153, 162, 169
  Fisher external and, 132
  and forecast bias, 81, 86n, 132
  and forecast horizon, 125, 126, 127, 168
  and forecast model, 125, 126, 127, 168
  and speculation, *See* Speculation
Melnick, Edward L., 121n
Model, 69, 78, 154, 156
  arbitrage-based, 4, 65–77
  balance of payments, 86n
  Box-Jenkins, *See* Box-Jenkins
  market, 85n
  martingale, 14
  monetary, 170
  multiple rational distributed lag, 77
  portfolio, 85n
  pure forecasting, 4, 65, 77–83
  random walk, 12, 13, 20
  structural, 14, 15, 65, 83n
  transfer function, multiple input, 77
Modern Theory of forward exchange, 72, 84n, 85n
Monetary Policy, and exchange rate volatility, 128–129
Monetary Theories, of exchange rates, 15, 84n, 170
Money, 15, 22n
  demand for, 21n
  supply of, 22n
Money Manager, 173, 175n
Montagu Monthly Review, 172
Morgenstern, Oskar, 37n
Moses, Ronald, 15, 17, 18, 131
Moving Average Terms, 103, 106, 109, 115, 122n
Moving Average Process, 120, 155n

Multiple Rational Distributed Lag
    (MRDL) Model, 77
Muth, John F., 78, 85n

Nelson, Charles R., 78, 81, 85n, 113, 155n
Netherlands. *See* Dutch Guilder.
Neutral Band, 4, 63n, 67, 82, 83
    and covered arbitrage flows, 113
    and deviations from triangular parity, 30
    empirical results, 46, 61, 62
    on exchange rate forecasts, 68
    and forecasting bias, 69
    forecasting errors within, 129, 136, 146, 154, 168
    around interest parity, 39, 40, 44
    limits on, 68
    and market efficiency, 49, 68–69
    and speculative flows, 72
    and transaction costs, *See* Transaction Costs
    and uncovered arbitrage, 43, 67, 68, 167
New York Interbank Market, 37n, 171, 172
New York Stock Exchange, 8, 37n
Norway, and snake, 121n

Officer, Lawrence H., 10, 22n

Parity Line, 40, 49, 69
    and taxes, 63n
    and transaction costs, 67
Pegged Rates, 3, 27, 30
    change to floating rate system, 92
    quiet peg, 167
    turbulent peg, 4, 90, 113, 167
Perfect Information Profits, 6, 160, 162, 168
Periodicity, 12, 21n
Pierce, David A., 106
Political Risk, 44, 83, 86n, 158
    and bias in transaction costs, 69
    and Fisher Open, 70
    market efficiency, 70
Poole, William, 11, 116, 120, 121
Porter, Michael G., 15, 18, 20, 22n, 84n
Portfolio, approach, 85n
    decisions, 12
    management and efficient market hypothesis, 170n
    measure of risk, 163
    of risk-free assets, 158, 159
    of risky assets, 158
    trade-weighted, 159
Portfolio Models, 70, 73, 84n, 85n
Portfolio Theory, 70
Predex Corporation, 21n, 22n
Premium, *See* Forward Premia and Risk Premia.
Price, 79
    Disequilibrium, and inside information, 8, 21n, 37n
    Impact of Informed Trades on, 24
    and Non-Pecuniary Returns, 70
Priestly, M. B., 121n
Profits, Arbitrage, 2, 3, 33, 47, 167
    and adversary theory, 8
    and deviations from interest parity, 43
    and forecasting errors, 82
    and forecasting model, 161, 162
    and forward rate bias, 151
    and hedging strategy, 169
    and market efficiency, 10, 47, 168
    perfect information, 6, 162
    speculative, 1–6 passim, 23, 74, 157, 160–170 passim
    and trading rule, 13, 48
    and transaction costs, 166
Purchasing Power Parity (PPP), 14

Q-statistic, 109, 122n, 146
Q-test, 112
Quadratic Loss Function, 81

Random Behavior, 11, 86n, 87, 115, 116, 134
   and market efficiency, See Market Efficiency
Random Shocks, 77, 79
Random Walk, 12, 13, 20, 85n, 104, 122n
   empirical evidence, 87, 106–120 passim, 153
   and exchange rate changes, 86, 86n, 116
   and exchange rate system, 167
   and market efficiency, 5, 154n–155n
   Model, See Models
   and time series analysis, 80, 179–181
Rate of Return, 3, 12, 79, 81, 83, 122n, 163n
Rational, 85n
   expectations, 78, 85n
   function, 103
   investor, 43
Rao, T. S., 121n
Regression Analysis, 10, 19, 21n, 155n
   for bias, 19
   to construct composite forecast, 152
   to estimate coefficients, 84
   of interest parity, 10
   for selecting weights, 79
Residual, autocorrelation of, 109, 122n
   and Fisher Open, 69
   from fitted models, 105
   and forecasting bias, 69
   profit opportunities, 46
   serial correlation of, 106, 109, 110, 112
   sum of squares, 106
   variance of, 109
Return, 14, 15, 18, 85n. See also Profit.
   risk-free, 14, 165
   speculative, 155n, 163
   unusual, 157, 158
Ricardo, David, 2, 37

Risk, aversion and transaction costs, 166
   Business, 86n
   comparability of assets, 11
   Covariance, 12
   Default, 64n, 158
   diversification, 70
   Exchange, See Exchange Risk
   Marketability, 8, 24
   Political, See Political Risk
   preference, 84n
   premia, systematic, 4
   pricing, 170
   Security, 8, 24
   and yields, quoted and realized, 63
Risk-free asset, 158, 159
Risk-free rate, 158, 159, 162, 168
Risk Neutrality, 160
Risk Premia, 4, 83
   and error term, 157
   systematic, 65
Roll, Richard, 157, 163n
Roper, Donald E., 84n
Rupee, See Indian Rupee

Salomon Brothers Monthly Bond Report, 173
Samuelson, Paul A., 21n
Scholes, Myron S., 21n
Schott, F. H., 21n, 37n
Securities, 4, 7, 8, 11, 43. See also Treasury Bills.
   and covered arbitrage, 48
   and deviations from interest parity, 60
   elasticities of demand and supply in markets for, 63
   risk comparability of domestic versus external, 4
   transaction costs and, See Transaction Costs.
Serial Correlation, 116. See also Correlation.

of deviations between forward and future spot, 169
of forecast errors, 6, 82, 123, 133, 168, 169
and market efficiency, 11–12
of residuals, 109
Shafer, Jeffrey R., 13, 38n
Sharpe-Lintner Model, 158
Siegel, Jeremy J., 84n
Skewness Statistic, 121n, 155n
Smidt, Seymour, 8
Solnik, Bruno H., 70, 73, 84n, 163n, 170
Spectral Analysis, 12
Speculation, 39, 85n, 157, 163n, 164n
 and deviations from interest parity, 10
 and forecast errors, 82, 83
 Forward, 2, 4, 6, 80, 157–163n passim
 and the neutral band, See Neutral Band
 Profitability of, 2, 19, 71, 72, 75
 and transaction costs, 11, 167
Speculative Returns, 158, 163, 164n, 165. See also Profits
 and market efficiency, 170
Speculators, 74, 112
 demand for forward contracts, 72, 73, 85n
 distinction from arbitragers, 84n
 and forward bid-ask prices, 77
 and market stability, 116
Spot Exchange Rates, 1, 2, 3, 83n, 109, 124, 171, 172, 174
 Box-Jenkins analysis of, 12
 Forecasts of, See Forecasting
 and interest parity, 40
 and market efficiency, 13, 167
 as predictor of future spot, 124, 168
 time dependence in, 155n
 time series behavior of, 5, 11, 14, 87–122, 122n
 volatility, See Volatility

Spot Market, 71
 spreads in, 27, 32
 transaction costs in, 32
Spreads, 7, 8, 9, 27, 32, 35, 37n. See also Bid-Ask Spread.
Stationarity, 121n
 of bias, 86n
 and Box-Jenkins technique, 104
 empirical results, 13, 31, 36, 90, 92, 106, 113, 166
 of forecast errors, 133
 and forecasting, 5, 87, 92, 102. See also Time Series Analysis.
 of forward rate series, 110
Stein, Jerome L., 10
Stiglitz, Joseph E. 5, 132
Stoll, Hans R., 21n, 84n
Stokes, Houston H., 37n
Structural Economic Relationships, 115, 116
 changes in, 86n
 and exchange rate models, 14–15, 83n, 84n, 85n, 170
 and time series analysis, 113, 167
Structural Forecasting Models, See Forecasting Models
Sun Spot Activity, in forecasting, 77
Sweden, and snake, 121n
Swiss Franc, 89, 92, 106–112 passim, 121n
 speculative profits in, 163n
Swoboda, Alexander K., 21n

Tanner, J. Ernest, 21n
Taxes, and interest parity line, 63n
 foreign exchange, 83
 and political risks, 86n
Thiel, Henri, 84n
Time Series Analysis, 12, 31, 37n, 77–78, 105, 113–121
 of Canadian exchange rates, 11, 116–121
 of exchange rate behavior, 5, 11–14, 19, 113, 165, 166, 171

Time Series Analysis continued
 and exchange rate system, 167
 of forecasting errors, *See* Forecasting Errors
 of forecasting horizon and accuracy, 134
 of forward premia, 113
 and market efficiency, *See* Market Efficiency
 and pure forecasting models, 4
 and random walk, *See* Random Walk
 and stationarity, 5, 36
 and volatility of exchange rates, 166
Time Series Models, 4, 13, 92, 122n, 155n
 Fitted, 113, 116
 forecasting in pegged periods, 92
 and random walk, 12–13
 for spot versus forward rates, 166
 and stationarity, 13, 102
Timing of Transactions, 46
Tinic, Seha, 7, 21n
Trade, balance, 21n
 flows, 14
 margins, 38n
Traders, competition among, 21n
 and inside information, 170
 speed of, and market efficiency, 2
Trading, 1
 Block, 8
 Informed, impact on prices, 24
 rule, 11, 12, 21n, 47, 48, 49
 and security prices, 1, 7, 8
 and transaction costs, 166
 volume, 7, 8–9, 21n, 24, 27
Trading Strategies, 11, 12, 13
 Buy-and-Hold, 11, 14
 Filter Rule, 11, 14
Transaction Costs, 3, 7–10, 23, 37n, 38n, 45, 60, 63n, 66, 159, 166, 167, 172, 173
 and arbitrage, 2, 3, 10, 42, 43, 47, 113.

 See also Triangular Arbitrage and Covered Arbitrage.
 bid-ask spread estimation of, 3, 20n, 23, 24–33, 36
 and changes in exchange rate systems, 46
 and covered interest arbitrage, 4, 42, 43, 67
 and deviations between forward and future spot, 169
 and deviations from interest parity, 16, 46, 49, 62, 64n, 69
 in Eurocurrency deposits, 131
 and filter rule profits, 120
 and Fisher Open, 70, 127
 and forecasting bias, 19, 169
 and forecasting errors, 65, 17, 73–77, 151, 153, 154, 157, 166
 in foreign exchange markets, 3, 8, 23–35 passim, 44, 62, 131, 165
 and interest parity, 39, 43, 66, 70
 and lags, 49, 116
 and managed float, 33, 46, 146, 166, 167
 and market efficiency, 3, 68–69
 across markets, 166
 and maturity of assets, 35, 44, 61, 85n, 166
 Negative, 8, 21n
 and neutral band, 4, 40, 67, 146, 167
 in quiet peg versus managed float, 3
 in quiet peg period, 33, 46, 167
 in security markets, 3, 33–36, 40–44 passim, 62, 165
 and speculative profits, 11, 146, 162, 163n, 167
 structure of, 30
 over time, 166
 triangular arbitrage estimation of, 3, 23, 28–33, 36, 166, 171
 during turbulent peg period, 46, 167
 and uncertainty, 33, 35, 166

in U.S. T-Bills. *See* Treasury Bills,
transaction costs in and volume
of trading, 35, 166
Transfer Function Models, multiple
input, 77
Treasury Bills, 3, 10, 11, 155n, 162,
174. *See also* Securities.
Bid-Ask Spread in, 37n
Bid-Ask Yields, 173
and deviations from interest parity,
62
transaction costs in, 3, 35, 36
Triangular Arbitrage, 3, 21n, 23,
28–33
deviations from, 31, 32
risk-free, 33
and transaction cost estimation, *See*
Transaction Costs
Triangular Parity, 28, 37n
deviations from, 37n, 166, 173
Tsiang, S. C., 22n

Uncertainty, 167
and Fisher Open, 70. *See also* Fisher
Open.
and Interest Rate Parity, 70. *See also*
Interest Parity.
United Kingdom, *See* British Pound
United States, *See* Dollar and Treasury
Bills
Uncovered Arbitrage Funds, profitability of marginal inflow, 68
profitability of marginal outflow, 67

Uncovered Interest Arbitrage, 65, 70,
73, 82
Unusual Profits, *See* Profits, speculative
Upson, Roger B., 12, 122n
Utility Functions, 81

Van Horne, James C., 83
Variance, 81, 163n
of residuals, 109
Vehicle Currency, in triangular arbitrage, 32
Volatility, of bid-ask spreads, 27
of earnings and hedging, 169
in exchange rate movements, 5, 12,
14, 27, 113, 128, 146, 166
of spot-forward ratio, 30
and time series analysis, *See* Time
Series Analysis

Wagner, Wayne H., 21n
Walras, Leon, 2, 37n
Wells, Chris, 37n
West, Richard, 21n
Westerfield, Janice M., 122n
"White Noise", 78, 103, 105.
See also Random Shocks.
Willet, Thomas D., 10
Working, Holbrook, 84n

Yield, 6, 43, 83

Zellner-Palm Identification Technique, 5, 105, 106